CESSNA
A MASTER'S EXPRESSION

By Edward H. Phillips

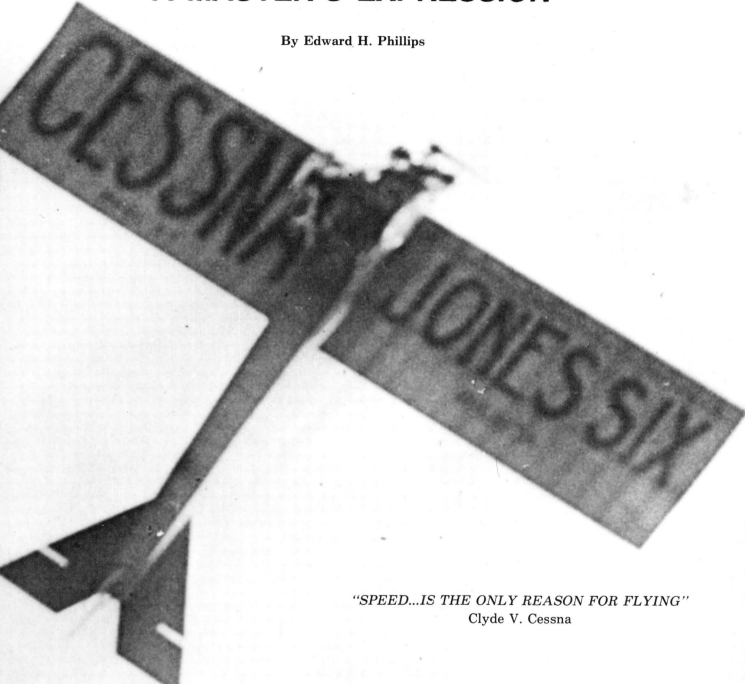

"SPEED...IS THE ONLY REASON FOR FLYING"
Clyde V. Cessna

FLYING BOOKS
Eagan, Minnesota 55122

FOREWORD

CESSNA!...That name has many meanings to different people. To the layperson it means 'all those little airplanes' at the local airport. To the flying fraternity it means the ubiquitous Model 150 and 152, or the ever-popular Model 120-140 that taught them how to fly.

And to the owners of more than 175,000 Cessnas produced since 1927 it's the company that has built more small airplanes than anyone else. But to the aviation history buff the name Cessna recalls memories of a young man in Enid, Oklahoma, in 1911. A young man who wanted to fly like the birds.

On many a hot, summer night that year, 31 year-old Clyde Vernon Cessna kept his neighbors awake as he tinkered with a cantankerous engine that kept him on the ground.

Sheer determination finally got Cessna airborne in 1911. By 1927 "Monoplanes Cessna" stood for high performance, modestly-powered, cantilever-wing airplanes much in demand by sportsmen, businessmen and racing pilots alike.

Resurrected from the Great Depression doldrums in 1934 by brothers Dwight and Dwane Wallace, the Cessna Aircraft Company began production of the classic 'Airmaster' series, and airplanes have been rolling off the production lines ever since.

Although much has been written about Cessna aircraft, little factual information has been accumulated about Clyde Vernon Cessna, the man, his companies and the machines that bore his name. In "CESSNA - A MASTER'S EXPRESSION", Ed Phillips has skillfully blended history with a highly readable text that represents the most thoroughly researched story of Cessna yet published.

Accordingly, much new ground has been covered in this book. The reader will quickly discover that many of the previously accepted stories of Cessna history will conflict with the information presented herein. Mr. Phillips has done much original and intensive research into the earliest days of Cessna's flying; a time period sorely lacking in reliable information until now.

He interviewed Cessna factory employees who were there when many of the company's historic events occurred. The author also talked with men and women who knew Clyde Cessna and his son, Eldon; a team that built the famous CR-series racers in 1932-1933.

As company historian at Cessna for the past 19 years, I have been looking forward to a publication that covers the history of Clyde Vernon Cessna and his tremendous career in aviation. It's my pleasure to welcome "CESSNA - A MASTER'S EXPRESSION" to the library of aviation enthusiasts and historians everywhere.

Bob Pickett
Wichita, Kansas
June, 1984

Copyright© 1985 Flying Books, Publishers & Wholesalers, Eagan, Minnesota 55122

Library of Congress Cataloging in Publication Data

Phillips, Edward

Cessna
A Master's Expression

85-81741

ISBN 0-91139-04-4

Printed in the United States of America
First edition

INTRODUCTION

Roy Cessna dug his heels into the hard, crusty surface of the Salt Plains. He gripped the fuselage struts of the Bleriot-type monoplane and turned his head to the side, closing his eyes tightly to keep out the salt dust as it stung his face. His pantlegs whipped back and forth. The shirt he wore flapped about as his brother Clyde brought the engine up to full power. The noise was deafening. Every piece of the machine was shaking. Wires vibrated wildly. It seemed to Roy as if the very being of the machine was protesting restraint by its would-be masters.

Then came the signal to release the ship. The eldest Cessna brother let go and the machine moved forward. Slowly at first, then faster until it broke free of the earth and flew.

In less than a minute the ascension ended. Aviator Clyde Vernon Cessna cut the throttle, eased back on the control cluster and immediately the airplane hit the ground, bounced, then hit and bounced again. Finally it settled, coasting to a stop.

Roy ran up to the cockpit. Brother Clyde was smiling. Almost immediately a broad grin spread across Roy's weathered face. They had flown. Their machine could fly. Only the whisper of the prairie wind could be heard, along with sounds of crackling cylinders and the hissing of boiling water from the overheated four-cylinder engine.

They talked enthusiastically about booking some exhibitions. The talked quickly died away. Clyde re-entered the cockpit and Roy stationed himself at the wooden propeller; one he had made himself. Clyde was ready with the controls. Roy took a deep breath, grasped the propeller with both hands and whirled it with all his might. The Elbridge two-stroke engine puffed smoke, then it erupted into a staccato roar.

Roy quickly took position at the rear of the ship, clutching the fuselage struts, looking away from the bullet-like salt pebbles. He dug his heels into the virgin flats, waiting for Clyde's signal...

That was the beginning in June, 1911, of Clyde V. Cessna's career in aviation. And yet, like the Wright Brothers before them, brothers Clyde and Roy Cessna worked side by side to make their airplane take to the skies. But it wasn't the shifting, faceless sand dunes of Kitty Hawk that witnessed those early flights. Instead, Oklahoma's Great Salt Plains saw the Cessnas earn their wings.

For months they had tried to fly. Then some very short flights were made, but only for a few hundred feet or less. The 40 hp engine was unreliable. It overheated constantly. But they were getting better at the game of aviating. From those trying and often troublesome flights of 1911, Clyde and Roy Cessna learned to fly and to foresee the possibilities of commercial aviation. Clyde never let go of that vision. He dedicated most of his adult life to making it a reality.

The next quarter century saw Cessna go from an inexperienced aviator to company founder, designer and chief engineer. He gained worldwide acclaim from the performance of his cantilever monoplanes. The tiny CR-series racers designed by Clyde and his son Eldon earned the respect of the racing fraternity as well.

Cessna built the most efficient monoplanes in the sky. His accomplishments in aeronautics were legion. He was a master of his art.

But perhaps the most lasting testimony to this quiet, genial man is his story. A story that deserves to be told. "Cessna - A Master's Expression" is the narrative of Clyde V. Cessna and how he conquered the air.

Edward H. Phillips
October, 1984
Wichita, Kansas

TABLE OF CONTENTS

ACKNOWLEDGMENTS

In compiling information for this book, the author was fortunate in having the assistance of many people who helped bring the story of Clyde V. Cessna and the Cessna Aircraft Company alive. I thank them all for their assistance: Bill Ellington and the Reference Section staff of the Wichita Public Library, Dean Humphries, Larry Wiggins and LeRoy Burgess of the Cessna Aircraft Company, Mike Sheets, Kenny Freeman and Barbara Harding of Beech Aircraft Corporation, the staff of the Kingman County Museum, Mary Moran of the Oklahoma Historical Society, Betty Smith, Georgie Throckmorton and Ruth Evans of the Enid Public Library, Bob Richman and the staff of the Kansas Historical Society, Phil Edwards, Jay Spenser, Dana Bell and Pete Suthard of the National Air and Space Museum Library, Tom Crouch, curator of the Aeronautics Department of the National Air and Space Museum, Deed Levy, Dwane and Velma Wallace, Mrs. Dwight Wallace, Walt House, John Underwood, Bob Resley, Marla Weyand, Les Forden, Gerald Deneau, Mort Brown, Bob Phelps, Karl Boyd, Tom Quick, Eldon Cessna, Wanda Cessna McVey, Monte Barnes, Truman Wadlow, Newman Wadlow, Gar Williams, Bill Koelling, Ray Brown, Robert Hirsch, Stephen J. Hudek, Peter M. Bowers, Herschel Smith, Truman C. "Pappy" Weaver, Delbert L. Roskam, V.G. "Doc" Weddle, John A. de Vries, Carol Hughes, Ted Hart, Kathleen Sullivan, Kathleen Snyder of the Wichita Chamber of Commerce, Ashley Moen, John Zimmerman, John Davis, Jim Thorn, with a very special thanks and appreciation to Robert J. Pickett, whose knowledge of Cessna history coupled with his extensive photographic collection contributed so much to this book.

CHAPTER ONE
From Buckboards To "Silverwing"

"Land in Kansas! 160 acres to every man!" James Cessna listened intently to the words of his friend John Burchfield. "Jim, it sounds like they're tryin' to get folks to homestead since they made Kansas a state. That's a lot of land. A man could make a new start with a piece of ground that size and feed his family, too."

Cessna nodded his head in agreement. He could tell that Burchfield was interested in the land offering. It sounded good. It was 1880 and America was still expanding to the west, settling the wide open prairie states by offering land grants to encourage homesteading and eventual communities.

But both men had wives and children to think about, too. The long, arduous trek across unfamiliar territory could be too much for the family to bear. Yet, James knew that Mary Vandora Cessna would follow her husband to the prairies of Kansas if that's where he wanted to go.

Both Cessna and Burchfield talked to their wives about the move. It would be a new life for them all, and the land was free. With the decision made to leave Iowa for Kansas, the two men bid farewell to family and started westward.

In a covered wagon drawn by oxen, suffering the whims of nature as they traveled, Cessna and

Louis Bleriot's popular Type XI monoplane was also offered as the Model XI-2, powered with a 50 or 70 hp Gnome rotary engine. A copy of the type was built by the American Aeroplane Supply House of Hempstead, New York, in 1911. (Bob Pickett Collection/Cessna Aircraft Company)

Burchfield reached Kansas and staked their claims in Canton Township, Kingman County in the south central region of the state.

Although Kansas was a relatively peaceful state by 1880, Indians still made raids on settlers occasionally, so Cessna and Burchfield chose acreage adjacent to each other for mutual defense.

The land was rich in potential, but poor in topographic appeal. There were very few trees sticking out of the endless prairie. Winds played their monotonous tones across the infinite miles of flatlands. Only the ubiquitous Buffalo Grass thrived on such surroundings. Yet, there was a certain beauty to the land, reinforced by the refreshing waters of the nearby Chikaskia River and its complement of bordering willow trees.

In this setting the two men from Iowa went to work building the Burchfield house first. The tiny sod house was soon finished, and James Cessna returned to Iowa. In 1881 James and Mary Cessna, with their two sons Roy and Clyde, left by rail for Kansas.

The family lived with the Burchfields in their soddy until the Cessna dwelling was built, a well dug and a crop of corn planted. By autumn of 1881 the Cessnas were comfortably settled in the sod house with a dirt floor that would shelter them until the spring of 1882 when a tornado tore off the roof and severely damaged the dwelling.

The Cessnas were taken in by their good friends the Burchfields once again. Another sod house was quickly built not far from the original homesite.

The International Aviators, formed by John B. Moisant in late 1910. Left to right: Rene Barrier, John B. Moisant, Roland Garros, Rene Simon and Charles K. Hamilton. Using Bleriot Type XI monoplanes and Hamilton's biplane, the group flew exhibitions in the United States as well as Central and South America. When the Aviators came to Oklahoma City in January, 1911, Clyde Cessna witnessed flights by Barrier, Simon and Garros in their Bleriot Type XI ships. He is believed to have learned about the Queen company in New York City from his conversations with one of the famed group of airmen. (Smithsonian Institution Photo #A32136D)

Growing up on the Plains must have been very exciting for three-year-old Clyde and his brother Roy. Their father was a good provider and taught the boys responsibility, respect, individualism and self determination.

Young Clyde and Roy didn't want for excitement in those early years in Kansas. Rattlesnakes, tornadoes and the fear of Indian attacks were typical of pioneer family risks. Fear of the Indians came from greedy ranchers who looked upon the settlers as a threat to their grazing lands. They would send cowboys racing through the countryside, screaming dire warnings that the Indians were coming. Many families packed up and left. But many more remained, like the Cessnas and the Burchfields.

Whenever a valid threat arose, James Cessna would gather his family together and move to the Burchfield house, where their combined numbers of guns could better deal with any raiders. However, no known battles ever took place. The warring Indians stayed in eastern Kansas and rarely disturbed the southcentral region of the state during the early 1880s.

Mary Cessna was admired for her cooking abilities and also served as a mid-wife in those years on the prairie. James Cessna often read aloud to the children from literary works like Pilgrim's Progress, Shakespeare and Longfellow.

Five more children were born on the Cessna homestead in Kansas. They were: Pearl William, Noel Miles, Bert David, Hazel Dell and Grace Opal, all members of a happy family.

The origins of the name Cessna had seen much turmoil before coming to America. During the days of Martin Luther's Protestant Reformation in 1517, the religious reformers banded together into a group known as the Huguenots in France. Among the members of this new sect were families carrying the name Cessna (French variation of the name was Cefna, the 'f' standing for a double 's').

Fierce fighting between the Catholics and the Huguenots occurred between 1525 and 1560. By 1569 the group had won some religious freedom but in 1629 the group had sustained great losses from many battles over the years.

Many of the Huguenots fled France instead of joining the Catholic faith. England, Holland, Switzerland and Denmark gave asylum to these people, one of whom was John Cessna I. Later, in England, a Count John De Cessna was known to be a member of a British brigade under the command of the Duke De Schomberg and William, Prince of Orange.

De Cessna fought with these two men at the Battle of the Boyne in Ireland in 1690 and remained there until 1718, when he came to colonial America and settled in Pennsylvania. One of his sons, John De Cessna, was a member of the Provincial Assembly and Constitutional Convention of 1775.

Of his descendants was one William Cessna, who lived in Kenton, Ohio. His son, George, was the father of James W. Cessna. There are many spelling variations of the name Cessna, such as Cisna, Cesena, Cisne and Cissna. This orthography is attributed to early day public servants, such as clerks and assessors who tried to spell a name that was unusual and unknown to them.

James William Cessna was born December 17, 1856 in Hardin Township, Cessna County, Kenton, Ohio. He was a farm boy very accustomed to hard work. At age 20 he married Mary Vandora Skates, who was born February 3, 1857, in Kenton, Ohio.

The young couple settled in Hawthorne, Iowa, where Cessna put in five years as a telegraph operator with the Chicago, Burlington and Quincy Railroad. Two of seven children were born at Hawthorne; Roy Clarence on December 25, 1877 and Clyde Vernon on December 5, 1879.

In Kansas, James Cessna and his sons worked hard to eke out an existence on the land; it was not easily subdued. Clyde and Roy spent many days of their youth out in the fields with their father. The family's team of oxen, named Jake, Duke and Brody, toiled along with their master, answering the commands "Gee" and "Haw" as they pulled the heavy plow through stubborn sod.

When the corn crop was harvested, the boys accompanied their father to Harper, 12 miles south of the homestead. That was also their post office. Clyde's education lasted only through the fifth grade. He attended the one-room schoolhouse 1 3/4 miles from home, near Raymond, Kansas. Roy was better at mathematics than Clyde, but couldn't match his brother when it came to ideas, coupled with a vision to make them reality.

By 1899 the Cessnas were comfortable residents of a new, two-story farmhouse nestled among a grove of cottonwood trees. Clyde had quite a reputation as a mechanic by this time. He seemed indwelt with a natural ability to innovate improvements to farm implements and could fix just about anything. His sister Hazel recalls that Clyde always seemed to have "a hammer in one hand and monkey wrench in the other."

It wasn't long before the neighbors found this out. Clyde was often called upon to repair machinery belonging to local farmers. One day the knotter malfunctioned on a farmer's self-binder. The knotter device was an intricate mechanism and not everyone understood its seemingly mysterious operation. It was designed to tie a sheaf of wheat with twine and finish the job with a knot. As far as this farmer was concerned, if the knotter wasn't working, no work got done.

A call for help quickly found young Clyde on the spot. He fixed the errant knotter with little difficulty. The word soon spread about Clyde and his ways with equipment.

But it wasn't just machinery Clyde Cessna found interesting. A young schoolteacher named Europa Elizabeth Dotzour also claimed much of Cessna's attention. Miss Dotzour attended McPherson College in Kansas and took up teaching in the rural Kingman area upon graduation in 1900 at age 18. For the next five years she taught elementary school subjects and attended many social gatherings. At one of these community get-togethers she met 26-year-old Cessna and courtship followed.

The couple were married on June 6, 1905. Cessna and his bride moved into Clyde's small house on his 40-acre piece not far from the original homestead. He had purchased the ground from brother Roy paying $400 and throwing in one Bay pacing horse as payment for the chicken house.

Roy had lived there as a bachelor for a number of years, giving music lessons on the guitar. He also became a proficient piano tuner that further supplemented his income.

Clyde farmed the forty acres but found that it was just too small to make a living on. It was time to find new pursuits, and brother Roy came up with just the thing...an automobile. He had been riding the Bay horse to Harper for quite some time. One of the merchants there kept telling Roy that what he needed was one those new horseless carriages.

After countless sales attacks Roy relented. His new mount was a one-cylinder, four horsepower, air-cooled 'buckboard' automobile with hickory wood springs and solid rubber tires. On the way home with his machine Roy was confronted with a problem; the river had to be crossed to get to his house and there was no bridge. He shut down the engine and went for Clyde who wasn't far from Roy's new property.

With Roy pushing and Clyde driving, the brothers got the auto across the river but it refused to climb the steep bank on the other side. Once again Clyde's talents met the challenge. Utilizing a block and tackle they got the machine up the bank. Fearing that James Cessna would disapprove of trading a horse for a four-wheeled contraption that couldn't cross a shallow stream, Clyde consented to keep the automobile at his house for the night.

Roy and Clyde were surprised the next day when their father did not express much disapproval over Roy's purchase. However, it was plain that the 'buckboard' wasn't very practical for the sandy soil that comprised much of Roy's land.

In 1907, Clyde bought a Reo automobile with eight horsepower.

It served the growing Cessna family well, as son Eldon Wayne was born that year. Clyde's experiences with cars ignited an interest in learning more about these new contrivances. He became acquainted with the Overland car dealer in Harper and became a very successful salesman in the Harper/Kingman area. By 1908 a lack of working capital and troublesome accounts forced the dealership to close. Clyde then went to Enid, Oklahoma that year and became a partner with Oscar J. Watson in another Overland dealership.[1]

Cessna was manager of the Enid Overland agency and by 1910 new Clark roadsters were also being sold. Clyde was so successful that in his first year he reportedly sold over 100 new automobiles. Soon he was general manager, and the agency's storefront

Interior view of the Lovelace-Thomas Aeroplane and Motor Works, St. George Park, New York City. By late 1910, it was known as the Queen Aeroplane Company, building American copies of the French Bleriot Type XI. Cessna went to the Queen factory in February, 1911, to learn all he could about airplanes and how to fly them, his experiences there culminating in the purchase of "Silverwing". (Wichita Chamber of Commerce)

sign was repainted to declare his success.

The Cessna Automobile Company continued to sell cars and make a profit. Clyde liked his work. Selling automobiles was an interesting vocation, but he had also become interested in flying machines.

Airplanes and aviation were not entirely new subjects to Clyde. He knew about Louis Bleriot's epic crossing of the English Channel on July 25, 1909; a flight that was made in a monoplane. Roy Cessna remembered that his younger brother was fired with enthusiasm after reading about the flight, and wanted to start construction of such an airplane.[2]

The elder Cessna reminded Clyde that it would be necessary to learn how to fly first--then a machine could be built. Clyde continued to nourish his interest in aviation. He believed the monoplane configuration was the only sensible design for an airplane.

When Cessna read of an upcoming aerial exhibition at Oklahoma City featuring monoplanes, he had to be there. It was a rare opportunity to see such craft, and Cessna was even more interested when he learned that three Frenchmen would be making ascents in Bleriot machines.

The trio were members of flyer John B. Moisant's International Aviators, a group of airmen who banded together in late 1910 for the purpose of flying exhibitions. Moisant was an American pilot who had learned to fly at Pau, France. A highly respected airman, he was killed in a flying accident in New Orleans on December 31, 1910, less than two months after forming the exhibition team.

The Oklahoma City air meet was held January 14-18, 1911. Pilots Roland Garros, Rene Simon and Rene Barrier performed, along with American Charles Hamilton in a biplane. Garros' Bleriot machine electrified the crowd with a 12 minute flight, circling the field while climbing his ship.

The Queen airplanes were well-built machines, although simplified in construction from their European counterparts. Three engines were offered; the Indian and Gnome rotaries of 50 hp and the three-cylinder Anzani of 30 hp. Earle Ovington, one of America's earliest pilots, flew an Indian-powered Queen monoplane similar to the one shown here. (Smithsonian Institution Photo #A18473H)

Simon and Barrier also made successful flights. Cessna was very impressed by the monoplane's maneuverability. Although the first Oklahoma City Air Tournament drew nearly 25,000 people, only $5000 in gate receipts made the event a financial loss for the International Aviators.[3]

While at the airmeet, Cessna sought out the Frenchmen and inquired about purchasing a Type XI. It was during this discussion he may have learned about the Queen Aeroplane Company of New York City.

Located at St. George Park, 197th Street and Amsterdam Avenue, the Queen company was one of the first American firms to build a copy of the Bleriot Type XI. Willis McCornick, a successful stockbroker and aviation enthusiast, founded the company in the fall of 1910.

The factory and its flying field had been property of the Lovelace-Thomas Aeroplane and Motor Works, which McCornick had acquired. Buildings were actually remnants of an amusement park, with the skating rink building utilized for primary assembly and other units housing woodworking and machine shops.

Queen was not alone in reproducing the Type XI design. The American Aeroplane Supply House also sold Bleriot parts and built a few full-scale machines, some of the two-seat XI-2 configuration.

The Queen airplanes were not license-built, but simply copies of the Type XI. Enterprising American businessmen saw a saleable product in the Bleriot. It was far cheaper to build a good replica than pay the high cost of obtaining a license from the French manufacturer.[4]

Although the Queen product was altered by modifications to the landing gear and rudder and featured simplified construction in certain areas, the New York airplane was a faithful reproduction of the little monoplane.

At least one Oklahoman tried his hand at building a Bleriot copy in March, 1911. M. S. Blackburn, of Chickasha, built what was reported to be a Type XI airplane that he called the "Albatross". An 'expert' aviator was to come and fly the ship before the Oklahoma Press Association but the flight was apparently never made.

BLERIOT TYPE XI

A classic view of the very popular as well as highly influential Bleriot Type XI. Louis Bleriot's flight across the English Channel in July, 1909, electrified the world and made the Type XI famous overnight. (Smithsonian Institution Photo #72-7963)

The name Bleriot is forever associated with the 1909 crossing of the English Channel. But Louis Bleriot also manufactured the most popular monoplane in the world between 1909 and 1912; the Type XI "Dragonfly" that was the basis for Clyde Cessna's "Silverwing".

Bleriot's first company built acetylene headlamps for automobiles, but he began aerial experiments with model ornithopters in 1901-1902. By 1908 his new company, founded to produce airplanes, had built several different designs of aircraft.

The Type XI monoplane made its debut at the Paris Automobile Salon in December, 1908. A small ship powered by a 30 hp, three-cylinder, fan-type Anzani engine, it first flew on January 23, 1909. In July of that year, Louis Bleriot piloted a Type XI across the English Channel, the first aeronaut to do so. His 23-mile trip thrilled millions of people. Only the Wright Brother's first flight eclipsed its importance. Louis Bleriot and the Type Onze had achieved a milestone in aeronautical history.

The little monoplane was extremely well known both in Europe and abroad by 1911. Rodman Wanamaker, whose department store in Philadelphia was a marvel to many, purchased a Type XI during the summer of 1909. He brought it to America in November and displayed it for all to see.

Many American aviators flew Type XIs. J. Armstrong Drexel and John B. Moisant, Harriet Quimby and Earle Ovington flew the type for exhibition work. Construction plans were drawn up and printed in various publications. Some examples were built strictly in an attempt to copy the monoplane's basic design.

French Type XIs could be purchased with the Anzani static radial or the Gnome rotary, the latter producing 50-70 hp. The Gnome-powered versions were popular because of the extra power and performance benefits.

The airplane bought by Clyde V. Cessna in New York City was a faithful American copy of the famous cross-channel airplane. But by 1911 the French versions had made some changes their Yankee counterparts did not share. Chief among these was the revised elevator structure. The older, fixed horizontal stabilizer with outboard pivoting elevators were on the Cessna machine, but not factory-produced ships, which had both a stabilizer and full-span elevator of conventional design. The rudder shape of the American copies made in New York City was also different, having a more rounded appearance. Cessna's airplane had this rudder.

Landing gear on the monoplanes made by the Queen Aeroplane Company also differed slightly in configuration. The pilot's cockpit control column did not have the French-type cloche (dome-shaped attaching point) over the control cable mechanisms for wing warping and elevator movement. Instead, Queen airplanes featured a simple bracket that performed the same function. Warping and elevator cables were routed to the bracket and attached to mounting points, permitting roll and pitch control in one mechanism. The Bleriot-copy bought by Cessna still retained the dual bipod support above the wing for attachment of flying and landing wires, but French machines resorted to a single pylon to anchor these cables by 1911. Still another feature of Cessna's "Silverwing" was the dual tail skid. French craft used a tailwheel initially but by 1910 they utilized a simple brace that greatly reduced the landing rollout.

1913 saw the Type XI fading from the scene. It was obsolete. But it was also famous. Today it is remembered as a classic aircraft of the pre-World War One era, and the airplane that taught Clyde Cessna to fly.

Clyde Cessna was determined to own and fly his own Bleriot. After returning from the Oklahoma City air meet, Cessna gathered his hard-earned savings and departed Enid for New York City in early February. Upon arrival, he made it clear to Queen officials that he wanted to learn all he could about flying machines.

For three weeks Clyde worked on the monoplane assembly lines, absorbing all he could about airplane construction; a subject he knew virtually nothing about. But he also spent time in the air. That was his primary goal...to fly.

Cessna flew with experienced pilots while at the Queen factory, with some flights lasting over a mile. He did not make any solo flights, but he did purchase an airplane. After inspecting and flying in several types of monoplanes, Clyde selected a special machine that was being custom-built for John B.

This closeup view of a Queen monoplane shows landing gear and engine details, especially the Bleriot-style bedstead frame that served as a support for the Gnome rotary and mounting point for wing brace wires. The original "Silverwing" also featured this design. (Smithsonian Institution Photo #85-905)

Moisant prior to his death.[5] Work had nearly stopped on the ship after Moisant's crash. Following considerable deliberation and negotiations with Queen officials, Cessna bought the airplane.

At least three or four potential buyers had tried to purchase the same aircraft. The ship incorporated unspecified changes to the standard Queen model, and was said by Cessna to be "the finest aeroplane of its type in America and the most powerful". The craft's name was "Silverwing."

Cessna also gave some details of this airplane in further correspondence with the Enid Eagle. Here are his comments:

"The cloth material used in the construction of the wings is a light silver sheen of silk and very strong. It is expensive, costing $2.75 per yard. The wings of the monoplane are 26 by 7 feet and the length of the fuselage is 30 feet."

Dimension details of the first airplane owned by Cessna were not certain before this description was obtained. The wingspan and chord of the airfoil and the length of the fuselage indicate that "Silverwing" was slightly altered from the standard Queen specifications given here:

1911 Queen Monoplane Dimensions
Wingspan: 26.9 feet
Length: Approximately 30 feet

Clyde also told the paper that two people could be carried in the machine if weight and balance changes were made, but that it was originally designed as a single-seat model (it was definitely not a Model XI-2, a two-seat version of the Model XI).[6]

Power for the airplane was to be an 80 hp, eight-cylinder, V-type inline, but the engine would not be ready for installation until a later date.[7] Cessna felt it was necessary to go to New York City for an airplane; "I went there for the experience", he said. After one of his flights, Cessna commented that he found flying so exhilarating he was moved to pen this poem:

"The Bleriot of Cessna is made in old New York,
It's 80 horsepower motor of no equal could we talk;
The wings of solid silver,
The tail made of gold,
A noise that sounds like thunder,
A speed that can't be told;
Above the clouds and under,
It tears the air asunder,
Just see it coming yonder,
Ah, Look it is a wonder."

On February 21, 1911, Cessna had the monoplane specially crated and shipped from the Queen factory to Enid. He paid $7,500 for the ship, including the engine.

The people of Enid were very anxious to see this aerial contrivance fly. Public interest ran high, and many citizens followed the progress of Cessna's trip back east very closely. Fred E. Botkin, Clyde's sales manager at the agency, was kept busy fueling anticipation of the airplane's arrival.

Before Cessna left for New York City, Botkin had reportedly signed an agreement to act as pilot of the monoplane for one year. He had been studying the problems of flight and engines with diligence in preparation for piloting his new mount.

Although Botkin had absolutely no experience with airplanes, he was very confident that his 11 years of driving automobiles would overcome any problems with flying the Bleriot (Botkin's ignorance toward the complexities of flying machines, in particular the whims of the Model XI, clearly indicate the naivete' of many would-be aviators of the era). He foresaw little difficulty in learning to fly, since the airplane seemingly demanded little more attention than the auto regarding control functions.

The Enid Eagle quickly pointed out the possibilities of car versus airplane races as soon as Botkin could handle the airplane, but the most exciting prospect was just seeing the machine. It was the talk of the town.

Cessna and Botkin had planned a way to get the Bleriot before the citizenry. The upcoming Garfield County stock show was the ideal event for such a purpose. Starting in early March, the annual exhibition drew thousands of people from Enid and the many outlying communities.

On February 20th, Botkin announced that an agreement had been reached between himself, representing Cessna, and the Chamber of Commerce for flights to be made by Botkin at the stock show. The Chamber of Commerce was very pleased to have such a calling card for their city's premier occasion, and March 5th was set as the date for the first flight.[8]

With the Bleriot enroute to Enid, Cessna entrained at New York City and settled down for the long trip home. He was confident of his purchase. "Silverwing" was the finest flying machine of its type.

The 31 year-old car salesman from Oklahoma was optimistic about his future. He had already made a highly successful transition from horse and buggy to the horseless carriage, but now all roads led to the clouds.

---

[1] Oscar J. Watson saw a good salesman in Clyde Cessna, the two men establishing the "Watson and Cessna" Overland dealership in Enid by 1908. Watson's name is still associated with truck body sales and service in Wichita as of 1984. He ran a profitable automobile agency in the prairie city during the 1920s.

[2] A story that still persists to this day, but cannot be substantiated, says that Clyde and Roy asked their father to fell one of the big cottonwood trees surrounding the homestead house, assuring him that only the first 10 feet of the tree would be needed to build an airplane and he could have the rest. No evidence exists to indicate that an airplane was ever built.

[3] Despite the large crowds, a total of only $6,500 was collected, and one day of the show was lost due to bad weather. The International Aviators said they lost nearly $7,000 attending the meet. The contract between the local committees and the aviators was declared void, with the flyers receiving about $5,000.

[4] Bleriot had set up channels for interested foreigners to license-build the Type XI, but the cost was so high that most of them simply built a copy of the airplane, including many backyard enthusiasts, who got plans for the airplane through aeronautical magazines.

[5] John B. Moisant was killed while flying a Bleriot Type XI at New Orleans. He was making a preliminary flight on the morning of December 31, 1910, in preparation for the Michelin Cup race. Winds blowing at 15 mph caused the ship to crash while he was attempting to land, hurling Moisant out of the craft. His neck was broken when he hit the ground, causing a quick death.

[6] The Bleriot Model XI-2 was specifically designed to carry two people aloft, but the Cessna machine was strictly a single-seat type. Only the fact that its V-type, inline engine was supposed to produce 80 hp led Clyde to believe it could carry more than one person. Perhaps with modifications, this may have been possible, but the engine did not live up to expectations nor did the airframe ever undergo any changes to accomodate two people.

[7] Had Cessna been aware of the trouble he would soon encounter with the powerplant, he may have elected to install the Indian or Gnome rotary engine, both of which were available from the Queen company.

[8] Enid's Chamber of Commerce was anxious to have an unusual drawing card for their exposition, and "Silverwing" fit the bill perfectly. Of course, the hoped-for flights, designed to promote the show, never materialized and the local officials soon lost interest in a flying machine that stayed on the ground.

CHAPTER TWO
On The Salt Plains

Clyde Cessna was a celebrity. No sooner did his feet touch Oklahoma soil before the Enid press surrounded him. It was February 25, 1911. The long journey from New York City had tired Clyde, but he answered questions about his new airplane to satisfy reporters.

For the next few days, all he could talk about was flying the Queen monoplane. Botkin, too, queried him about its every detail. People on the street wanted to know when it would arrive, when flights would be made. But time was against Cessna and Botkin.

Both men knew March 5th had been stated as the day a flight would be made. They completed plans to display the machine at the stock show. Advertisements were printed in the Daily Eagle urging people to come see the flying machine.

On Tuesday, February 28th, "Silverwing" arrived in a special freight car. It was carefully unloaded and whisked away to a large exhibition tent at the show grounds. By March 2nd Cessna and Botkin were busy assembling the airplane.[1]

The V-type engine was not included in the ship-

"Silverwing", now sporting the four-cylinder Elbridge "Aero Special", rests at Cherokee, Oklahoma. Brace wires attached to front spar limited wing deflection in flight, while smaller cables controlled wing warping and were attached to a bellcrank that pivoted on kingpost under fuselage. Note dual tailskids. (Bob Pickett Collection/Cessna Aircraft Company)

ment, but was due to arrive any day. A mechanic was to accompany the powerplant all the way from New York City. His orders were to help with details of installation and adjustment before returning east.

With the stock show in full swing, Cessna opened his tent to spectators. Flanking the Queen monoplane were two Clark "30" roadsters from Cessna's dealership. Like the airplane, the torpedo-type Clarks were exciting vehicles. They represented the latest in driving technology. With such attractions in hand, Clyde's tent was crowded, despite a small admission fee.[2]

On March 5th, Clyde fought off flurries of questions as to when he would fly the monoplane, assurring his peers that an ascension would be attempted as soon as the engine arrived and was installed in the silver and gold airplane.

A 'flight' and an 'ascension' were far from being the same. Cessna knew he couldn't make a true flight, defined (in 1911) as a takeoff, traverse of the ground for some miles with one or more turns followed by a successful landing at the takeoff point.

But he could make an ascension; meaning a takeoff, very brief period of flight and a landing; all straight ahead, no turns. The reason Clyde Cessna could not make a true flight was simple: he didn't know how to fly. He had received some basic instruction in handling the Bleriot-type controls, but his personal flying experience was extremely

limited.[3]

However, nothing could happen until the engine arrived, yet, "Silverwing" continued to be the exhibit's center of attraction. Clyde spent hours every day answering questions about the ship. How fast will it go? Is it hard to be an aviator? Are airplanes really safe? Patiently, and with respect for their inquiries, Cessna satisfied each person's curiosity.

The fee was revoked on March 8th, probably at the request of the Enid Chamber of Commerce. They feared the charge would inhibit attendance at the stock show, so Cessna complied with their wishes. He could not, however, comply with the relentless desire for flights voiced by the people.

At the close of the stock show in mid-March, the monoplane was still without an engine. The daily flights that had been advertised during the show never occurred.

In late March or early April, the engine arrived...without a mechanic. It was taken to the Cessna home at 520 South Buchanan where test runs commenced. By April 16th Cessna was having little success making the engine behave. It was, according to the Daily Eagle, "out of adjustment".

And Cessna was almost out of patience. To make matters worse, neighbors didn't appreciate the sudden increase in the community's noise level. For days Clyde grappled with the recalcitrant apparatus, sometimes working long into the night with very little success.[4]

Louise Beerbower, 10 years old in April, 1911, lived two houses from the Cessnas. She remembers the engine's staccato roar very well. It kept her awake many nights and also caused problems for her friend, Mary Bass. Miss Bass, who took music lessons across the street, often found her virtuoso sounds competing with the cacophony of an airplane powerplant.

Slowly, however, Clyde made progress. He worked on the engine until it finally ran and then installed it on "Silverwing," although it still refused to produce full power. It ran rough and vibrated terribly. To make matters worse, when the propeller finally arrived in mid-April, it was damaged in the crate. Cessna immediately shipped it back to New York City for replacement.

One problem after another delayed any flying attempts. The newspaper lamented along with Cessna. Enid's population read all about the engine trouble. It was the chief reason Cessna could not fly his "great cloud piercer".[5]

About April 20th, an alternate powerplant was considered. With it, Cessna could at least get airborne. He was acquainted with W. D. Lindsley of Waynoka, Oklahoma, who was also struggling to get airborne. His biplane was already on the Salt Plains, being prepared for trial flights.[6] Cessna bought a four-cylinder, two-stroke, Elbridge "Aero Special" from Lindsley that month, but the 8-cylinder engine would suffice for the initial flights of "Silverwing". Lindsley, who was having his own share of trouble with engines, found a sympathetic ear in Clyde Cessna. The two men planned to make flights together, supporting each other's efforts.

On May 12th Clyde packed up the family and moved to the Great Salt Plains. "Silverwing" was disassembled and carefully crated, then loaded aboard a freight car for shipment to Jet, Oklahoma, a small town five miles southeast of the Plains. Prior to departing Enid, Cessna had made out his last will and testament. Botkin, who had been so enthusiastic about aviating, was not among the group to depart. He apparently changed his mind about flying and disappeared from the scene.

The Cessna clan soon set up camp on the southeastern edge of the flats, in an area that became known as "Aviation Heights" to the people of Jet.

The Salt Plains were both a blessing and a curse to would-be aviators. A vast expanse of flat, arid land, the Plains were beneficial since there were no obstructions to hinder maneuvering while airborne, but the sun reflecting off the surface made it very difficult to judge altitude. Later, Clyde would admit it was the wrong place to fly, but under the circumstances of the time it seemed the only logical choice.

In early May, after a new propeller had been received and installed on the V-type engine, the Cessnas were ready to try their wings. They made successful flights of very short duration, attaining only a few feet of altitude. The engine continued to give trouble. Cessna, in discussing his tribulations with the press, blamed the lack of horsepower as the culprit; it produced only 30 hp, he said, not 80 hp as was claimed.[7]

During mid-May, "Silverwing" was grounded for an engine change. Clyde and Roy worked out the details for installing the Elbridge powerplant in the Queen airframe. Wooden beams served as mounts.

The V-type engine was removed and reportedly installed in Lindsley's homebuilt biplane. His machine had barely attained more than a few feet of altitude in early flights, and caused its designer/pilot untold frustration. With 8-cylinders for power, it was hoped the biplane would finally perform, but on a test hop in mid-May, the engine blew up.

Clyde traveled to St. Louis to obtain new parts that he believed would breathe new life into the troublesome powerplant. However, the parts

Closeup of "Silverwing" powerplant installation shows wooden engine bearers (visible below propeller), bedstead frame, landing gear springs and handmade propeller crafted by Roy and Clyde Cessna. Wing warping bellcrank is also visible at bottom of kingpost tubing. Engine coolant radiator can be seen immediately above rear cylinders. (Bob Pickett Collection/Cessna Aircraft Company)

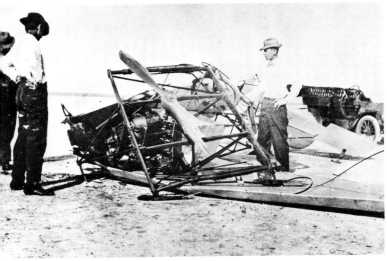

Crackup! "Silverwing" after it smashed into the salt flats on Wednesday, September 13, 1911. While the airplane was virtually destroyed, Cessna escaped without serious injury. The monoplane sustained heavy damage to its forward structure, but the aft fuselage and empennage were salvaged and later used to rebuild the ship. Behind the man on the right is a wooden ground stake with a rope tied to the airplane. This was necessary to keep the wreckage from being blown across the salt flats by gusty winds. (Bob Pickett Collection/Cessna Aircraft Company)

apparently did nothing to improve performance. Realizing that the engine was an expensive failure, Clyde abandoned it. Lindsley's ship, dubbed the "Waynoka Awfulplane" by the papers, was placed in storage after the engine incident and its owner faded into oblivion by 1912.

With the Elbridge engine installed, the brothers accomplished more short flights. The water-cooled inline overheated very easily. Once the engine was started, the pilot took off without delay.

The overheating problem was primarily caused by poor airflow through the small heat exchanger. It was mounted aft of the engine. Ram flow was minimal in flight...almost non-existant on the ground. "Silverwing" had a maximum airspeed of approximately 60-65 kph (40-45 mph), and while this speed was adequate it did not provide generous airflow to cool the water. Since full power was necessary to fly safely, cylinder head temperatures were always very high, taxing the coolant severely.

Day after day Cessna flew except when the ubiquitous winds kept him on the ground. The monoplane couldn't be safely flown if winds exceeded 15 mph. Clyde was forced to select early morning and late evening to make his ascensions.[8]

Journeys of 1/4 mile at 50 feet altitude were soon achieved. Partial turns, with very shallow bank angles, came next. Strictly trial and error methods were employed up to this point, as Clyde Cessna had no books, no tutors, and no training on how to fly an airplane. Only the brief trips made with aviators in New York City had provided him with any knowledge of controlled, heavier-than-air flight.[9]

In a letter written to selected businessmen of Enid and the Commerical Club of Cherokee, Oklahoma, Clyde invited the group out to witness his first public, sustained aerial attempt. He told the newspapers that anyone else could also attend if they desired. Cessna remarked that the engine problems

seemed to be solved, with the Elbridge performing satisfactorily.

June 18, 1911 was the big day. The invited groups came, as did some citizens from Enid and Jet. Conditions were safe for the flight. Clyde manned the cockpit, Roy started the engine. The monoplane's nose pointed into the gentle wind. With throttle fully advanced, the Elbridge roared and Roy released the ship.

Slowly the machine gained momentum. Then it was free and flying. Suddenly, without warning, the airplane dipped and struck the ground. The engine stopped immediately. No crash ensued, but the propeller was badly smashed from its impact with the flats.

With regret Clyde advised the crowd that no further attempts would be made that day. "Silverwing" was wheeled back to the camp while Clyde returned to Enid. A new propeller was expensive. Lacking cash, he sought help from Carl Evans of Wichita.

Evans and Cessna were friends and both sold cars. The two men had met when Cessna went to Wichita to pick up Overland automobiles. Occasionally, Evans journeyed to Enid on sales trips. After discussing Cessna's need, Carl approached his employer, J.J. Jones. They agreed that Cessna should have his propeller and provided the $65 required.

The brothers, by June of 1911, were in poor financial condition. Clyde labored long hours on his airplane, but spent very little time at the automobile agency. Expenses quickly mounted; shipping costs, fuel and oil, a new engine, parts for the original powerplant, transportation costs, not to mention money required to care for his family. On top of all this came the inevitable mishaps. Crackups, that's what Clyde called them. Crackups cost money.

Late in June the Cessnas experienced another, more serious crash. According to Clyde, he was flying "Silverwing" at an altitude of about 60 feet. An updraft of wind caused the machine to climb rapidly. The pilot retarded throttle, thinking the ship would quickly regain level flight.

Instead, the Elbridge stopped cold. Without power and with airspeed decreasing, lateral control vanished. The right wing dropped. Cessna pushed the control column forward and applied full left warp with no effect. His ship essentially out of control, all Clyde could think about was the right wing; wings were hard to build. Wings cost a lot of money. Fortunately, the landing gear struck the ground first, damaging it but saving the precious right wing panel. The propeller was also spared and Cessna was unhurt.

The propeller had been made by the brothers themselves. They had decided to produce their own after realizing how often they might break one. Both men had woodworking tools at their disposal and the craftmanship to do the job.

Although Clyde Cessna had not made a public flight by June 30, 1911, he and Roy were confident that the time had come to do so. Their flying wasn't perfect, but Clyde could get the machine off the ground, make very shallow turns and land again.

They wrote to Enid City Railway Manager Clarence Kline, offering to fly at Lakewood Park on the Fourth of July. Kline accepted. The brothers arrived in Enid on July 3rd to evaluate the proposed flying field.

Upon inspection, Lakewood Park was deemed un-

THE ELBRIDGE "AERO SPECIAL"

The Elbridge Engine Company of Rochester, New York, was well known for its reliable marine powerplants by 1908. In 1910 it offered a series of two-stroke, lightweight, inline-type engines suitable for aircraft use. The company took aeronautics seriously. Officials attended many air meets and trial flights. Two airplanes were used by Elbridge for experimental work. They also conducted tests of propellers, fuel, lubricants and heat dissipation. Their products were well received by pilots.

The first of these 'Featherweight' designs featured three cylinders, 30-45 hp and weighed only 68 kg (150 pounds). In 1911 a modified four-cylinder version called the "Aero Special" was introduced. Producing up to 60 hp, it was advertised as weighing less than 68 kg (150 pounds) without magneto.

Company dynamometer runs showed the engine developed 57.8 net bhp (brake horsepower) at 1500 rpm, with 40 bhp available at 1050 rpm. The engine was capable of 2000 rpm; very high revolutions for 1911. To absorb this power a propeller with at least a 75 inch diameter was required.

Construction of the "Aero Special" was typical for the era. Crankcase of aluminum, cylinders of combined steel and grey iron, a forged steel crankshaft and die-forged steel connecting rods riding in bronze bearings. Water jackets were of brass. The crankshaft/connecting rod bearings were splash lubricated.

To accomodate either a tractor or pusher configuration, Elbridge designed the engine with propeller thrust bearings at each end of the crankshaft. High-tension ignition was used, with the magneto mounting plate cast integral with the crankcase.

Improved intake and coolant manifolds were welcome features of the 1911 model. Elbridge advertised the "Aero Special" as being able to sustain 40 bhp for at least 8 hours.

On "Silverwing", Cessna bolted the engine to wooden mounting frames, supported at the front by a bedstead crossmember. A small, heat-resistant pad was placed against the forward cylinder. It acted as a anti-chafe guard for brace wires.

Fuel from the small tank was gravity-fed to the carburetor, and then via curved intake manifolds to the four cylinders. No intake valves were used. The fuel/air mixture was drawn in by the descending piston, then compressed and ignited on the next stroke. Every stroke produced intake, compression, power and exhaust events.

Top end lubrication was by fuel/oil mix; one pint of oil for five gallons of fuel. An inherent drawback of the two-stroke design was poor scavenging. On each stroke when the piston descended, exhaust gases were expelled through small openings to atmosphere. The incoming mixture was often contaminated by remaining gases, reducing its combustability.

The single carburetor on the "Aero Special" featured a conventional throttle valve design. A mechanically-operated control was mounted in the cockpit and connected to the carburetor for adjusting power. Cessna was very careful when increasing or decreasing power; full throttle was applied slowly to avoid overloading the engine with fuel, while retarding the throttle required the same care to preclude stalling.

Flying behind a two-stroke powerplant was a dirty affair. Some unburned fuel always escaped with exhaust gases. This combination was blown back on the pilot, soiling his face and clothes. Goggles were a must. Oil leaks caused further uncleanliness. Exhaust noise was nearly unbearable at full power. Cessna, along with many of his contemporaries, experienced some hearing impairment from exposure to such damaging decibel levels.

The "Aero Special" served Clyde Cessna well for nearly 2 1/2 years, but in 1914, a six-cylinder Anzani static radial replaced the obsolete Elbridge.

The Elbridge "Aero Special" was designed for aeronautical applications, producing up to 60 hp at 2,000 rpm. Gearing on rear of the engine turned the water pump and magneto. Exhaust gases escaped through openings above the intake manifold. Device below rear cylinder was a hand-filled oil reservoir for lubricating the crankshaft. Four more reservoirs were located on the right side of the crankcase for lubrication of the main bearings. Water jackets surround top portion of each cylinder. Elbridge designed the Aero Special for use with either tractor or pusher aircraft configurations. (NASM and Smithsonian Institute Photo)

SPECIFICATIONS - ELBRIDGE "AERO SPECIAL"

Type: Inline, four-cylinder
Bore and Stroke: 4 5/8 x 4 1/2 inches
Horsepower: 40-45 bhp at 1050 rpm
Weight: 150 pounds without magneto

satisfactory because of its rough surface, so a ravine to the west was selected for the flight. Reporters queried "the Cessna boys", as they were known, about the exhibition and what it was like to fly.

Clyde, who did virtually all of the public relations work, told the press that the Bleriot-type monoplane was more difficult to handle than a Wright or Curtiss machine. He said the monoplane was "showier, worth more to see than any of the biplanes." He referred to biplane pilots as "amateurs", saying that the slower-flying machines made it easier to control them.

When asked how he liked flying, Clyde said he would "enjoy it after I get it learned," indicating just how much of a struggle Cessna was having in mastering "Silverwing." He had often mentioned the sensitivity of the pitch and yaw controls, especially the elevator. "The machine is very sensitive to any movement of the steering apparatus", Cessna said. "In going up," he continued, "if one tips the machine a little too much he will be caught by the wind and he can't stop going up; that's what happened to me."..."If the engine stops for any reason, you are due to tumble, and that's all there is to it.

One reporter asked Cessna when he was in the most danger. He replied, "Oh, at the start; when you are getting off the ground." "You see, when you are well up in the air and get started away, if anything happens you can glide; but when her nose is pointed up, and you have not got speed, nor your equilibrium established, if anything happens you can't get her pointed down; there is no chance for that and so it's a fall." Concluding the interview, Cessna told reporters, "If she goes right this time, we are off for good."

Words of a true aviator. Words chosen from bone-jarring crashes and feelings of helplessness in the air. Words of a man who flew monoplanes.

In addition to the proposed flight, Roy and Clyde planned to set up a tent housing damaged parts of the airplane. They would explain how each piece was broken, going into as much detail as the listener desired. There was no charge for the explanations, but a fifty cent fee would be required for admission to see the Enid aviator fly.

The Fourth of July celebration promised to be an exciting time for everyone. Great anticipation of Cessna's flight seemed to all but secure a large attendance. With manager Kline's men stationed at the gates to the field, the boys felt certain that people would come out to see them fly.

They were wrong. As time approached for takeoff, only $40 in receipts had been collected. Many people remained outside the area, jeering and laughing at Clyde and Roy. They joked about businessmen who were foolhardy enough to support the Cessnas.

The brothers had made it clear that they were sincere in their desire to fly before the public. Kline's men held all the money at the gates, and a full refund was guaranteed by Cessna if no flight could be made. Yet, the people showed little faith in the brothers' claim that they were aviators. $40 was simply insufficient inducement to risk a flight. They refused to fly.

"I don't want to talk about it," said Clyde the next morning. He was very disappointed about the whole matter. To him, such an investment of thousands of dollars plus the months of training should have meant something to the public.

Later that day, Cessna was more receptive to reporters. He told them, "We will go right on. But there is nothing in flying that justifies a flight unless we get the money back that we have spent." He was right. While the Cessnas needed money, they had no choice but to continue their flying. Clyde had divested himself of his Overland/Clark dealership, and in his own words, had "burned all bridges behind me". It was airplanes and aviating or nothing at all.[10]

For the City of Enid, the Fourth of July had yielded profits. While the two flyers went home with empty pockets, city officials had sold over 360 cases of soda pop and more than 300 gallons of lemonade.

Clyde Cessna continued to fly on the Salt Plains. He flew farther and higher than ever before. Every week brought more confidence in himself and his machine. Roy Cessna, while in the background compared to his brother, was a critical cog in the wheel of fortune.

Roy often made the propellers, plus he made suggestions for numerous improvements to the engine and airframe adopted by Clyde. He was good with mathematics and also possessed mechanical skills. Europa Cessna supported Clyde's aeronautical efforts throughout the tough months on the Plains.

The brothers' activities attracted others to the flats. During August, A. C. Beech, already an accomplished aviator, was in the Cessna camp. He made numerous flights in "Silverwing" with little problem, being familiar with the Bleriot-type monoplanes from earlier flying experience.[11]

Also there was Herman Dvry, from Tulsa, Oklahoma, who was said to be the first Oklahoman to build and fly an airplane. Like Clyde, he had great foresight when it came to the future of aviation. Dvry envisoned a flight school and airplane factory on the Salt Plains, and was formulating plans to build such facilities by late 1911. The plans were never carried out.

Clyde Cessna made a two mile flight on Thursday, August 17th, that impressed his fellow airmen. Flying at 50 feet altitude, Cessna handled the ship with skill. A new propeller had been fitted to the Elbridge engine. It improved performance, and Clyde believed the time had again come to attempt a public exhibition.

With optimism for the future, the Cessnas, A.C. Beech and possibly Dvry formed the Cosmopolitan Aviators in August, 1911. They planned to fly as many county fairs, picnics and holiday celebrations as possible.

Their first engagement was at Cherokee, Oklahoma, on Saturday, August 19th. Clyde and Roy Cessna shipped their monoplane from Enid to Cherokee, assembling it and testing the engine. They were ready. The stands were filled with spectators, paying spectators. Things were looking up at last.

Mr. Beech was to fly the airplane. As Roy worked to start the two-stroke Elbridge, he tripped over a wire and fell into the wing cables, injuring himself. Clyde got the engine running.

Beech, perhaps in his haste to be airborne before the coolant overheated, fell from the cockpit and was hurt. He couldn't fly. So it was left to Clyde to take the ship up. He eased the engine to full power, his assistants released the airplane and "Silverwing" was rolling. After takeoff, however, the craft flew only 100-150 yards before making a hard landing.

Cessna later said that the presence of telephone

wires directly in his flight path caused him to land. The wires could have been avoided, but that would have meant making a turn close to the ground, and Cessna wanted no part of that risky maneuver.

The landing gear was damaged when Cessna set the ship down, one wheel being sprung from the impact. No further attempts to fly could be made that day. Disappointed, people emptied the stands, murmuring to each other about pilots who couldn't fly and airplanes that broke so easily. Spectators weren't the only ones upset.

Disgruntled officials from the towns of Alva and Carmen, who were at Cherokee to see Cessna fly, were very hesitant to discuss contracts for flights after seeing another failed exhibition. Just when success was in their grasp, the Cessna boys couldn't hold on.

Facts stared Roy and Clyde in the face; they were still neophyte flyers. They needed more practice. Clyde began making flights with complete 180 degree turns and attained higher altitudes than before. Finally, he was certain that it was time to hit the show circuit and leave the flats behind.

To demonstrate his confidence, he invited the citizens of Enid and Jet to the Cessna camp to see him fly. On September 10th, before more than 1,000 observers, Clyde V. Cessna attempted a flight but the wind now conspired against him, gusting too much for a safe ascension. Then the Elbridge engine rebelled, refusing to run smoothly.

By early evening the winds had abated and the engine was successfully adjusted. Cessna flew three short flights at no charge to the few hundred people who remained to witness the event. Although he hadn't made a long flight, he did make a good showing and received congratulations and applause for his efforts.

Clyde and Roy were riding the crest of a wave. They were flying higher and further than ever before, their monoplane was behaving well, the engine was reliable for up to three mile trips...and most impor-

tantly, controlled turns were being made.

Then came Wednesday, September 13, 1911. Weather was good for aviating, and Clyde was out early making short hops in "Silverwing." Today, he would attempt a three-mile odyssey, including a course reversal at the 1 1/2 mile point. The wind increased as the day wore on, but Cessna believed he could handle the airplane safely.

Takeoff was uneventful. Clyde's hand guided the control column as the ship climbed. He made quick, direct warp inputs as soon as the wind tried to lift a wing. The engine roared along at nearly 2000 rpm, leaving a trail of smoke behind. Wind gusts jolted the craft, but the pilot flew steadily on, concerned only about the upcoming turn.

At the mile and a half point, warp was applied carefully to enter a right turn. Lazily the ship came around, answering the command of its master. Suddenly, Cessna had a problem; the right wing was warped down too much. Without warning the nose started dropping. Bank angle increased rapidly.

Clyde gave the left wing full down warp. He confirmed full throttle, but nothing helped. Roll rate accelerated as the wind lifted the left wing. The ground was coming up fast.

"Silverwing" passed through 90 degrees of bank, continuing toward an inverted attitude. Cessna could think of nothing but survival. He waited until the last

Clyde Cessna piloting the rebuilt "Silverwing", April 14, 1912, from the Val Johnson Farm south of Enid, Oklahoma. The new landing gear design eliminated the bedstead frame and incorporated a transverse wooden beam for shock absorption. Cessna retained the four-cylinder Elbridge engine and made modifications to it that increased horsepower. It was in this airplane that Clyde Cessna made his first, known successful flight. He took off from Val Johnson's farm on December 17, 1911, made a seven mile flight and landed in the same field without damage to his ship or injury to himself. (Bob Pickett Collection/Cessna Aircraft Company)

second, leaping from the cockpit into space.

The airplane smashed into the flats on its back. Wood cracked, fabric ripped, cables snapped and the Elbridge was silenced. It was all over in a few seconds. Man and machine lay still on the Salt Plains, one injured, the other destroyed.

Clyde slowly picked himself up. Dazed and in great pain, he moved lethargically toward his machine, gazing upon the wreckage, glad to be alive. It wasn't just the loss of an expensive airplane, but the loss of nearly $4,000 in booked exhibitions that hurt the most.

Clyde was hopitalized and his injuries diagnosed. He wouldn't be flying airplanes for a month or more, the doctors said.

"Silverwing", decided the brothers, would require no less than complete rebuilding. Fortunately, the aft fuselage and empennage was virtually intact, but major damage was inflicted on the forward fuselage/cockpit section and engine mount. The wings were broken toward the roots and would require extensive repair.

On September 16th, Roy and Clyde hauled the remains of the monoplane back to Enid. They told the press that a new ship would be built, using assemblies and parts from the wrecked Queen.

The two men had spent five months on the Great Salt Plains. Their education in the flying game had been painful and hard. Nobody laughed at them anymore. They were respected men...they were aviators...they were broke!

And the people of Jet responded to their latest mishap. 26 people contributed $30.50 toward cost of repairing the aircraft. Although the amount was miniscule compared to the cost of the airplane, the brothers published a note of thanks in the Jet Visitor, expressing their appreciation.

During the remainder of September, the brothers worked on the Elbridge engine. The crash caused external and internal damage to the little powerplant. Main bearings were sprung loose and the intake manifold needed repair.

Both men worked many long hours rebuilding the airframe and engine of their craft. The wings and fuselage were repaired, and the landing gear totally redesigned. Clyde intended for the reborn "Silverwing" to be lighter than the original model. The Elbridge was coaxed to produce nearly 25% more horsepower.

By October 11th the ship had made its first flight, and Clyde was anxious to make every exhibition possible in the remaining weeks of good flying weather.

"Silverwing" made an unannounced flight on November 19th. Clyde had moved flying operations to the Val Johnson farm located south of Enid's baseball park. Johnson was a well-known rancher and friend of the Cessna family. A large wheatfield on his farm was offered to the aviator for his flying needs.

After transporting the airplane to Johnson's property, Cessna assembled it and ran the engine. Everything seemed ready. Only a few selected people had been invited to observe the flight. Clyde manned the cockpit and ran the engine to full power. Acceleration was slow across the rough, soft earth, but after a takeoff roll of only 200 feet, the craft was airborne and climbing into the cold, north wind. 100 feet altitude was gained easily. Upon reaching the Frisco

tracks, the ship was turned west and completed the half-circle to a heading of east.

Turning north again, the pilot sensed he was in trouble. Even with full power the monoplane was steadily descending to the ground. Attempting to roll out of the bank with opposite warp, Cessna found little response from his mount. He was going to crash again.

With full warp against the bank and maximum power all the way to impact, the monoplane crashed into a dry creek bed and flipped over, breaking the right wing. Shaken but unhurt, the aviator emerged from the wreck as frightened friends arrived on the scene, relieved to find Clyde moving about.

Weeks of hard work had put Cessna in a creek bed. The brothers once more hauled their damaged creation back to the shop. A successful flight, with controlled turns and a landing in the same spot as takeoff, still eluded Clyde Cessna.

There was no doubt, however, that the machine outperformed its predecesor. The Cessnas quickly set about repairing the right wing. Within 30 days they were ready to fly again. Transporting the airplane by horse-drawn cart to the big flying field, Clyde and two assistants began assembly of the aircraft.

The wings were moved into position and bolted, warping cables were attached and their function checked. Flying and landing wires carefully installed and turnbuckles drawn up tight. With the rudder installed, the entire airplane was perused, with nothing being found amiss.

Fuel and coolant tanks were filled, and the propeller was closely inspected. Cessna then surveyed the soft, plowed ground he would use for takeoff. He checked the wind...easterly, but light.

Cessna whirled the large propeller once, then twice. On the third pull, smoke belched from the engine's exhaust ports and the monoplane shuddered as the Elbridge increased rpm, then settled into its rough, discordant song.

Clyde quickly ran to the cockpit, climbed in and was off. For 100 yards the monoplane bounced and jinked, struggling to gain airspeed. Then it was airborne.

Climbing out to the east, 200 feet of altitude was attained and a turn made to the west. People on the ground were awed by the smooth, graceful arc described by the airplane. Even from two miles away they could clearly see the aircraft, trailing its ever-present black plume of exhaust smoke.

Clyde turned the machine back toward the field. As he approached to land, the crowd of about 100 people cheered him on. Men waved their hats. Ladies gave conservative gestures that belied their true excitement.

At 50 feet altitude, Cessna cut the ignition. The propeller coasted to a stop. Only the subtle tremor of wind in the wires could be heard as the aviator glided downward. In a few moments the airplane landed and rolled to a stop.

People quickly crowded around the monoplane, everyone wanting to congratulate Enid's pilot on a spectacular show. Wiping the oil from his face, the aviator turned and said with a broad smile, "Well, boys, you see, Cessna can fly."

No one would dispute that statement. Clyde V. Cessna had reached a milestone in his brief, troubled and costly aviation venture. That Sunday, December 17, 1911, marked his first known, true aerial flight. He had taken off, flown five miles in seven minutes and landed where he had departed, without damage to his airplane or injury to himself.[12]

Cessna told the press that he had spent almost $5000 and a year of his life making "Silverwing" fly. He intended to incorporate changes into the airplane that would improve performance and reliability. The Elbridge engine had performed superbly on the flight, but the aircraft still lacked horsepower.

During the winter months of 1912, Cessna refined his ship and by spring he was ready for a profitable season of exhibition flying. On April 14th, Clyde flew eight miles at Enid, landing safely. He made turns, becoming intimately familiar with every idiosyncrasy of the modified "Silverwing".

The Cessna Exhibition Company was formed to handle all accounts and contracts for flights. Home office was located in Enid with a branch office in Rago, Kansas.

On June 3rd, Cessna contracted with The Pond Creek Boosters Club of Pond Creek, Oklahoma, to make a flight on the Fourth of July. Clyde was very careful in negotiating his contracts. Remembering how much money had been spent learning to fly, he intended to recoup his expenses. But he would also give a good show.

At Pond Creek, Cessna was to receive 75% of the gate receipts, in cash, immediately after a successful flight. A successful flight meant, according to the Booster Club, that man and machine had to stay in the air for a minimum of five minutes.

The Booster Club agreed to pay all transportation and lodging costs for Cessna and his assistants, both in getting to Pond Creek and returning to Rago or Enid.

When the Fourth of July came, Clyde was ready to fly. But the wind was just too strong, and kept Cessna grounded until 8 P.M. Crowds watched every step of preparation given to the monoplane. Then Cessna waved, the engine was started and quickly the ship was airborne. It flew a mile and a half, when suddenly it descended, struck the ground, then bounced back into the air, followed immediately by the unmistakable sounds of a crash.

Officials drove with reckless abandon to reach the site. They helped Clyde from the wrecked machine. Again, he had escaped serious injury, but was badly shaken up. His airplane was severly damaged. No mechanical malfunction could be blamed for the accident; it was simply loss of control by the pilot. Cessna went home empty handed, but full of resolve: he was determined to fly an engagement without crashing.

It wasn't long before he had another chance to prove himself. The folks at Kremlin, Oklahoma hired Cessna to make flights for a carnival to be held August 14th. Cessna, the aviator, really put on a show. Not only did he fly successfully, but navigated his machine over the town of Kremlin itself, flying at an altitude of 150 feet. "Silverwing" stayed aloft for six minutes without mishap and $200 was paid to Mr. Cessna upon his landing.

Hot on the heels of the Kremlin success came another contract for flights at Jet. On September 16th, Clyde flew at the Old Settler's Reunion Celebration, where the weather, often his nemesis, cooperated beautifully. Never before had Cessna had

conditions so favorable for flying.[13]

Cessna's increasing prowess in the air was evident that day. He took off and began describing a figure eight. The eight required back-to-back turns with constant bank angles. The first half of the eight went well, but during the second half a leaking fuel tank caused a forced landing in a plowed field, but no damage occurred.

By flying a complex maneuver like the figure eight, Clyde Cessna was giving the crowds what they wanted; to see airplanes do circles, volplane (glide) and perform steep banks. He was admittedly a conservative flyer, not attempting any maneuver beyond his, or the airplane's, capabilities.

Following the Jet exhibition, Cessna made "important improvements" to the monoplanes' powerplant. Exactly what changes were made is uncertain, but when "Silverwing" flew at Cherokee, Oklahoma, in October, it obviously had better performance than ever before. Clyde took the ship up to 2,000 feet, flying circles around the field, thrilling the audience below. He had rarely been able to reach such heights and the exhibition proved to be a great success.

Returning to Enid, Cessna continued his tinkering to improve performance. His confidence was flying as high as his airplane. To demonstrate the monoplane before Enid's citizenry, he made an unannounced flight over the city on November 25th. Taking off from a field a quarter mile west of the high school building, Cessna cruised over the city at midmorning. Flying 1,000 feet high, the noise of the engine brought people out of houses and buildings, everyone craning their necks to see the first aircraft

Wichita's first airmeet was held on May 4, 1911, and featured 19 year-old aviator Jimmy Ward, along with C.C. Witmer, R.C. St. Henry and Eugene Ely. Held at Walnut Grove Park north of the city, thousands of people turned out to see the birdmen fly. Ward was very popular with the crowds, and gave his new bride her first airplane ride during the show. The apparel being worn by Ward and his wife are most interesting and typical of flying garb used by early-day flyers. Note belt around Mrs. Ward's legs to keep her dress and coat in place during flight, also total lack of safety belts. Fuel tank for Curtiss engine is under the top wing, with large coolant radiator behind Ward. (Courtesy J.E. Thorn)

to fly over city square.

Turning to the south, Enid's flyer landed back at the departure field. 15 minutes had elapsed since takeoff...a long flight for Oklahoma's airman. He continued making flights, each one giving Clyde valuable experience.

On Christmas Eve, 1912, Cessna planned a holiday flight over the town. It was his personal gift to the city and accordingly, at 5 P.M. on Christmas Day he took off and flew a large circle around the southwestern section, where thousands saw him. After a 10 mile, 20 minute flight, he landed and answered reporters questions about his immediate plans.

Clyde told the Daily Eagle that he was going to Kansas for about two or three months, where he planned to make as many aerial exhibitions as possible, despite the cold season that was rapidly setting in. The monoplane was shipped to the railroad station at Rago, Kansas.

After assembling the airplane at his farm near Adams, Clyde made a flight at Rago on December 29th. To celebrate the holidays with his parents, (he had not seen his mother in two years), he flew five miles to his father's homestead near Belmont, Kansas, on December 30th. To please public demand, Cessna flew once on January 1, 1913 for the people of Belmont, despite a stiff wind that caused him some concern.

During the remainder of January, six flights were made in Kansas towns. Cessna had stopped depending on gate receipts for income, and contracted for a set amount of money, usually $100 to $400, for each engagement.

The Cessna family moved to Adams at the end of January. "Silverwing" was stored while Clyde returned to Enid at the end of the month. The purpose of his return was to work on a new monoplane, under construction with little fanfare since December, 1912, until the opportunity to make flights in the Sunflower state caused work to stop.

Cessna returned to Adams by February 1st, making a flight at Norwich, Kansas, on the 15th with "Silverwing." The crowd raved about how high the airplane flew, while others were excited by the fancy aerial circles drawn in the sky. Cessna's Kansas tour was winding down. He flew at Kingman on March 3rd, then disassembled the monoplane and shipped it back to Enid. Clyde and his family left Rago by train, and after settling in once again in Oklahoma, it was time to get back to his new project.

"Silverwing" was, however, reassembled and ready to fly by March 26th, and Clyde flew the ship on the 30th. The "old tub", as he called it, had taught Cessna how to fly, but her days were numbered. After two years of hard flying, crashes and countless repairs, the airplane was retired.

As winter gave way to spring, 1913, the new monoplane being built in Cessna's shop was nearly finished. Using the Queen aircraft as a pattern, the first Cessna airplane took form.

Control and handling improvements were paramount considerations in this design. Wingspan was increased slightly along with chord. A single, vertical tripod forward of the cockpit anchored the landing wires. Wing warping was retained, with control cables running around pulleys mounted on the landing gear assembly. The fuselage was also longer and completely covered with fabric. A small vertical stabilizer was included in the empennage assembly, capped off with a rudder of much greater area operated via crossed cables. Left rudder movement required pushing the right side of the cockpit rudder bar.

For right rudder, the left rudder bar was pushed (Cessna would always prefer this arrangement). Horizontal stabilizer area was also augmented, with a curved leading edge that blended nicely with the tapered, aft fuselage. Each elevator was of standard configuration and hinged to the trailing edge of the stabilizer.

For landing gear, two large, curved struts bolted to the lower fuselage longerons. The struts were cross-braced with wire, and an axle was fixed to the lowest point of the struts. A single, wire-spoked wheel was mounted at each end, without benefit of any bearings or brakes.

Mounted on wooden bearers ahead of the cockpit sat the four-cylinder, smoke-belching, hot-tempered, but faithful old Elbridge. Oil and fuel tanks were located behind the engine and extended into the forward cockpit area. The coolant heat exchanger was positioned to receive improved ram air flow.

Cessna would have preferred a radial engine like the six-cylinder, 60 hp Anzani, but admitted he couldn't afford one until more exhibition flights earned him enough money for one of the popular French powerplants.

In early June, the monoplane was rolled from the shop. Final details were completed and on June 6th the ship was transported to a field southwest of Enid. The maiden flight started out without mishap. Handling was very good, especially around the longitudinal axis. Clyde finally had adequate roll control; an ability sorely lacking in his first ship.

Flying along effortlessly, the pilot suddenly noticed telephone poles and high tension wires dead ahead. Making a low altitude turn to avoid them, Cessna was forced downwind. He guided the ship to a landing, but it flipped over when the wheels hit a dry creek bed. One flight, one crackup.

A consoling fact was that the ship flew well. Repairs were made in the next few days and Cessna was soon to be off for his second Kansas flying tour, taking the new monoplane with him. The schedule was a busy one, with the first stop at Englewood.

Clyde flew five minute flights, earning $200 for the first one and $100 for the second. On the Fourth of July he was in Harper, providing the holiday's top entertainment. Next destination was Nashville, Kansas, on August 22nd and 23rd, where he received $400 for two flights.

Taking time from his busy schedule, Cessna rested and worked on the monoplane at his home near Adams. One Sunday he decided to attend church in Kingman, 14 miles to the north. Donning his go-to-meeting duds, Clyde fired up the engine and took off, intending to arrive for services in his own, unique way.

The pastor had just started his sermon when a growing noise outside rose to an unbearable crescendo. He stopped preaching as the church emptied, following his flock outside. Everyone stood back as the noisy, vibrating flying machine trundled up to the churchyard, blowing dust and dirt everywhere as it taxied. When the pilot vacated his seat, a man of

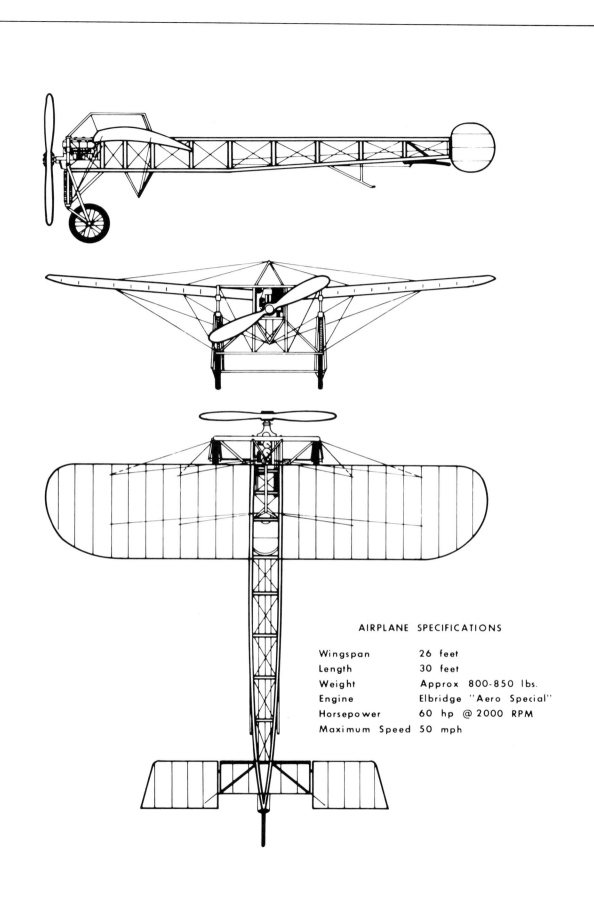

AIRPLANE SPECIFICATIONS

Wingspan	26 feet
Length	30 feet
Weight	Approx 800-850 lbs.
Engine	Elbridge "Aero Special"
Horsepower	60 hp @ 2000 RPM
Maximum Speed	50 mph

1911 Cessna-Queen Monoplane "Silverwing"

the cloth greeted a man of the clouds, then all went inside to hear the Word.

By September Cessna was in Liberal, flying there on the 17th, 19th and 20th of the month. This exhibition made $600. He flew for seven minutes at Stafford on October 2nd and 3rd, collecting $400. His profits were growing, and so were his dreams.

Cessna's interest in aeronautics went beyond flying. He believed people were ready to buy airplanes and learn to fly them. Such an attitude was visionary for 1913. When he traveled to Wichita for a three day exhibition, Clyde realized that the 'Peerless Princess of the Prairie', as the city was known, held great potential; it could be the right place to make his dreams come true.

Cessna was not the first aviator Wichitans had ever seen. On May 4, 1911, the city held its first airshow. Jimmy Ward, C.C. Witmer, R.C. St. Henry and Eugene Ely flew their Curtiss biplanes. Ward, known as the "boy aviator" at age 19, gave his wife her first airplane ride at the meet. Ward returned for another exhibition on July 4th.

The first monoplane flight was made by J. Hector Warden on May 29, 1912. He flew his Bleriot copy from Walnut Grove Park, remaining airborne for 10 minutes despite a bad cylinder on the 50 hp rotary engine.

Clyde Cessna, along with Roy and another assistant, arrived in Wichita on October 14, 1913. Clyde informed the press that he had come there to seek a location for building airplanes and training aviators. He met with Charles Bell, superintendent of the Arkansas Valley Interurban Line, to discuss a flight schedule.

October 17th, 18th and 19th were set for exhibitions. Roy needed help with distributing handbills advertising the flights, so Clyde took to the streets. He hadn't gone far when J.A. Blair, superintendent of street cleaning, arrested him. The charge: unlawful distribution of handbills on city streets.

Hauled into court, Cessna explained that he wasn't aware of the law and asked that the charge be dropped. Judge W.D. Jochens disagreed, levied a $1 fine and suggested dropping handbills from airplanes next time. There was no ordinance against that!

Still smarting from his brush with justice, Clyde quickly began preparations for the first flight. In the late afternoon of October 17th, he climbed to 4,000 feet, aiming for the downtown area. Cessna became the first aviator to fly over the city, yelling to people below as he glided downward with the engine at idle. Pedestrians crossing the Douglas Avenue bridge were startled to see an airplane descending toward them, and waved enthusiastically as Cessna "opened 'er up" and climbed back to altitude. After a flight lasting 16 minutes and covering about 20 miles, he landed and informed the crowd that tomorrow another exhibition was planned.

The next day's success was hampered by a water leak in the engine that got the magneto wet, forcing Clyde to land after only 10 minutes in the air. While airborne, he carried out one of his attention-getting gimmicks; anyone who caught a football dropped from the monoplane won $5. If not caught, then whoever possessed a football first received $2.50. Considering that admission was only 25 cents, grabbing or scrambling for the pigskin was well worth the effort.

H.H. Burnside, after realizing how hard it was to catch a football dropped from 1000 feet up, managed to corral one and was duly rewarded by the Cessnas. Before leaving Wichita, aviator Cessna made two things very clear: he wanted to build airplanes there and train pilots to fly them.

The public reaction was undetectable, but the city fathers and other officials were keen on the idea. It would promote their city as progressive, modern and open to new concepts.

By November, the Cessnas had returned to Oklahoma and Clyde continued to make flights there, including one on Thanksgiving Day in Enid, which would be the final flight of her native son in that town.

Clyde packed up the house, family and airplanes on December 23, 1913, and moved back to the forty acre farm near Adams. As the Christmas season began, Clyde was already thinking about building another, more powerful, airplane. 1913 had been a good year; 1914 promised to be even better.

---

[1] Fred E. Botkin is a bit of a mystery man; he was Cessna's sales representative at the auto agency and seemed to possess a true interest in flying, but no evidence could be found that even suggests he carried out his desires.

[2] The admission fee was Cessna's first attempt at recouping some of his expenses in buying and shipping "Silverwing" to Enid. How much was charged for admission to the tent is not known, but it was probably less than 30 cents.

[3] Cessna apparently understood enough of the fundamentals taught him in New York City that he could takeoff, fly straight ahead and land again without difficulty under ideal weather conditions.

[4] The monoplane's engine was definitely not in working order when Cessna received it. On initial attempts to start it, nothing would work, and soon it was apparent that the powerplant was in need of an expert mechanic familiar with its bad manners. Since none was available, Cessna tackled the job himself with only minimal success.

[5] The Enid press was always asking Cessna what kind of troubles he was having with his airplane, and were quick to report such news as he would give them.

[6] Lindsley was a good example of the early experimental aircraft builder. He apparently had no education regarding airplane structures or flying technique, and his biplane seemed to prove that out since it never flew successfully.

[7] Exactly how Cessna determined that the engine was only producing 30 hp is not known, although devices were available in 1911 for testing power output of reciprocating powerplants. He may have obtained one or built some apparatus that served the same purpose.

[8] "Silverwing" was difficult to fly, even in good weather with little or no wind. Elevator control was extremely sensitive, while the rudder was very ineffective until an airspeed of 30 mph or more was attained and, more importantly, maintained. Roll control from the wing warping system was poor at best, again depending on a sustained airspeed above 30 mph for control. With winds above 15 mph, all three controls were taxed to their limits in controlling the aircraft.

[9] Cessna often commented to the press (both in 1911 and in later years) that he was 'starting from scratch' on the Great Salt Plains. It seems apparent that he really had little conception of how difficult it was to master his machine.

[10] Having sold his interest in the Overland/Clark automobile agency, Clyde Cessna had chosen to follow aviation instead of cars, and found the going very tough, especially in the area of finances. He had to sell aviation to the public to make it pay.

[11] A.C. Beech is reported to have had some experience flying Bleriot-type monoplanes, and Cessna allowed him to fly "Silverwing" on the Salt Plains. Cessna had confidence in Beech's ability to handle the whimsical monoplane, and intended to have him act as pilot in upcoming exhibitions, however, Beech fades from the picture after the failed flight at Cherokee, Oklahoma.

[12] After an exhaustive search of all available references, no other flight made by Cessna, prior to Demember, 1911, consisted of a takeoff, traverse of the ground (including turns of 180 and 360 degrees) followed by a landing in the same location where takeoff was made until the December 17th event. Cessna's remarks to reporters after landing attest to this fact.

[13] "Favorable for flying" usually meant absolutely no wind. Cessna often estimated his chances for a successful flight on the the wind's velocity.

CHAPTER THREE
Wichita's Aviator

Everyone in the little towns of Adams and Belmont, Kansas, were glad to see Clyde Cessna back home again. Almost five years had passed since he had left the rural neighborhood of his youth.

As the cold of a Kansas January swept down on the prairie, Cessna was busy building a home for his family and a hanger for his airplanes, both on the little forty acre farm north of his father's homestead.

The hangar was situated on the east side of a dirt road that ran in front of the house. Taxiing across the road was no problem, but some trees had to be felled to permit access to the flying field.

During the winter of 1914, Cessna began designing and building his second monoplane. It was very similar to the 1913 ship, but the empennage was smaller, with an all-moving, stabilator-type pitch control (no fixed horizontal stabilizer was used.)

Two other improvements appeared on this ship: a small windshield and a 60 hp Anzani static radial engine, turning a propeller almost 84 inches in diameter to absorb the horsepower. Cessna's successful 1913 exhibition season enabled him to buy the powerplant. Landing gear remained identical to the 1913 configuration.[1]

The new monoplane made its first flight in June, 1914, with Clyde flying from his farm to Adams and

Clyde Cessna poses beside his new monoplane at Kinsley, Kansas, June 9, 1914. Built during the winter of 1914, the ship featured a 60 hp Anzani radial engine, V-braces above the fuselage for anchoring wing wires and an all-moving, stabilator- type pitch control. Fabric covering over the wheels was intended to reduce drag but often separated from the wheel, exposing wire spokes underneath. (Bob Pickett Collection/Cessna Aircraft Company)

return. Performance was good, with a maximum speed of nearly 90 mph. That summer, at least 11 towns were visited with over 25 flights being made.

Propeller ground clearance was minimal with the Anzani engine installation, especially when the terrain was rough, and Cessna installed small, wood extensions on the leading edge of each landing gear strut, along with a nose-over skid that extended forward of the axle.

For the 1915 flying season, Cessna's machine was essentially unchanged, although he told the local press that some "remodeling" of the monoplane was done the previous winter (no details were given.)

On May 15th, Clyde made one of his test flights over Belmont, easily attaining 2,000 feet altitude. He was ready for a busy show schedule, and was off for Blackwell, Oklahoma, on July 5th. On August 12th, Cessna made an unannounced (and unscheduled) appearance at the Anthony, Kansas, fair. He had never been to the town's annual event and decided to fly over for a visit.

Just as the afternoon horse race was galloping to completion, someone in the grandstands caught the shape of a flying machine approaching and yelled, "An airship!" Instantly, all eyes abandoned the racetrack and peered skyward.

Cessna cruised over the field at 500 feet altitude, then landed in a nearby pasture. Officials, knowing a good attraction when they saw one, spoke to Clyde and offered him $100 for a flight the next day. On Friday he gave the crowds a good demonstration of what his airplane could do, then he flew home, 28 miles away, in just 18 minutes. He rolled the airplane into its hangar, washed up for supper and was enjoying the meal with his wife 25 minutes after taking

By August, 1914, the front landing gear assembly was modified with small, wooden extensions in an effort to prevent propeller breakage if the ship nosed over on takeoff or landing. Most of the fields Cessna operated from were little more than cow pastures, with lots of holes and soft spots that could trip the airplane up on its nose. This view also shows the first (confirmed) use of a windshield on a Cessna airplane. Note assist stirrup for entering the cockpit on lower fuselage longeron, below the right wing. (Bob Pickett Collection/Cessna Aircraft Company)

off from Anthony.

On August 30th, Clyde took off for Woodward, Oklahoma, flying the 105 miles in 1:55 at a reduced power setting. He made the long flight without incident, and was highly pleased with the monoplane's cross-country performance.

After making two flights in Woodward, Cessna pointed the airplane north toward Kingman, where he was to fly at the 17th Annual Old Settler's Picnic. A leak in the fuel tank caused a forced landing near Alva, Oklahoma, that damaged the airframe badly enough to prevent completion of the trip.

Two days were required for repairs, this being the first serious mishap with the new airplane and the first engagement missed by the pioneer aviator in almost six years. In the previous eight days, Cessna had flown over 800 miles from town to town, making exhibitions. 1915 was a very good year for the Cessna Exhibition Company.

Despite his obvious mastery of the air and his machine, Clyde still had his bad days at the stick. In the first week of July, 1916, he crashed near Adams, substantially damaging the airplane and slightly injuring himself. In only three weeks he was back in the air, flying the show circuit once again.

Cessna's interest in building airplanes and training pilots to fly them never abated. He was certain such a venture could succeed...all he needed was the right combination of time, place, people and money to help him get established.

In late August, help arrived. George Sherwood, production manager for the J.J. Jones Motor Company, visited Cessna at home. Clyde already knew Sherwood from his friendship with Mr. Jones, whose successful "Light Six" automobile was built in Wichita.[2]

Sherwood represented a small group of businessmen who wanted Clyde to build airplanes and train aviators in their town. Most of them belonged to the local aero club, but their only flying machine was a hot air balloon. While it did get them into the blue, some members believed airplanes were the only practical course to pursue.

One member of the group, Jack Turner, a local lumber, hay and coal distributor, espoused that belief with vigor. He was very anxious for Cessna to relocate in Wichita because he wanted to buy an airplane and learn to fly it.

His zest for aeronautics bred considerable influence among the group, and Sherwood echoed these sentiments along with other details about the proposed move.

As Cessna listened intently, his guest explained that a vacant building at the Jones factory would be made available for the manufacture of airplanes, and that a large tract of ground adjacent to the site would serve as a flying field.

To drum up local interest and publicity, a flight from Hutchinson, Kansas, to Wichita was discussed for September 1st. Plans called for Cessna and Sherwood to depart Hutchinson in a race to the Jones facilities in North Wichita. Airplane against automobile, Clyde knew he would win, but Sherwood intended to keep the Jones flat out all the way.

On September 1st, Roy and Clyde Cessna were in Hutchinson preparing the monoplane for the next day's flight. At exactly 11 A.M. the Anzani-powered ship took off as Sherwood was upshifting the Jones. Roy, having launched his brother, climbed into his own Ford and sped southeast toward the prairie city.

After flying 35 minutes at less than full power, Cessna landed in an alfalfa field near the Jones factory. The flight had been uneventful, with the road below providing a groundbound airway to his destination. Sherwood, of course, was no where to be seen. He arrived 30 minutes later.

Having rested briefly and reserviced his mount, Cessna took off at 11:55 A.M. Flying over the downtown area, he circled four times, once each over the Schweiter, Eagle and Fourth National Bank buildings and the sales offices of the Jones company.

To cap off the trip, Cessna reduced power and glided down to within 300 feet of the streets, then gave the radial full throttle and zoomed skyward. Dipping down once again, he flew along Main Street toward North Lawrence Avenue, landing in the same field near the Jones factory.

Both flights had provided the desired public impact, as hundreds of people began gathering at the Jones facility for a closer look at Wichita's aviator and his flying machine. Roy had now arrived, and joined his brother answering questions about the airplane.

Soon, the brothers were ushered off to a special luncheon given in their honor. The Wichita Aero Club members were there in force, including Jack Turner, C.C. Bayless, Jerome Herington, Elmer Reese, Hal Black, Henry Lassen, Sherwood, and Charles E. Becker, publicity manager for Jones.

They reaffirmed their desire to have Cessna move to the city, and offered financial and logistical support for establishment of an airplane factory and flying school. Clyde was agreeable to the offer, but no formal announcement was made that day.

On September 5th, Cessna and the Aero Club told the press that Wichita now had her own aviator, with a factory and pilot school coming soon. Nearly 40 men had already expressed an interest in taking flying lessons, although no starting dates for classes had been set. Cessna estimated it would take at least six months before the school was organized.

Of all the men who wanted wings, Jack Turner was the most outspoken. He intended to fly as soon as Clyde could sign him up. Turner was quick to approach Cessna about building a monoplane expressly for his use. No definite agreement was reached between the two men, but Clyde knew he had a potential sale in the wealthy and erudite Wichitan.[3]

The brothers inspected building "I" in the Jones complex, finding it very satisfactory for building airplanes. It was a large, rectangular structure, approximately 80 feet in length and 50 feet wide. Production of at least 10 airplanes was expected in the first year, and Mr. Jones had granted 73 acres of ground adjacent to the factory for a flying field.

Cessna's newest endeavor seemed full of promise. There was no incorporation, no stockholders, no capital investment. He was simply invited to Wichita, given a place to build airplanes and operate a flying school, supported in small measure by a handful of businessmen. The Cessna Aeroplane Exhibition Company, as it was now known, continued to operate essentially as it had before. Only the location, facilities and possibilities for the future had changed.

With details wrapped up, the brothers prepared for an upcoming exhibition at the Cowley County Fair on September 7th. Flying from Wichita, the 60 hp monoplane cruised at one mile per minute enroute to the host town of Burden. It was, according to Clyde, capable of twice that rate.

After making his required flights, thrilling the crowds with "fancy tricks in the sky," Cessna flew home to Adams. He covered 64 miles in one hour, despite being momentarily lost twice. Although his navigation abilities were improving, he occasionally became disoriented since all course guidance was primarily by pilotage (reference to ground features and landmarks only).[4]

In September, 1915, Cessna had an accident with his monoplane that caused some changes to be made during the rebuilding process. Within a few days the repairs were completed, and Clyde was back on the show circuit, giving flights in Wakeeney, Trago County, Kansas, on September 20th when this photograph was taken. Most obvious change made to the ship is the landing gear arrangement, with the front, curved pieces being replaced by straight members of increased width and thickness. Cessna stated that he could fly up to two hours non-stop with this monoplane, permitting him to fly to engagements instead of shipping the machine by rail. (Wichita Chamber of Commerce)

1914 ANZANI ENGINE

Of the aero engines used during the period 1909-1919, the Anzani series of small, dependable static radials were among the most popular. The firm's founder, Alessandro Anzani, switched from bicycle racing to aviation, finding a ready market for his products.

Louis Bleriot used a fan-type, 3-cylinder Anzani of 25 hp on his cross-channel Type XI, and by 1913 the French company was manufacturing five models, ranging from a 3-cylinder, 30 hp model to a 10-cylinder, 110 hp version.

Clyde Cessna was attracted to the radial powerplant because of its simplicity and availability. Most aircraft engines in 1914 were of the inline or V-type, and the static radial was just emerging as a practical design. The Anzani series (which were never considered to be technically-sophisticated engines) were exported to the United States in large numbers, costing about $2,000 in 1914 for the 60 hp model.

All of the company's designs used automatic intake valves until 1922, when cam-operated assemblies were incorporated. While automatic intake valves were simple, they caused a rapid power loss with altitude and a high specific fuel consumption of 0.66 lb/hp/hour (0.3 kg/hp/hour).

Another technical drawback of the type was crankshaft design, which limited the engine to three cylinders per row. If more power was desired, another row of three cylinders had to be added, increasing engine weight.

The exhaust valve was located forward of the intake valve, and this undesirable feature allowed hot exhaust air to flow over the intake ports, overheating the incoming fuel/air mixture.

Improvements were made to the lubrication system by 1913, using a pressure oil pump and cored passageways for delivery to critical bearing areas and the propeller thrust bearing.

Ignition was provided by a single magneto mounted on the rear of the crankcase, and a Zenith updraft carburetor, complete with throttle, hung between the two bottom cylinders.

By 1928, Anzani's designs had fallen into disuse, being surpassed by the new generation of static radials like the Wright J4, Warner 'Scarab' and the German Siemens-Halske. The world of aviation does, however, owe much to this elementary, dependable, engine, since it was used extensively in those early years of heavier-than-air flight.

Specifications for the 1914 powerplant, as used by Clyde Cessna, are included here:
Type: Static radial
Cylinders: Six, in two rows of three
Bore/Stroke: 4.1/4.7 inches (105/120 mm)
Weight: 200 pounds (160 kg)
RPM: 1,300

Cessna flew at the Hutchinson State Fair during the third week of September, and by the end of the month, Clyde and Roy, along with their brother Noel, moved to Wichita and began arranging equipment in the new facility. While his two brothers set up shop, Clyde was busy flying.

Officials of the upcoming Wheat Exposition, to be held the first week of October in Wichita, hired Cessna to make a series of flights. They were anxious to reap the harvest of publicity from aerial excursions, and Clyde received a handsome fee for his efforts and brought the citizenry out in droves.

He flew nearly every day at 5 P.M., wind and weather permitting. To alert people attending the show that a flight was about to start, a siren at the nearby milling company sounded for several minutes.

Hundreds of spectators quickly gathered outside the pavilions. They could clearly see the aviator and his ship passing over them, the rattle of the engine reverberating in their ears.

As a result of his flights, Clyde Cessna again found himself a celebrity. Interviews, questions and answers never seemed to cease. Everyone wanted to know about airplanes, how they were built and how hard they were to fly. To educate Wichitans, the brothers decided to hold an open house.

On October 5th, the doors of building "I" were opened to all. Inside, woodworking equipment, tools and airplane parts were displayed. Outside, Cessna stood beside his monoplane, answering torrents of questions about its performance while crowds milled around the ship, peering inside the cramped, spartan cockpit.

Inside view of the Jones automobile factory where Cessna and his brothers were given work space in September, 1916. The airplane on the left was the first one built in Wichita. In the rear, left of the shop is the 1913 monoplane that still has the Elbridge engine installed. Workers are building the fuselage and empennage of the 1917 "Comet". Note Jones "Light Six" fenders hanging from the ceiling, tires, wheels and propellers strewn about the shop. (Bob Pickett Collection/Cessna Aircraft Company)

In walking around the airplane, many people noticed that the machine had recently become a flying billboard. Jack Spines, a clothing merchant, paid Cessna to paint "111 West Douglas-SPINES-111 West Douglas" under the left wing (the sign was retained during the fall season while Cessna completed his exhibitions).

Others were fascinated by the Anzani and its seemingly-odd arrangement of cylinders. The Eagle newspaper hailed it as the "mighty French engine", extolling its 60 horsepower rating as one of the highest in the United States.

An overwhelming success, the open house lasted all afternoon. Many inquiries were made about flying lessons and how someone could get enrolled in a pilot class. Public interest in aviation remained very high as the brothers continued to prepare the factory for business.

As Cessna completed his last flight for the exposition, the advance group for another flyer was in town. Miss Ruth Law, well known aviatrix, was coming October 10th. Her show would include the 'bombing' of city hall, the Forum building and the court house as well as aerial stunting.[5]

Such demonstrations were popular in 1916. America was holding fast to its isolationism, but news of devastation in Europe reached its shores daily. Airplanes, which had been a novelty for field commanders to toy with in 1914/1915, were now viewed as a potent offensive and defensive weapon by all combatants. To show people how vulnerable defenseless cities would be to air attack, many pilots added bomb dropping stunts to their repertoire.

Miss Law and Cessna were scheduled to fly together over the city during her visit. For unknown reasons, Clyde did not make the flight. The afternoon of October 10th found Law racing against Jerry Wonderlick in his fast Marquette Buick in a two-mile race, which she won easily. Cessna found such antics unpleasant and detrimental to the furthering of aeronautics. But he had to admit it was profitable; Ruth was paid $750 per day for her flying, plus a certain percentage of gate receipts.

While Ruth Law and others like her sensationalized the airplane, Clyde Cessna was trying to commercialize it. By Thanksgiving Day, the final pieces of machinery were installed in building "I".

With temperatures outside dropping as winter approached, flying activities slowed down. The cold, winter months would afford time to construct airplanes for the 1917 exhibition season, and at least two ships were anticipated to handle the growing demand for engagements.

To promote his airplane designs, Clyde planned a long cross-country flight from Wichita to New York City in the spring or summer of 1917. He believed the trip could be made in 18 hours, with three fuel stops enroute. If all went well, he would land on Manhattan Island the same day he departed the Sunflower State.[6]

A new airplane and more powerful engine would be required for the flight, and Cessna hoped to convince some of his business associates to consider $2000 for a 100 hp powerplant. He estimated that two months would be consumed building the airplane. Increased fuel and oil capacity and more instrumentation were paramount design considerations before any construction began. "From Wichita to New York" became the slogan around Cessna's facility and the brothers started design layout and preliminary construction in early December.

Financial support for the idea was not forthcoming, however, and the Cessnas certainly couldn't afford the high costs involved themselves. Reluctantly, they dropped plans for their aerial marathon.

Sharing disappointment with the brothers was Ms. Avis Van Hee, who had been employed by Clyde to help with construction of the Wichita-New York City ship. No newcomer to aviation, Van Hee had reportedly flown with the famous Arch Hoxsey. She expressed a great desire to learn all about airplanes, and wanted to learn to fly them, too. Apparently, her spunk and determination impressed Clyde Cessna to the point that he allowed her to assist the brothers

Aviatrix Ruth Law came to Wichita in October, 1916, flying her Curtiss biplane modified with Wright-type controls. Law and Cessna were scheduled to fly in formation, but this never took place for unknown reasons. She is shown here wearing her non-commissoned officer's uniform in 1917 (she was the first woman authorized to wear one) during a campaign for Liberty Loans in World War One. (Smithsonian Institution Photo #A5532)

Clyde Cessna (sitting, second from right) poses with a few members of the Beaver Boosters in Beaver, Oklahoma, and the first airplane built in Wichita. It features a horizontal stabilizer with conventional elevators, 60 hp Anzani radial and a single kingpost above fuselage for anchoring wing wires. Cessna retained wing warping for this ship, with the control cables and bellcrank arrangement being the same as earlier airplanes. Jack Spines, Wichita clothing merchant, paid Cessna to advertise his store with writing under left wing. (Bob Pickett Collection/Cessna Aircraft Company)

as the first airplane built in Wichita, Cessna's seventh aircraft since 1911, took shape.

In February, 1917, Cessna traveled to New York City as a representative of the Wichita Aero Club to attend the National Aviation Congress, held in the Grand Central Palace. While there, he met other aviators and discussed the trends in American aeronautics. He diligently examined the many types of aircraft on display, naturally paying close attention to the monoplane models. In between meetings and dinners, Clyde went shopping.

He purchased spruce and other woods needed to build airplanes, and investigated the purchase of engines, tools and special hardware. Returning to Wichita, he commented to the press that there were literally hundreds of aircraft designs shown at the huge convention. A person had only to decide which type he liked best, whether it be a 'limousine' style or an open cockpit monoplane or biplane, all were represented there.

Returning to work with much needed materials in hand, Cessna and his brothers made rapid progress on the new monoplane and started construction of a second ship on February 26th. It was designed from its inception to incorporate two seats, as Cessna intended to better his exhibition profits by carrying a passenger aloft.

By March, Clyde had received a dozen inquiries about his airplane factory, pilot school and flying ex-

Cessna opened the first flying school in Wichita in June, 1917. He is shown here with W.E. True, Joseph J. Smitheisler, Edgar B. Smith, Marion McHugh and E.F. Rickabaugh, his first students, outside the Cessna factory/flight school housed in Building H of the Jones complex. The veteran 1913 monoplane on the right was employed as a basic trainer for the would-be airmen. The new, speedy "Comet" is at the left, with the first Wichita-built monoplane in the center. (Bob Pickett Collection)

hibitions. One letter came from a Kansas pastor who asked if Cessna could build him a four-place biplane for personal use. He couldn't, but the request supported Cessna's contention that people were interested in buying airplanes.

Spring soon rolled around and the new monoplane was nearly finished. Anzani-powered, it flew late in March and Clyde scheduled a bomb-dropping demonstration for April 10th, but high winds prevented the flight.

Cessna's bombing display, even though it didn't take place, pointed out his interest in military applications of the airplane. The widening war in Europe was threatening America by the spring of 1917. President Woodrow Wilson did not want war. He vehemently protested Germany's unrestricted submarine warfare that claimed American lives, but Yankee involvement in the Great War was inevitable. Congress approved a declaration of war against the Central Powers on April 6th.

The public rallied around the President...young men and women rushed to the aid of their country. Clyde Cessna was too old to enlist, but he could help the war effort in another way; he wired the Defense Department that his two airplanes were at their disposal. Both monoplanes were "ready for action" according to Clyde, and he believed the two-place ship would prove ideal as an aerial scout, providing valuable reconnaissance information.[7]

He also told the government that his factory stood ready to produce one airplane per week if required. All of the equipment had recently been moved into building "H" of the Jones complex, where there was more room for expansion. If production contracts came along, the brothers stood ready with adequate facilities.

Cessna was also concerned about America's near total lack of trained airmen and had read about how

Closeup view of the "Comet" cockpit/passenger compartment shows details of the fuselage cowl built to enclose the second occupant. Pulley for wing warping can be seen at top of the kingpost. (Bob Pickett Collection/Cessna Aircraft Company)

ill-prepared the country was for war, especially in air-power. On April 24th, Clyde sent a telegram to Kansas Congressman William A. Ayres requesting assistance authorized under the recently-passed National Defense Act.

He wanted the politician to wield his influence on Capital Hill for one purpose: to get Cessna the equipment, vehicles and airplanes he needed to set up a pilot training facility. Clyde proposed that he and his brothers give flight instruction to primary students, teaching them the technical aspects of airplanes and giving them basic rudiments of flight before they applied for formal army training.

Cessna's hopes were dashed when he received word that the government, although appreciative of the offer, declined his help...the army would train its own pilots. Disappointed, the brothers still hoped the government would change its attitude in the near future. Meanwhile, they continued to prepare for the exhibition season. Work on the two-place airplane progressed smoothly.

It was a slightly larger monoplane than earlier Cessna designs, primarily because the ship would carry two people; the pilot and a passenger. Wingspan was 32 feet and fuselage length 25 feet. Wing warping was retained, and the empennage area was enlarged.

A streamlined fairing, with one small window on each side, swept aft from the engine to the cockpit, completely enclosing the forward passenger compartment. The pilot's station remained exposed, although the forward fairing afforded some protection from the elements.

Sea Island cotton fabric was used for covering the entire airplane. Small shock absorbers were installed on the landing gear, each one costing Cessna $11.00. The higher gross weight required larger wheels than the other ships had used, with each wheel costing $45.00 (Clyde openly complained about the high price of building airplanes. Nearly $6,000 would be spent on the monoplane before its first flight).

For power, Cessna again used an Anzani. He purchased a new 60 hp engine and in mid-April it was installed on the uncompleted airframe. The six-cylinder powerplant swung a hand-made, eight-foot diameter propeller of silver-grained spruce and white oak. At least six more weeks would be required to finish the aircraft.

Since the government pilot training program was not to be, Cessna renewed his efforts for civilian classes. He circulated advertising about the new flight school, claiming it was the very first private flying institution west of the Mississippi River. Response was good, with over 25 applications being

Clyde Cessna and the 1917 two-place monoplane later called the "Comet". Cessna considered this ship his best design, and its performance proved him correct. He flew it from Blackwell, Oklahoma, to Wichita in 36 minutes, 35 seconds at an average speed of 107.5 mph in July, 1917. A new, 60 hp Anzani engine powered the craft. Wing warping was still used but the control cables were routed through the kingpost above the fuselage and connected to the upper surface of each wing. (Bob Pickett Collection/Cessna Aircraft Company.)

Overall view of the "Comet" clearly shows Cessna's progress with airplane design from 1911 to 1917. The airplane was still flying as late as 1922, but was reportedly destroyed by Cessna sometime in the late 1930s or early 1940s. (Bob Pickett Collection/Cessna Aircraft Company)

received by June and more were expected. Cessna now had two feathers in his cap; one for the first airplane factory in town, and the second for Wichita's first flight school.

It cost money to set up the course, and Clyde bore all expenses himself. Applicants were required to pass a physical and mental examination (administered by qualified physicians) that was equivalent to the army's in content. On June 4, 1917, the Cessna Aeroplane Exhibition Company held it's first aviator class, with but five eager, air-minded students reporting for training.

W.E. True, Joseph J. Smitheisler, Marion McHugh, Edgar B. Smith and E.F. Rickabaugh were the first to sit under Clyde Cessna's tutelage. True worked as a mechanic for the Jones company, while Smith, a student at Fairmount College, was also first assistant to Homer Harden, a commercial photographer in Wichita. McHugh worked with canvas at the Ponca Tent and Awning Company in town.

Cost for the course was $400, the period of instruction to last six to eight weeks, and by graduation day the neophyte flyers would be capable of making solo flights.[8]

Each day of class, the rookies arrived at 4:30 A.M., while the air was cool and still. After attending lecture on the theory of flight, engine operation and control movements, the students got a chance for some 'hands on' experience.

For initial instruction and ground handling practice, Clyde used the 1913 monoplane, still sporting the Elbridge engine. To give the student as realistic a flight environment as possible, the ship was suspended off the floor by a block and tackle arrangement in building "H".

Taking turns in the cockpit, each student was drilled on the purpose and movement of each lever, the control column and rudder bar. Every detail of the airplane was memorized by the five young men.

Finally, Cessna was satisfied they knew the airplane technically and the group was ready for ground handling. The ship was moved outside, and the fine points of pre-flight were explained.

Each student learned how to start the engine by whirling the wood propeller, and made low speed taxi runs across the ground. Throttle was gradually increased until very short takeoff runs were attained. After three weeks of these fundamentals all of the boys were doing well.

Clyde watched his charges with care; he evaluated their growing prowess as pilots. Two of them could become exhibition airmen, traveling around the nation, as Cessna had already contracted for over 30 flights during the upcoming season. With three airplanes and pilots to fly them, business was expected to boom.

Smith and McHugh were the likely candidates for Cessna's troupe, and they hoped to work off most of the $400 tuition by flying. True and Smitheisler intended to apply for army pilot training when they graduated.[9]

From June through October, the busy flying schedule, coupled with construction of the two-place ship, kept Clyde Cessna occupied, but he still found time to get his fledglings into the air and proceed with their training.

By July, three of the students were progressing so well that Clyde was ready to let them solo. By the middle of the month they each took the airplane up for a short hop, staying a few feet above the ground, flying straight ahead and landing.

McHugh is the only one of the five men known to have completed the entire course of instruction. He was chosen by Cessna to join the company, and reportedly made a flight at Coldwater, Kansas, while working for the exhibition company. However, Clyde's flying commitments began to compete with flight training, and time became so scarce that the would-be pilots complained. Despite Cessna's efforts to finish their education and complete the contracts, the pupils finally rebelled against their mentor.

To bring pressure on Clyde, Smith, True, Rickabaugh and McHugh filed suit for breach of contract. They claimed Cessna had not provided eight weeks of training, nor did he set up demonstrations of the student's flying as called for in the contract [the case was never tried and actual settlement is unknown. Cessna may have simply refunded tuition money to the individuals, thereby solving the situation peacefully].

Perhaps flight training wasn't Clyde's most successful venture, but the maiden flight of his latest design, the two-place monoplane, couldn't have been better. On June 24th, he made a short flight to check basic performance and control. Everything about the airplane was right; it climbed well, maneuvered easily and had a small surplus of power. Landings were gentle. With a few minor adjustments to the engine and airframe, the best Cessna yet would be ready for the show circuit.

Clyde was very enthusiastic about the ship, and wanted to take some of his business associates up for a ride. Although the airplane was outfitted with a second seat ahead of the pilot, it is uncertain if Cessna carried any passengers aloft during during the next four months.

As the Fourth of July holiday approached, the brothers were deluged with offers from 17 towns, each one offering good money for an exhibition. Clyde had already contracted with officials in Blackwell, Oklahoma, for a $500 flight there, although he had a later offer of $1,000 if he came to Jefferson City, Missouri.

On July 3rd, Cessna took off and flew to Blackwell in 41 minutes. The flying time enroute afforded him a chance to peruse every aspect of the airplane's behavior.

A crowd of 11,000 turned out for the Independence Day celebration. Clyde flew once in the early morning, then again at dusk. He really put on a show each time. Climbing to 1,000 feet, the aviator turned his craft first one way then another, increasing the bank until the wings appeared to be vertical.

Easing the ship into a dive, Clyde cut the throttle and glided down toward the masses below. Within a few hundred feet of the ground, he suddenly applied full power and zoomed directly over the spectators, causing many to scream, duck their heads and scatter in every direction.

He had earned his money, and everyone got a thrill from Cessna's flying. That night, he prepared the airplane for a return flight to Wichita early the next morning.

Taking off at 5:30 A.M., Clyde climbed above the airport and checked the engine's systems. With the Anzani's reassurring rattle ringing in his ears, Cessna pushed the throttle full forward as he passed over downtown Blackwell.

It was a speed dash to Wichita, 65 miles to the north. Cessna wanted to know just how fast the ship would go, and the air was silk smooth. With the chill wind whipping against his cheeks, the pilot glanced at the earth and easily determined that the airplane's ground speed was very high.

The engine continued its relentless din...time passed quickly. Soon, the destination appeared ahead. At 6:22 Cessna and his monoplane flashed over the Jones factory. They had made the trip in just 36 minutes, 35 seconds for a speed of 107.5 mph.

That was fast for 1917 and Clyde was justly proud of his ship. It had the speed of a shooting star; it left its mark in the sky like a...like a Comet! The name stuck.[10]

Two weeks later, Clyde and the "Comet" were airborne again, this time to check improvements made to increase speed further. These changes were minor, being limited to streamlining the airframe. The words "CESSNA MONOPLANE - MADE IN WICHITA" were painted in black under the right and left wings, respectively, along with "JONES SIX".

In the fall of 1917, Cessna and his brothers moved their flying activities from the Jones factory to a small field 1/4 mile north of Fairmount College, but the airplanes were still housed in building "H".[11]

Between August and October, the Comet was placed in Cessna's shop. Modifications were made to the airplane, including a new Anzani engine of 70 hp. Cessna said the machine would easily carry two people, and demonstrated this capability on October 9th. He made three flights, each time carrying a heavier person aloft, with 130, 150 and 165-pound individuals being carried.

All three flights were successful, with no surprises

On July 18, 1917, Clyde Cessna and Fred DeKor flew their airplanes at the West Side Racetrack to benefit the Ladies of the Federal Guard, a Wichita organization dedicated to raising money to help American servicemen. DeKor's Gnome-powered biplane and Cessna's Comet monoplane are poised wing-to-wing in this photograph. DeKor was reported to have performed loops with his biplane, but Cessna refused to attempt such maneuvers, considering them foolhardy and unnecessary. Note "CESSNA" and "JONES SIX" painted under the wings of Cessna's ship. (Wichita Chamber of Commerce)

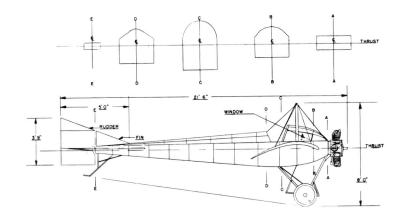

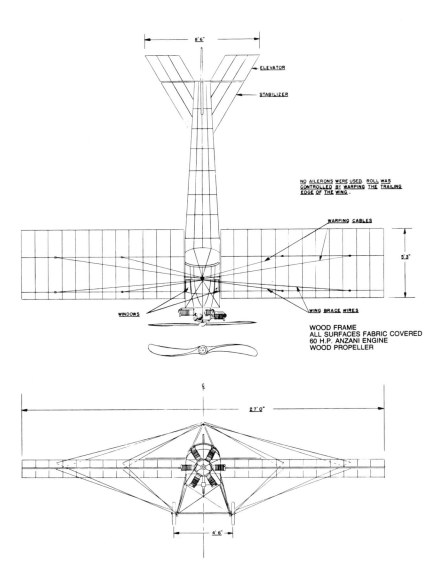

THRUST

RUDDER

FIN

WINDOW

THRUST

ELEVATOR

STABILIZER

NO AILERONS WERE USED. ROLL WAS
CONTROLLED BY WARPING THE TRAILING
EDGE OF THE WING.

WARPING CABLES

WINDOWS

WING BRACE WIRES

WOOD FRAME
ALL SURFACES FABRIC COVERED
60 H.P. ANZANI ENGINE
WOOD PROPELLER

1917 Cessna "Comet"

aerodynamically. Cessna claimed the airplane landed at only 35 mph and had exceeded all design expectations.

Clyde was so confident his monoplane could outperform other airplanes that he went looking for a worthy competitor. The only one in town during October was Louis Gertson, hired to fly at the 1917 Wheat Exposition.

Cessna went to the press and made a direct challenge to Gertson and his biplane. He proposed a race from Wichita to Hutchinson, with the victor

Later photograph of Cessna and the "Comet" shows that "JONES SIX" has been deleted from under left wing and the passenger compartment cowl has been noticeably shortened. This change is believed to have been made in the fall of 1917, when Cessna modified the Comet to more comfortably accomodate a passenger. (Smithsonian Institution Photo #81-12610)

receiving $1,000. There was no response from his fellow aviator...if the race had occurred, the Comet probably would have won easily.

Since America's entry into World War One, civilian flying had continued, but as 1918 drew closer, the picture changed; fuel rationing measures threatened to curtail most flying.

The Cessna brothers, too, found that civil aviation had little future until peace returned. For now, it was wasn't airplanes that were important, it was food. Shortages of bread were acute throughout the country...there wasn't enough to feed Americans and their comrades in arms.

Clyde Cessna still knew how to farm, so he returned to Adams and tilled the soil, helping to feed the Doughboys while doing his part to support America's war effort. Threshing wheat under the hot, Kansas sun, however, airplanes and the future were never far from his thoughts.

[1] Newspaper references state that Cessna bought the Anzani engine from John Sloan, in New York City, but positive confirmation of this could not be made. The new powerplant enabled Cessna to fly further, higher and longer than ever before, and was a welcome change from the temperamental Elbridge.

[2] The J.J. Jones Motor Company began production of the "Light Six" automobile in 1914, eventually relocating on the site of the old Burton Car Works in north Wichita. Burton was well known for construction of quality railroad cars in the late 1880s.

[3] J. H. Turner was a solid advocate and friend of aviation. He supported Cessna's 1916-1917 aircraft business and later invested money in other Wichita airplane companies that started in the 1920s.

[4] By 1915, evidence suggests that Cessna had at least an altimeter and magnetic compass in his airplanes for basic navigation and altitude control. He apparently navigated well, as he rarely became disoriented on his many trips to fly exhibitions, although much of the cross-country work was done within a 75-mile radius of Adams and he knew the country intimately. It is also interesting to note that the Hutchinson newspaper, covering the state fair in September, 1916, reported that Cessna's monoplane had a wing span of 34 feet and a length of 25 feet, weighing about 800 pounds, but these figures cannot be confirmed.

[5] Ruth Law was one of America's most celebrated female pilots in 1916-17. Her most memorable flight was a cross-country journey of 590 miles in November, 1916, flying her Curtiss pusher biplane (modified with Wright-type control levers) from Chicago to Hornell, New York, non-stop in just over five hours, setting a distance record. Miss Law campaigned rigorously for 'Liberty Loan' drives on behalf of the Red Cross and the military services.

[6] Cessna firmly believed the flight to New York City was feasible. He had already flown his 1916 monoplane "more than 400 miles" and felt very confident of flying longer distances non- stop.

[7] Although the airplane had two-seats, it is very doubtful if it could have performed the military role Cessna envisioned for it. Altitudes of 10-15,000 feet were required for good reconnaissance photographs and the little monoplane simply could not have attained such heights when light, let alone with heavy camera equipment. It is also interesting to note that Cessna quoted a price of $4,000 for each of the monoplanes he was offering for sale to the government.

[8] Edgar B. Smith later became one of Wichita's most respected and sought-after commercial photographers. He took thousands of photos for Travel Air, Cessna, Swallow, Lark, Laird and other aircraft companies in the city. He owned a Standard J-1 biplane and used it for aerial photography, often flown by local pilots like Walter Beech or Ted Braley.

[9] Except for Smith, it is unknown if the other four men continued flying after completion of the Cessna school.

[10] The Comet survived in Cessna's possession until the 1930s, when he is reported to have destroyed it when he grew tired of people asking to see the old monoplane. Unfortunately for future generations, he destroyed the last and best of his original designs.

[11] Reasons for Cessna's moving away from the 73-acre alfalfa field are unknown. There is no evidence of a problem between Cessna and Jones at any time during 1916-1917 that could have precipitated such a move.

CHAPTER FOUR
Travel Air Days

When it came to selling, Walter Beech had no peer. One day in February, 1922, Clyde Cessna was on the receiving end of a spirited Beech sales pitch. Every sentence had a punch to it; each word possessed a certain alacrity that was skillfully administered to listening ears.

Walter, along with E.M. "Matty" Laird, chief engineer of E.M. Laird Company of Wichita, flew to Clyde's farm intent on selling him a biplane. They weren't successful, but the trip did prove useful for cementing relations between the aviators. Laird and Beech had no doubt that Cessna was an ally. He shared their desire to see airplane manufacturing succeed as an industry. Since World War I, Cessna had concentrated on farming but had never lost his affection for flying.[1]

Laird had been instrumental in bringing airplane manufacture to the prairie city, starting in 1919. Oilman Jacob Melvin Moellendick had provided the cash and Matty the plans for the genesis of a new industry.

Although Cessna had been the first to actually build and attempt to sell airplanes in Wichita, the "Swallow" produced by Laird's company was hailed as the first commercially-produced airplane in the United States.[2]

It was a successful design, although it greatly resembled and barely out performed the ubiquitous JN-4 "Jenny". One advantage of Matty's double-bay wing, OX-powered ship was its ability to carry two passengers in the front cockpit. The emerging crop of gypsy pilots known as 'barnstormers' made money with those two front seats.

Although Cessna was well aware of the biplane's existence, he still clung firmly to the concept that one wing was better than two.

During Laird's tenure in Wichita, two personalities well known in American aviation came on the scene. The first was Lloyd Carlton Stearman. Working as an architect in town, he answered Matty's employment advertisement in the newspaper. Hired by Laird in 1921, Stearman started his aviation career working as a mechanic in the final assembly area at the North Hillside factory.[3]

Moellendick, ever the cavalier entrepreneur, was in need of part-time help and hired Walter Herschel Beech the same year, in Matty's absence and without his approval. Beech had been flying with Pete Hill in Arkansas City since 1919, but a disastrous hangar fire had put them out of business.

Walter was, in Laird's words, a flyer "of limited experience" when he was hired. Beech totally wrecked a Swallow his first week with the company, but the young pilot soon proved his mettle in the air.

The Laird "Swallow" biplane, powered by a Curtiss OX-5 engine of 90 hp, was the company's first and only product. Featuring room for two in the front cockpit, the Swallow sold well and its future looked good, but Moellendick and Laird parted in 1923 after about 19 ships had been sold. (Les Forden)

Left: Jacob Melvin Moellendick was a Kansas oil tycoon who believed in aviation and Wichita. He is largely responsible for starting the aircraft manufacturing business in the prairie city in 1919. (Wichita Chamber of Commerce)

Right: Matty Laird was a self-taught engineer who also possessed an inate ability to design good flying airplanes, a trait he shared with men like Clyde Cessna and Lloyd Stearman. Laird came to Wichita in 1919 to form a partnership with Jake Moellendick and Billy Burke, forming the E.M. Laird Company. (Wichita Chamber of Commerce)

Left: Kansas-bred Lloyd Carlton Stearman went to work for Jake Moellendick in 1921, then became chief engineer upon Laird's departure in 1923. He designed the New Swallow biplane late that year. It was an instant success and thrust the young engineer to the forefront of American aeronautics. He later joined forces with Walter Beech, William Snook and Clyde Cessna in founding the Travel Air Manufacturing Company in January, 1925. (Bob Pickett Collection/Cessna Aircraft Company)

Right: Flashing a rare smile for the camera, Walter Herschel Beech stands beside the Travel Air C-6 "Special" in August, 1925. Beech worked part-time at Swallow in 1921, then became general manager in 1923. Beech and Stearman wanted to build the New Swallow fuselage of welded steel tubing, but Moellendick vetoed the idea. Undaunted, the duo decided to strike out on their own and sought Clyde Cessna's help in forming a new company. (Beech Aircraft Corporation)

He won a number of important air races that kept the coffers from hitting bottom.[4]

Swallows sold well. Orders kept increasing during 1922 and 1923, but so did friction between Moellendick and Laird. Matty was the sole authority at the factory; Moellendick had no say whatsoever regarding its operations. That didn't stop Jake. He ordered a new building erected without Matty's consent and hired workers at will. A clash of personalities was inevitable.

By September, 1923, relations between Laird and Moellendick were irreconcilable. The two men were of different molds, and Jake's bold personality rubbed Matty wrong once too often. Taking two airplanes and about $1500 for himself, Laird departed Wichita for his native Chicago. He reestablished his

company there and prospered as a builder of high quality, custom-made airplanes.

Moellendick now took the reins. He changed the firm's name to "Swallow Airplane Manufacturing Company" and Stearman was made chief engineer. Beech became a flying salesman and general manager of the company. 1924 saw the introduction of the "New Swallow", a single-bay, OX-powered biplane of clean, esthetic lines.

Designed by Stearman, the ship was instantly recognizeable by its metal cowling that completely enclosed the engine. Lloyd used a welded, tubular steel engine mount to support the Curtiss powerplant. An overnight success, the New Swallow prompted orders from dealers all across the United States, and one of those orders came from a flying farmer named Cessna.

The monoplane man from Adams, Kansas, took delivery of a New Swallow biplane in January, 1924, powered by the often cantankerous OX-series eight-cylinder engine. Clyde Cessna liked the ship. He gave

Lloyd Stearman (center) left Travel Air in October, 1926, joining forces with Fred Day Hoyt (right) and George Lyle (left) to establish Stearman Aircraft, Inc., in Venice, California, late that year. Mac Short came west to join the group, and the first ship, known as the C-1 and powered by the ubiquitous OX-5 engine, looked and flew great. Unfortunately, sales were hard to get, but friends in Wichita collected nearly $60,000 to finance Stearman's return to Kansas. He set up shop in the Bridgeport Machine Company (old Jones automobile complex) in September, 1927, and found great success building mail planes and custom sportsman models. (The Boeing Company via Jack Wecker)

Not content to build only biplanes, Cessna designed and constructed this five-place, semi-cantilever wing monoplane in the winter of 1926. Powered by a 110 hp, 10-cylinder Anzani radial engine (note automatic intake valves), it first flew in June. Wingspan was 44 feet, gross weight approximately 1,200 pounds and maximum speed was about 100 mph. For 1926, this aircraft was an advanced design but still lacked the full cantilever wing Cessna advocated so strongly. Photograph taken at Travel Air Field on East Central Avenue, summer, 1926.
(Bob Pickett Collection/Cessna Aircraft Company)

nephews Dwight, Deane and Dwane Wallace their first flights in it and Dwane Wallace remembers the day very well. His mother, Grace, was Clyde's sister. She had full faith her brother's pilot abilities, but another relative cautioned her against letting all three of the boys go at once, lest she lose them all in a crash.

Grace Opal Wallace ignored the plea. There would be no accident, not with Clyde flying the ship. When the biplane landed there were three big grins in the front cockpit.

Between 1918 and 1925, the Cessnas worked their farm and also operated a custom threshing business that, according to Eldon Cessna, netted between 20 and 30 thousand dollars per season. That was big money in those days, and when Walter Beech and Lloyd Stearman decided to strike out on their own to build airplanes, they went to see Clyde Cessna.

Both men knew him well. Stearman said the first

Closeup view of cabin area shows removeable seats that transformed the airplane into an aerial ambulance in five minutes. Note shock cord detail on landing gear, cabin skylight and fuel line against right side windows. Walter Beech also flew this ship and liked its performance. As a result, Travel Air soon had a monoplane on the drawing boards that became the prototype for the Model 5000 cabin monoplane. (Bob Pickett Collection/Cessna Aircraft Company)

airplane he ever saw was flown by Cessna during one of the many exhibitions he gave during 1913-1916. Beech had sold him an airplane. They respected the seasoned aviator and sought his counsel and assistance in their new venture.

For Clyde, the opportunity to re-enter the airplane manufacturing business was too good to ignore. His abortive attempt in 1917-1918 hadn't soured his outlook on aviation. Then, conditions weren't conducive to selling aircraft, but now the rage of flight had changed the public's attitude from one of apathy to serious interest.

The three men discussed details about the new company. Cessna knew it would take large amounts of cash to get the business established, and he agreed to join the duo. No name had been chosen for the firm, and other men were still being enticed to invest money.

Beech put up $5,000, Stearman $700 and his plans for a new biplane design utilizing steel tubing for the fuselage. Cessna, in addition to being assured of the presidency, eventually loaned Travel Air almost $25,000 to help establish the firm.[5]

On January 26, 1925, Walter J. Innes, Jr. announced the formation of "Travel Air, Inc.". Innes, along with William "Bill" Snook and Charles Yankey, had joined Cessna, Beech and Stearman in their bid for the burgeoning airplane sales market.

Innes was formally announced as president of the company on February 25th. Despite Cessna's claim to the post, he was not elected president until May, serving as vice president in the interim. One possible reason for this was that Innes, a successful Wichita merchant, had invested more money than anyone else. He was also treasurer during the first five months.

Many problems faced the infant company. Foremost of these was a factory. A small, cramped portion of the Kansas Planing Mill was leased from the Breitwiser family, owners of the mill. Located at 471 West First Street, the building was soon humming with activity.[6]

Clyde loaned Travel Air some of his woodworking equipment from the farm, and by January the machinery was hard at work fashioning the company's number one airplane.

One of Cessna's first jobs as vice president was finding a company secretary. One of the applicants was a young, attractive woman named Olive Ann Mellor. The vice president told her that he wanted someone experienced in handling lots of phone calls, letters of inquiry and the other mundane tasks associated with the position.

Miss Mellor assured the vice president she could handle that requirement. Her schooling and abilities made Olive Ann Mellor the logical choice.

After deliberation with his peers, Cessna announced that Travel Air had a secretary, even if she didn't know one end of an airplane from another. She soon learned. And Walter Beech soon found Olive Ann more interesting than airplanes. Although he was quiet and reserved about his feelings, he thought highly of the hard-working gal in the front office.[7]

Cessna sensed Beech's attraction to Olive Ann and minced no words in telling him so, exhorting Walter to just go ahead and marry the girl instead of pretending he didn't care. It took Beech another five years before heeding that advice. Cessna was an active worker at the factory. He roomed in Wichita during the week and returned to the farm on weekends. Slowly the biplane took shape. Stearman had designed the ship with even more graceful lines than the New Swallow. The engine cowling concept was retained. Wings were of single-bay type, with mass balance overhang on each aileron.[8]

Designated Model "A", Travel Air's first product was completed and ready to fly by the second week of March. Irl Beach, an experienced pilot, was in command on the maiden flight. Stearman, along with L.S. Seymour, observer for the National Aeronautics Association, witnessed the highly succesful event.[9]

Cessna and Beech had insisted that safety be paramount in the new airplane. They had both flown ships that were very marginal in roll and pitch control. To make the Model A as safe as possible, the ship could be flown with only one aileron and landed with the pitch trim alone if an elevator jam arose. The elevator featured dual bellcranks and control cables for redundancy should one cable break.

O.E. Scott, of St. Louis, bought Travel Air #1 in the spring of 1925, and the company was busy trying to cope with an ever-increasing backlog of orders. Stearman had sent out over 1,000 pamphlets describing the ship to prospective buyers.

Eleven airplanes were under construction by April, with 15 ships on order a month later. The backlog was getting too great for just 15 men to handle, so the company refused any new orders until August.

Meanwhile, to keep Travel Air in the public eye (and fatten the slender treasury) air races were entered. Cessna was one of the airmen who attended the Tulsa Air Meet held August 30th through September 6th. Beech was flying a sleek, new biplane powered by a six-cylinder, 160 hp Curtiss C6 engine.

Travel Air's Model 5000 monoplane was used by National Air Transport on their Chicago-Dallas route. Featuring heated and ventilated cabins, they were popular with passengers and served NAT well until replaced with more advanced aircraft. (Beech Aircraft Corporation)

Designed by Stearman with assistance from Mac Short, the airplane was resplendent in its stunning paint scheme of gloss black and silver. Beech easily won the free-for-all event, while Short and Stearman each clinched a victory in other races.

Clyde was content to observe, not wanting to get into any throttle-bending competition. His personal ship was a stock Model A with minor drag reduction cleanup and featured the crossed rudder control cables he always preferred.

His reasoning for this configuration was simple: when one rides a bicycle and desires to turn left, the right handlebar is pushed out, not the left. A right turn is made by pushing outward on the left handlebar, not the right.

In flight, turns were made by pushing the rudder in the same fashion. As long as Clyde was the only pilot flying the craft there was no problem, but the cables were returned to the normal configuration when Cessna wasn't at the stick.[10]

Cliff Mans (far right) obtained Cessna's 1926 ship after Clyde had thoroughly tested the monoplane's safety and structural integrity, installed a different radial engine and changed the original enclosed cockpit into an open style. The ship was destroyed sometime in 1927 or early 1928. Photograph taken at Stinson Field, San Antonio, Texas. (Harry B. Adams via Bob Pickett)

38

At the end of 1925 Travel Air had sold 19 airplanes, and the order book was stuffed full of firm sales. Another facility was obtained on West Douglas Avenue to accomodate the increased production rate.

In August of 1926, Walter Beech and Brice Goldsborough won the second annual Ford Reliability Tour in a specially-built biplane. Financed by investors in New York City and Wichita, the airplane was fully equipped with the latest in flight and navigation instrumentation furnished by the Pioneer Instrument Company.

Beech sought outside financing because of Cessna and Stearman's opposition to building a costly airplane at Travel Air's expense. It was a rational decision based on the financial tightrope the firm was on during its first two years of existence. However, when Walter produced the $10,000 required, nobody objected to construction of the ship by Travel Air employees.

Clyde was a cautious and pragmatic businessman. He had already invested thousands of dollars in the company since its beginning. Much of the funds had been consumed by hiring new workers, buying equipment and tools as well as purchasing a stock of war-surplus OX-5 and OXX-6 powerplants.

With the advent of modern, but expensive static radials, Cessna, Beech and Stearman decided to design the standard biplane craft into the Model BW, powered with the Wright J-4 engine of 200 hp. The company's first radial-powered ship was sold to W.B. "Skipper" Howell and cost a whopping $9,800.

Although Cessna was president of a successful, growing enterprise, he was restless. Biplanes were everywhere; monoplanes were not to be seen on the assembly lines. Walter, while favoring the biplane, was well aware of Clyde's preference for one-wing aircraft.

The problem was production. Biplanes were selling while monoplanes were still something of a novelty. They required different design considerations and manufacturing techniques untried by the company up to that time.

In the winter of 1926, Cessna approached Beech and Stearman about building a monoplane for his own use. He wasn't asking for help in any way from Travel Air; he would pay all cost and use another building for construction.

His two partners had no objection, so Clyde started

Travel Air built nearly 800 OX-5-powered biplanes from 1925 through 1930. Initially known as Model A, then Model B, the type was designated Model 2000 by 1927. Many were used for flight instruction, like this example belonging to the Wichita-based Braley School of Flying. (Bob Pickett Collection)

work along with the help of Guy Winstead, a long-time Wichita pilot and skilled craftsman. Renting a small shop on Wichita's west side, construction was well underway by March.

This latest design, (the ninth since 1911) would feature a completely enclosed cabin for five occupants, surrounded by generous window area. A 300-pound, semi-cantilever wing, spanning 44 feet, was mounted above the fuselage, with dual lift struts on each side.

Entry/exit from the ship was through a large door installed on the left side, complete with a viewing window. The wicker chairs could be quickly removed to convert the aircraft into a flying ambulance, with only five minutes required to make the change.

Seated up front, the pilot had excellent all-around visibility. Landing gear was of coventional design with shock cord in tension on vertical strut assemblies. Powered with a 110 hp, 10-cylinder, air-cooled Anzani static radial, the monoplane could carry 1,000 pounds and land at only 45 mph. Gross weight was estimated to be 1,200 pounds. In May the ship was completed and groomed for its first flight.

On June 14, 1926, Cessna test-flew the airplane for 20 minutes and was very satisfied with its initial performance. Next day he flew the machine with two passengers aboard, and then Walter Beech took the controls.

Beech was quite impressed. Although he and Clyde had their disagreements about monoplanes and biplanes, Walter admitted that the ship flew well and was very promising. It was so promising that it became the basis for Travel Air's first monoplane, the Type 5000.[11]

In October, National Air Transport invited the company to enter competition for a new airplane to be used on the Chicago to Dallas route, day and night. Air mail, passengers and express would be carried, and at least eight airplanes would be ordered from the winning manufacturer. Timing was very fortuitous for the young Wichita company. Clyde's monoplane was already a successful design, so Beech and Cessna began discussing how a new airplane could be built quickly and still retain the virtues of the Anzani-powered ship. There was no time to waste...less than 70 days remained until NAT wanted a demonstration flight.

Cessna, working along with company engineers, began revamping his concepts to satisfy the needs of National Air Transport. Lloyd Stearman had resigned on October 8th, so Clyde spearheaded the project with his usual determination to succeed. He told the newspaper that the new monoplane was his creation, indicating that he was given considerable, if not complete, freedom in developing the design.

Many of Clyde's monoplane theories, proven on the five-place craft, were incorporated into the new design. In the cabin, four passengers were seated in cushioned, metal chairs. Two windows on each side of the cabin could be easily opened for cooling, while cold temperatures were handled by a complete heating system.

The pilot was seated in a separate cockpit forward of the cabin. A removable, cupola-style canopy, jettisonable in flight, covered the cockpit (it was often removed for summer flying).

Two sets of wings were built and flown on the prototype airplane. One set featured a reduced span that decreased drag but also increased wing loading and stall speed. Since many airports NAT anticipated operating from had short runways, the higher approach and landing speeds would be a liability.

A larger set of wings, using the M-6 airfoil, were constructed and stall, landing and approach speeds were lowered, much to the satisfaction of Travel Air and NAT officials. After further flight testing, the big wing was selected for future production models.

Knowing that servicing of the engine would be important to an airline, Cessna designed the engine and its mount to swing away from the fuselage for maintenance. In fact, complete engine changes could be accomplished in less than 30 minutes with experienced mechanics doing the work.

A Wright J-4 of 200 hp graced the nose, moving the ship through the air at more than 100 mph while lifting 1,100 pounds with its semi-cantilever wings. Clarence Clark, chief test pilot, was very enthusiastic about the airplane when he made the first flight in early December. Only 69 days had elapsed since construction began.

Cruising speed was 105 mph and stability was good about all three axes. Visibility for the pilot was very good, even during approach and landing. After some adjustments to the airframe and engine, Walter Beech and Clyde Cessna flew the airplane to Kansas City on December 20th, landing at Richards Field.

National Air Transport pilot Egbert P. Lott inspected the ship and then flew it. He liked it. Cessna stressed the salient points of its modern construction, while salesman Beech emphasized how comfortable passengers would be in the spacious, heated cabin. Lott was certain the Type 5000 was right for NAT. Winging their way back to Wichita, the two air pioneers knew they had a good chance for a contract. Meanwhile, there was pressing business back at the office.

Cessna was a very busy man that December. Not only had he led the way to monoplanes for the company but he also helped supervise layout of a new factory.

Thanks to the Booster Building Association, a group of aviation-minded businessmen in Wichita, arrangements had been made for six acres of ground at the East Central flying field to be purchased.

A sorely-needed factory complex was to be built on the site, the first unit being 75 feet wide and 275 feet long.

Cessna and Beech closely supervised floor plan details, and $30,000 worth of stock issues would pay for the new facility. With the West Douglas building bursting at the seams, it was paramount that the company move into the factory as soon as possible, but it was June 27th before production was shifted to the new location.

On January 7th, NAT awarded Travel Air a contract for eight Type 5000 monoplanes, worth $128,676. To meet NAT's requirements, the production airplanes would be larger overall and feature the production wing plus Wright "Whirlwind" J-5 power.

Beech and Cessna continued to discuss further monoplane developments, but Clyde was still anxious to seek his own path. Although the NAT ships had proven the merits of monoplanes to Walter Beech and the board of directors, it seemed unlikely that they would acquiesce to Mr. Cessna's true desire: to design, build and produce a full-cantilever wing monoplane.

Clyde informed Walter about his intention to start a company. Beech understood. He encouraged his friend and wished him success. There were no hard feelings between them, as each man respected the others' beliefs about airplane design.[12]

The catalyst for Cessna's decision came in late January. Three Wichita businessmen offered to buy Clyde's 179 shares of stock for $90 per share. Richard M. Gray, John Rigby and J.A. Woods purchased the issues. Profits from the sale enabled Cessna to seriously consider his personal re-entry into airplane manufacturing. News traveled fast, and Clyde's departure from Travel Air was quickly the talk of the town.

Reporters sought him for interviews, wanting to know all about his immediate and future plans. Cessna told them, "Monoplanes are the only worthwhile type of aircraft", his convictions ringing clear and true in every word.

With that statement he set his course. Cessna was in Wichita to stay...he intended to design, build and sell monoplanes with a full-cantilever wing. For 16 years he had believed such a structure was technically feasible. Now, he would turn his beliefs into reality.

---

[1] The years between World War I and 1922 found Cessna busy with his son, Eldon, in a custom threshing business. But Clyde never stopped thinking about building airplanes. He still flew the Comet, and Eldon remembers flying with his father in the ship to Wichita in 1924 to visit the Swallow company.

[2] Virtually all of the post-war airplanes used for commercial purposes were military surplus types, usually the Curtiss JN-4 'Jenny' or Standard J-1 biplanes. Laird's Swallow was one of the first airplanes to be built specifically for use in the infant commerical airplane marketplace.

[3] Lloyd Carlton Stearman saw his first airplane at Harper, Kansas, flown by Clyde Cessna. The two men later became good friends and remained so through the years, teaming up to begin Travel Air in late 1924.

[4] Moellendick's hiring of Beech was not well accepted by Laird initially, although Walter was soon viewed as an asset to the company.

[5] Cessna's successful threshing business enabled him to keep the cash flow at Travel Air in the black. Local banks were hesitant to loan the company any money until an acceptable profit margin was established.

[6] The Breitwiser brothers offered Travel Air the small space to work on the first biplane. They had recently built the shop at 471 West First Street for their expanding business, and eventually the building served as the starting point for a number of other budding airplane firms in the late 1920s.

[7] Walter Beech and Olive Ann Mellor were married in 1930. She became president of Beech Aircraft Corporation in November, 1950, after Mr. Beech succumbed to a heart attack.

[8] Stearman designed the Model "A" Travel Air biplane to use steel tubing for the entire fuselage structure and the engine mount, as well as part of the empennage assembly.

[9] Beach (no relation to Beech) was an expert aviator and highly respected among Wichita's flyers. He made several flights on Travel Air's production prototype, with the ship lifting 1,119 pounds of bagged sand...an amount almost equal to the airplane's 1,300 pound empty weight.

[10] Cessna flew the monoplane extensively in 1926, wringing it out until he was certain of its safety before selling it. By 1927 or 1928, it was in the possession of Cliff Mans, flying out of Stinson Field in San Antonio, Texas. Mans installed another engine and continued operating the aircraft, but it was reportedly destroyed that year in an accident.

[11] Clyde Cessna continued to use this rudder cable configuration, and always maintained that everyone else flew airplanes with rudder cables connected wrong. Carl Evans, Cessna's long-time friend since his earliest flying days, also remarked that Clyde feared patent suits if he used the conventional rudder cable configuration.

[12] The long-standing story that Beech and Cessna came to an argument over biplanes and monoplanes, causing Cessna to leave Travel Air is without foundation. Beech believed in monoplanes, so much so that he conceived and initiated a market research program to define exactly what pilots wanted in such a ship. He ordered his engineers to develop the powerful A6000A with its Pratt & Whitney 'Wasp' engine, pushed hard to get floats approved for both the Model S6000B and the SA6000A versions, and by June of 1929, fully one-half of the Travel Airs delivered had one wing.

CHAPTER FIVE
Flight of the Phantom

The lights at 615 South Green Avenue in Wichita burned far into the night during February and March, 1927, as a man with an insatiable desire to build monoplanes pursued his goal.

Clyde Cessna did not remain idle after leaving the Travel Air company, but plunged himself into long, hard hours of detailed design work on a full-cantilever wing airplane, spending over 60 days developing its basic layout.

On April 19th, he declared (in name only) the beginning of the Cessna Aircraft Company, with assets of two airplanes, one employee and lots of optimism for the future.

Both aircraft were full-cantilever wing monoplanes, one designed to carry five people and the other only three. The five-place ship, unofficially called the "Cessna Common", had a wingspan of 47 feet and was intended to be powered by a 200 hp Wright J-4 radial, while its sister ship, tagged the "Cessna All Purpose", featured a wingspan of 36 feet with a 100 hp engine.

Useful load for the two aircraft was expected to be 1,000 pounds, with maximum speeds of 120 mph for the "All Purpose" and 140 mph for the "Common".[1]

Clyde Cessna smiles proudly from the cockpit of his latest design, the "Phantom", in August, 1927. A very clean design from spinner to rudder, the full-cantilever monoplane was powered by a 90 hp, 10-cylinder Anzani radial engine swinging a wooden Hamilton propeller. Cabin was configured to seat three, including the pilot. First flown on August 13, 1927, with Romer G. Weyant at the controls. (Bob Pickett Collection/Cessna Aircraft Company)

Although Cessna intended to form a company soon, no formal incorporation nor sale of any airplanes would occur until both designs were completely tested and analyzed. A 50' x 75' workshop at 1520 West Douglas Avenue was obtained, and by the end of the month tools and equipment were being moved in.

Clyde knew he had an uphill battle ahead with the Department of Commerce regarding the full-cantilever wing structure, so he decided to build the three-place ship first as a proof-of-concept airplane.[1]

Construction began in May, with Cessna, Carl Winstead and Johnny Hiebert comprising the workforce. The 23-foot long fuselage outline was carefully chalk-lined on the workshop floor, then the tubing was tack-welded to check alignment. Final welding was done slowly, since only a simple jig was used to hold the tubes in place.

Bob Phelps, who had been with Travel Air since its very early days, was wooed away by Cessna and paid $15 per week for his talents with wood and metal (working adjacent to Clyde's table, Phelps remembers how Cessna worked out control movements and reactions using small wooden sticks, with the nails holding them in place acting as pivot points).

Wing construction followed a simple, empirical rule: overbuild it. Cessna did, with a 12-inch thick center section tapering along the 37-foot, four inch span to two and one-half inches at the wingtips. It was designed to be shoulder-mounted on the fuselage, with the front spar face acting as a headrest for the pilot and right-seat passenger.

To satisfy the strict government requirements for issuance of an Approved Type Certificate, a thorough stress analysis was necessary on the entire airplane, and Cessna knew the wing would receive a particularly tough evaluation.

Since Clyde could not perform the analysis himself (Carl Evans said Cessna's engineering "was in his eye") because he had no formal education to tackle the task, he engaged Joseph S. Newell, professor of aeronautical engineering at Massachusetts Institute of Technology for that purpose. Technical drawings and data on the new airplane were sent to Newell so he could commence his analysis (although Cessna could not sell any aircraft until receiving government approval, he could build and fly prototype models).[2]

Meanwhile, the group of workers were proceeding at a feverish pace with final assembly of the little monoplane. If all went well, it would be completed and flight tested in time for the upcoming New York to Spokane Air Derby in September with George I. Myers as pilot.[3]

Refusing to rush the project just for an air race, Clyde supervised the final construction details of the ship with care. He was also occupied with locating a possible factory site since he estimated the company would build almost 100 ships the first year.

The ten-cylinder, 90 hp Anzani engine was hung on mounts ahead of the open cockpit, and the airplane was ready for its maiden flight. On Saturday, August 13, 1927, Romer G. Weyant, (who was hoping to have his own Cessna monoplane for the air derby) climbed into the single-seat cockpit, checked the Anzani's instruments and taxied across the makeshift airfield at 13th Street and Hydraulic Avenue.

After a short pause to recheck controls and the engine, Weyant eased the throttle forward, feeling the airplane accelerate as it bounced gently over the sod. At 40 mph the trim monoplane broke ground, eagerly climbing into the wind.

For nearly an hour Weyant checked every handling characteristic of the craft, doing stalls, full throttle dashes along with turns, climbs and glides. When he landed, the first Cessna company test pilot reported that Clyde's creation had no serious problems, but that some wing torsional vibration was felt in flight. Dwane Wallace, who witnessed the event, remembers this condition being caused by inadequate brace wires in the wing structure. Maximum speed observed during the flight was almost 100 mph...good performance on only 90 hp.

Cessna now dubbed his monoplane the "Phantom", with a gross weight of 1,200 pounds and a payload of 722 pounds. He was very pleased with the machine's performance, and so was Victor H. Roos, a motorcycle dealer from Omaha, Nebraska, who wanted to talk with Cessna about a possible partnership between the two men.[4]

Roos was a good salesman, and liked what he saw in the Phantom. It was a fresh and different design, one that held promise in the growing commercial airplane market. Informal announcement of the joint venture was made August 22nd, and soon thereafter Cessna and Roos finalized paperwork for their new company.

By the end of the month, materials were on hand to build 12 Phantoms, and a second ship was already taking shape. It would be very similar to the first, but had its wing mounted on top of the fuselage and

Serving as a prototype for the "A"-series airplanes, the first ship was used as a testbed to prove out Cessna's full-cantilever wing structure. Internally-braced wings were not new to aviation, but the Department of Commerce demanded very thorough stress analysis and testing on the wing before approving it for production. (Bob Pickett Collection/Cessna Aircraft Company)

featured right and left side cabin entry doors with a nine-cylinder, 200 hp Wright J-4 up front.

In early September, 15 men were hard at work getting the Phantom and the second airplane ready for the air derby. Chances were slim that either ship would be completed in time, but the $200 Clyde paid for entry fees wouldn't be lost; if neither airplane made the derby, then at least one of them would be entered in the National Air Races held in conjuction with the derby contest.

September 9th found the second airplane nearing completion, with the engine and propeller installed. It was a madhouse at the workshop, everyone scurrying to finish the ship, so much so that Cessna finally put a halt to it, withdrawing both monoplanes from competition. There simply wasn't sufficient time, and rushing to meet deadlines didn't appeal too much to Clyde...he was in business to sell airplanes, not to win races.

One week later monoplane number two was ready to take wing. It was painted red overall, with race number 5 in white on the fuselage sides. The cockpit was covered by a Pyrolin windshield, open on each side, to afford some streamlining.

Trucked out to Swallow Field (this was Wichita's first true airport, located at 29th Street and Hillside

Man and machine. Cessna poses with his monoplane inside the workshop at 1520 West Douglas Avenue. Metal fairings on top of the center section cover 16 bolts used to secure the wing assembly to the fuselage. (Bob Pickett Collection/Cessna Aircraft Company)

Public relations, Cessna-style! 17 men standing on the prototype's wing was good advertising and worked wonders with the public's image of an airplane without wing struts. (Bob Pickett Collection/Cessna Aircraft Company)

Pre-production "A"-series wing is shown here before fabric covering was applied in this October, 1927 photograph. The tapered front and rear spars show up well, as does the plywood covering around the leading edge. Of special interest are the wire braces used to give torsional stiffness to the wing structure. (Bob Pickett Collection/Cessna Aircraft Company)

Avenue. It was an active flying field as early as 1919), a careful preflight inspection was done while fueling was completed (using metal buckets to pour gasoline into the wing tanks) and last minute details double-checked.

Romer Weyant, again doing honors at the stick, took his seat and fired up the mighty J-4.

Soon, man and machine were ready to go. 200 horsepower pulled the ship faster and faster across the grass, then it was airborne...for ten seconds. The Wright's ear-splitting roar suddenly changed to an erie silence, and Weyant's mount changed from an airplane to a bulldozer.

As the tires hit ground, first one and then two wire fences were torn asunder, followed by a stubborn hedgerow that snagged the gear, tripping the airplane up on its nose with the left wingtip dug in the dirt.

As the dust settled, Weyant, unhurt, bolted from the ship to observe the damage; one blade of the micarta propeller was broken, and the wingtip was slightly crushed. Engine damage was confined to smashed cooling fins and the valve mechanism on one cylinder.

Clyde, arriving on the scene almost immediately,

Design #2 is believed to have been modified with cabin side windows and 10-cylinder Anzani radial engine as a production prototype of the "A"-series monoplanes. It is shown here in early December, 1927. Note single cabin entry door on right side; production airplanes had another door at the front. (Bob Pickett Collection/Cessna Aircraft Company)

surveyed the situation and estimated $300 would fix everything except the cylinder. That would be a problem, since Wright Aeronautical couldn't possibly ship a new unit for weeks. Cessna was having great difficulty procuring engines from Wright, as was just about everybody else who wanted one. Their powerplants were in extreme demand and supply, including parts, was short.

Cause of the accident was incredibly simple; the buckets used to fuel the airplane were not properly cleaned before use, permitting a small amount of dirt to contaminate the fuel, starving the J-4 at the worst possible time.

Repairs to the wing and cylinder were underway by the next day, with men working through the night to accomplish the task. With regret, Clyde informed George Myers that no racing would be done with Cessna #5 during the fall season.

Weyant and Myers, whose interest in Cessna airplanes centered around glory and winning big bucks, lost enthusiasm, but Weyant stayed on as company test pilot. Cessna, however, needed more than one man for flying duties.

He soon found another one: Francis "Chief" Bowhan. Part Osage indian, Bowhan hit the big money when black gold was found under his property, and, with nothing better to do with his cash, took up flying in the early 1920s. He was a flamboyant individual, with an occasional irreverance for authority, rules and regulations, but possessed natural skill as an airman. Both men already knew

each other from their tenure with the Travel Air company, and Chief, as he was universally known, was a welcome addition to the company payroll.[5]

At the first company meeting, held on September 26th, the Board of Directors was elected, with their shares of stock as follows:

Clyde V. Cessna - 387 1/2 shares
Victor H. Roos - 237 1/2 shares
George H. Siedhoff - 123 shares
C.A. McCorkle - 1 share
J.D. Fair - 1 share

Cessna and Roos, since they had only a partnership in effect prior to incorporation, had equipment and materials on hand that needed to be absorbed into the new company. They proposed to sell these assets to the firm for the sum of $75,000.

Assets included 67 10-cylinder, 90 hp Anzani radial engines, including spare parts; all wood, sheet metal and tooling on hand at the 1520 West Douglas workshop as of August 22, 1927; patents and applications for patents and the good will of the Cessna Aircraft Company, along with two Cessna monoplanes.

Based on Clyde's interest in the property, he was later voted 512 1/2 shares of capital stock. The official name of the new business was voted as "The Cessna-Roos Aircraft Company", with Cessna and Roos each receiving $50 per week salary.

On October 5th, Arthur "Art" Goebel, winner of the Dole race to Hawaii the previous summer, turned the first spade of dirt for a new factory complex at First Street and Glenn Avenue on Wichita's west side.

Known as the Swartz tract, it comprised 27 acres of land, with ample room for flight operations north of the factory. Plans were drawn up by the architectural firm of Schmidt, Boucher and Overend, receiving approval from Cessna and Roos in early October.

The main building would be 100′ × 150′, facing First street, housing primary and final assembly areas, with a second structure, 50 feet square, to be used for all dope and painting, located 20 feet west of the larger building in case of fire. Cost was estimated to be $35,000 to erect the facility, and George Siedhoff's company got the contract, starting work that month.

The land for the factory was large enough that Cessna offered to share it with Lloyd Stearman and

Clyde Cessna cranks the inertia starter on Cessna-Roos Design #2. Closeup view affords good detail of J-4 installation and landing gear shock cord. (Bob Pickett Collection/Cessna Aircraft Company)

Mac Short, who had recently returned to Wichita from California. Stearman, along with Short and Fred Day Hoyt, had been struggling to sell their biplanes on the Pacific coast since November, 1926, with little success.

Walter Innes, Jr. had drummed up almost $60,000 cash in one afternoon on the telephone, and then called Lloyd to ask him about coming back to the Plains. He and his partners agreed to the offer, and the Stearman Aircraft Company set up shop in the old Jones Motor Company buildings, then housing the Bridgeport machine works.

The airplane shown in this February, 1928 photograph is believed to be Cessna Design #2, after rework from the Anzani-powered version to the Wright J-4 ship shown here. Cessna may have been using the aircraft for prototype testing of the Model BW series. Note registration number-- X1627. (Bob Pickett Collection/Cessna Aircraft Company)

43

Six key men of the Cessna Aircraft Company pose before Cessna-Roos Design #1. Left to right: Romer G. Weyant, test pilot; George Bassett, Wichita financier; Clyde Cessna, George Siedhoff, building contractor and member of the Cessna board of directors; Francis "Chief" Bowhan, test pilot; Meade Hargiss, assistant sales manager. (Bob Pickett Collection/Cessna Aircraft Company)

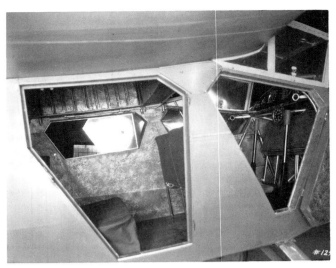

Interior view of X1627 showing early cabin appointments and instrument panel. Note aft sliding window, fuel lines and wing spar carrythrough, just above front seats. Entry into the pilot seat was awkward at best, while rear seat passengers had a much larger door. Levers with rings on the end below instrument panel are throttles, designed for use from either seat. Airspeed indicator hangs below center of panel. (Bob Pickett Collection/Cessna Aircraft Company)

Although he would have liked to accept Clyde's offer, Lloyd declined; it was just too soon in his company's short life to think about a factory complex. Stearman's California venture may have been unsuccessful, but in Wichita he was soon prospering as a builder of quality, high-performance biplanes. The C-3-series ships (the first Wichita product) were an instant favorite with many small contract air mail (CAM) operators.

As concrete foundations were being poured for the Cessna-Roos factory, Bowhan flew the third production prototype monoplane on October 9th from Swallow Field. Whirlwind-powered, the airplane's wing area had been increased by 50 square feet, new Cessna-designed wing ribs used and four seats were installed in the completely upholstered cabin. Fuselage length was now 25 feet, and all production models would incorporate this and the interior improvements as standard.

Further tests were conducted on the new ship to check how the increased wing area affected performance, with results indicating a lower stall speed benefit and payload increase to 1,200 pounds.

With the company's first design approaching production status, Newell (and the students who worked under his supervision) were working hard on the stress analysis. Clyde had received word from Newell that the original wing was overbuilt and overweight; he commented that production wings could be lighter without sacrificing strength or safety factor.

The Department of Commerce allowed Cessna to proceed with any initial deliveries of his monoplanes to customers with the Approved Type Certificate pending.

Cessna reported three orders in hand as November approached, one of them coming from famed pugilist W.L. "Young" Stribling. He and his father contacted the company about buying an airplane as well as becoming a distributor in their home state of Georgia.

Stribling did not know how to fly, but he had taken numerous flights in Travel Air and Swallow airplanes during his visits to Wichita for boxing matches. Cessna intended to deliver the first production monoplane to him by December if the cramped workshop permitted the ship to be built in time.

One thing was certain: without a new factory to build airplanes quickly and efficiently, nobody would get a Cessna product. As Thanksgiving day drew closer, bricklaying was finished, roofing was in progress and new equipment was arriving daily, being installed as fast as Siedhoff's men moved out.

Four hangars, each one 50′ × 25′, were also being built just north of the main complex, and the Standard Oil Company placed two, 500 gallon storage tanks, with pumps, on the site.

On November 23rd, the exodus from 1520 West Douglas to First Street and Glenn Avenue began. The first two weeks of December were spent setting up the final tooling and machinery, preparatory to commencing production.

Finishing touches were being put on the personnel roster, too, with the Board of Directors being brought up to full strength of nine members. Henry J. Allen, William B. Harrison, William Floto and Meade Hargiss rounding out the group. G. Curtis Quick, well-known for his engine expertise in converting LeRhone rotaries to static radials and T.T. Maroney, previously a California flyer, were hired to help organize sales territories and keep the factory in contact with its far-flung distributors. Quick would also serve as an engineer in the powerplant section of the factory.

Roos, staying in the background publicly up to this point in time, now became openly displeased with the manner in which Cessna and other directors were handling company affairs. At a meeting held November 15th, he declared his objections to "proposed plans and changes" for the firm, namely discussion about changing the name to "Cessna Aircraft Company," as suggested by other board members. No action was taken on this sensitive issue during the meeting, but tensions were beginning to run high between Roos and his colleagues.[6]

When the next meeting was held on November 22nd, the subject again came up and this time sparks flew. Roos vehemently objected to any change in the company's name, claiming it would be detrimental to the firm just when production was about to begin in earnest and was also an "injustice" to him personally.

As far as Roos was concerned, if the directors were going to change the company's name, then he was entitled to remuneration for such an action. The board disagreed and Roos tendered his resignation on the spot.

On December 22nd, the Charter Board of the State of Kansas approved the corporate name change to "The Cessna Aircraft Company". Victor Roos went across town to become manager of the Swallow Aircraft Company.[7]

There was peace on earth and peace within the Cessna company that Christmas, as 20 employees labored to complete 6 airplanes. Only four monoplanes had reportedly been built and flown since the company began nearly five months earlier (it is interesting to note that as of December, 1927, 974 airplanes had been built in Wichita aircraft factories since 1919).

Along with Stribling, who was taking flying lessons from Bowhan, Edmund A. Link of Pittsburgh, Pennsylvania, was waiting to take delivery of his monoplane. As of February, 1928, no airplanes had yet been delivered to a customer. Vexing problems with procurement of the new Wright J-5 now began to plague the production line.[8]

There was a solution to this problem: install the old Anzani radials. Clyde's stock of the French powerplant numbered 67, but they required major rework before being considered a satisfactory engine for production airplanes.

Cessna, with technical and engineering help from Curtis Quick, began transforming the pre-World War One design into dependable powerplants. Aluminum alloy pistons were installed. The automatic intake valves (identical to Clyde's 1914 engine) were replaced by a cam-activated mechanism that permit-

ted more horsepower to be developed up to a higher altitude.

Lubrication was vastly improved by use of a scavenge return in addition to the pressure delivery system already on the engines, and a crankcase ventilation tube was also installed. Dual ignition, using Scintilla magnetos, completed the transformation from 90 hp to an advertised 120 hp. These modified radials were very reliable, and although the company didn't sell airplanes using them in large numbers, it was not because of the engine's performance; customer acceptance of the 'old-fashioned' radial was generally low and hindered sales.

It took more time and money to incorporate such improvements into the powerplant, causing further delivery delays. Cessna ordered one Siemens-Halske radial in January, planning to install it for exhaustive testing before making a purchase commitment for more examples to T. Claude Ryan, who marketed the German-designed product.

Mounting one of the first modified Anzanis on a production airframe, the Cessna Aircraft Company finally delivered its first monoplane to E.A. Link and Richard Bennett on February 28, 1928. Link paid $6,500 for the ship, flying it home at a leisurely pace a few days later. Bennett, who had signed up as a Cessna distributor for New York state, remained behind to learn all he could about the technical aspects of the monoplanes.

Stribling, however, tired of waiting and bought a Swallow biplane in March, forfeiting his hoped-for rights to a Cessna distributorship. Clyde didn't want to lose Stribling as a customer, but there were many more to replace the boxer as people began to line up at the factory door for airplanes. To boost things along even more, the upcoming Detroit aviation exposition would afford the company widespread exposure.

Mr. H.H. Linn, whose company built the popular Linn ten-ton truck, placed an order for a special monoplane with dual controls, special interior appointments and a Wright J-5 engine; it also came with price tag exceeding $10,000. This ship was flown

Loaded and ready to go, X1627 displays the entry doors and somewhat cramped cabin common to all of the early Cessna monoplanes. Note the inward/upward-folding right side cockpit window. (Bob Pickett Collection/Cessna Aircraft Company)

Closeup view of landing gear and Wright J-4 on X1627. No brakes were installed, and 16 loops of shock cord were used to absorb taxi and landing loads. The long exhaust stack on the bottom cylinder was routed to avoid drawing fumes into the updraft carburetor and the cabin. (Bob Pickett Collection/Cessna Aircraft Company)

to the Detroit show in April and displayed there, drawing much attention. Clyde, who attended the event, reported back to the factory that he had been flying many demonstration flights, some resulting in sales by closing day of the exhibition.

As April came to an end, the company had delivered another Whirlwind-powered monoplane to W.T. Ponder of Fort Worth, Texas, who also became a Cessna distributor for the area, while Beacon Airways of Kansas City, Missouri took delivery of a Siemens-Halske-powered ship, the first one delivered by the company.

This airplane was put to work during the Republican National Convention, held in Kansas City that August, flying newsreel film to St. Louis for Pathe News. It was also good advertising for Cessna and Beacon Airways, since the passengers liked the speed and comfort the monoplane had to offer.

Orders for the J-5-powered airplanes continued to roll in, but a lack of engines continued to prevent more than a few deliveries. As late as July, only five were in customer's hands. Clyde wrote letters and wired Wright Aeronautical about shipping schedules, pressing them about their promise to send him a quantity of engines. Finally, when Clyde was called about the shipment, he was alotted only one engine per month.

Cessna wasn't alone, though; every airplane company in the city was crying the blues over the radial's scarcity. Travel Air and Swallow, along with Charles Laird's company building the "Whipporwill" cabin biplane, couldn't get the highly reliable powerplants in sufficient numbers.

Testing with the improved Anzani engines was accelerated to help fill the void. Curtis Quick and his

Cessna "A"-series stripped of its fabric cover shows the rugged chrome-molybdenum steel tube fuselage/empennage assembly and all-wood, full-cantilever wing. (Bob Pickett Collection/Cessna Aircraft Company)

brother, Tom, climbed to 15,500 feet with an Anzani-powered Cessna and found that the modifications produced significant increases in the powerplant's performance, especially in climb rate and cruise regimes. Further flights were needed to confirm cylinder head and oil temperatures, plus fuel and oil consumption, but at least the program showed promise and development continued.

New, lightweight engines were making their presence felt by late July, and Cessna was quick to use them. The following list shows the engines used on production ships by late summer:

- 120 hp Anzani, 10-cylinder
- 110 hp Warner; seven-cylinder
- 220-225 hp Wright J-5, nine-cylinder
- 118-125 hp Siemens-Halske, nine-cylinder
- 115-150 hp Floco, seven-cylinder (Axelson after August, 1928)
- 130-150 hp Comet, seven-cylinder

The rugged, reliable Warner 'Scarab' proved to be the most popular of all these engines, not only because of its small frontal area, but because it was miserly with a gallon of fuel, could be maintained in the field easily and the manufacturer backed up the product with good parts and service support.

Cessna recognized a good engine when he saw one and quickly became a valued customer for the Warner company (by 1929, almost all "A"-series ships were powered with the seven-cylinder radial).

Everyone of Cessna's employees at the factory was working at maximum capacity to meet delivery dates. With all the hustle and bustle going on around the facility, little thought was given to air racing. There was both monetary and advertising value in competing and winning races (Cessna recognized that fact), but it would take a special event, with a good chance of seeing a Cessna monoplane in the winner's circle, before the company's president would go for the glory.

That special event did come in September, 1928. The National Air Races were to be held in Los Angeles, with four cross-country dashes to liven up the annual competition:

Class A: Open to all airplanes with engine displacement not to exceed 510 cubic inches.

Class B: Open to all airplanes with engine displacement more than 510 cubic inches but less than 800 cubic inches.

Class C: Open to all airplanes with engine displacements exceeding 800 cubic inches.

The fourth classification was a non-stop race across the continental United States. Cessna planned to enter every category, believing the speed of his monoplanes could put him in the winner's circle.

Cessna and the board of directors decided that eight airplanes would be entered and then selected pilots to fly them. As of August 28th, the lineup looked like this (listed with airframe series, engine and pilot):

Class A Division: "A"-series, 110 hp Warner, Earl Rowland; Class B Division: Five "B"-series, 220 hp Wright J-5, Francis 'Chief' Bowhan, F.J. Grace, Jay Sadowski, Edward G. Schultz and J. Warren Smith; "A"-series, 120 hp Anzani, Clyde Cessna and G. Curtis Quick (flying together); Cross Country Division: "B"-series, 225 hp Wright J-5, Owen Haugland. No entrants were posted for the Class C Division.

Sadowski, Smith, Grace and Haugland were Cessna distributors. Haugland's airplane was specially fitted with cabin fuel tanks holding 350 gallons, and was expected to cruise at 130 mph for the entire transcontinental dash. On August 30th, he departed the California Section (the only field in Wichita big enough to allow the fuel-laden ship sufficient takeoff distance. The tanks were not filled to capacity on this flight) for a night journey to become accustomed to his racing mount.

Haugland had very little night flying experience, so he flew around in circles for 90 minutes before aiming the ship north toward his home in Buffalo, Minnesota. All night the J-5 purred away, small tongues of blue exhaust flame licking at the windshield.

By morning, a combination of headwinds, a new engine and the pilot's unfamiliarity with the

The Model BW was powered by a Wright J-5 radial engine of 220 hp, and was a real performer with or without a load. The Department of Commerce would not grant Cessna an Approved Type Certificate based on the "A"-series stress analysis, so the company obtained Group Two approval for the design as a four-place airplane, but it was often flown as a three-place ship. (Bob Pickett Collection/Cessna Aircraft Company)

airplane's fuel consumption forced the ship down near the Minnesota/Iowa state line, the tanks empty. Back in Wichita, Clyde Cessna was concerned about Haugland's safety, because no word had been received about his planned arrival in Buffalo. Haugland, in all the excitement of the unexpected landing, made matters worse by failing to inform Cessna of his situation.

Finally, after the Western Union Company spent hours tracking down the missing pilot, Clyde was informed that all was well. Cessna politely reminded Mr. Haugland to keep the factory informed of his every movement, and to be certain he was at Roosevelt Field in New York City to join the other company entrants not later than September 3rd to qualify for the race.

The aerial armada of monoplanes winged its way from Wichita, and joining Haugland at Roosevelt Field, were ready for the pre-race inspection by September 2nd. The next few days would be challenging ones for the band of airmen from Kansas...before them stretched 3,000 miles of rough, tough, competitive flying.

CESSNA MONOPLANES - A TECHNICAL LOOK

Airplanes are usually judged by their appearance and performance, and Cessna monoplanes were no exception. When introduced in 1928, they were recognized as a step forward in technology for light aircraft, primarily because of the full-cantilever wing. Let's take a look at Clyde Cessna's efficient aircraft from the inside, and discover how they became "A Master's Expression."

BASIC STRUCTURE AND STRESS ANALYSIS

Joseph S. Newell completed the stress analysis for the the "A" series in June, 1928, including data for the Wright J-5, Warner 'Scarab', Siemens-Halske and Anzani engine mounts.

Cessna Design #1, the "Phantom", was used for some of the certification tests required by the Department of Commerce on the flight control surfaces and operating mechanisms. It is shown here undergoing landing gear sideload tests in the First Street and Glenn Avenue factory, November, 1927. (Bob Pickett Collection/Cessna Aircraft Company)

Information used by Newell and his associates was based on the original drawings as provided by Clyde Cessna, after preparation by draftsmen and engineers at the factory. This information was revised as necessary during the analysis period to reflect changes to the structures. The "Handbook For Airplane Designers", first issued in October, 1927, was produced by the Department of Commerce to guide manufacturers as to methods of distributing loads and analysis of structures before the proposed design was submitted to the department for approval (this publication was used by Cessna engineers in preparing the engineering data for all models, and supplemented the Air Commerce Regulations that took effect December 31, 1926).

After the conference of manufacturers and the Department of Commerce, held at Washington in December, 1927 (attended by Clyde Cessna) load factors, as originally published in the handbook were increased from 6.0 to 6.5 in the high angle of attack condition (such as pulling out of a high-speed dive), 4.32 for the low angle of attack and 2.66 for inverted and nose dive configurations. For the "A" and "B" series stress analysis, 6.7, 4.4 and 2.7 were used.

Newell traveled to Wichita for all static tests done on the wing, fuselage, empennage and landing gear, which were conducted at the Cessna factory under the direct observation of a government inspector. The original "Phantom" (c/n 112, Department of Commerce number 1626) was used for some aileron, empennage and landing gear load tests since it was no longer in flying status.

WING

An NACA (National Advisory Committee for Aeronautics) M-12 airfoil was selected for the wing. Span was 40 feet, two inches, with a total area (including ailerons) of 240 square feet. Chord at rib #1 was 87 inches, decreasing to 58 inches at the wingtip, and MAC (mean aerodynamic chord) was located at 66 inches from the wing root.

Both the front and rear spars were made of built-up spruce laminations, with spruce and mahoghany built-up ribs, the wing being constructed as a single,

continuous unit bolted to the upper longerons of the fuselage. The leading edge of the wing was covered with mahogany back to the front spar, the entire wing being covered with cotton fabric and doped for tension and color.

The most critical condition for the front wing spar was the high angle of attack condition, while for the rear spar it was the dive mode. Bending moments for both spars were carefully calculated, each exhibiting a safety factor above that required.

For the static load test, the wing was arranged on a special fixture to simulate the high angle of attack condition, with the wing divided into six sections along the span, and three sections along the chord, using strings to designate each area. This was necessary so that the loads could be applied in accordance with the loading curve requirements worked out on paper, accurately simulating inflight stresses.

There were no failures of any kind in the structure until a factor of 6.0 was applied, when a four-foot section of the leading edge, located about three feet from the root, protested the load but remained intact until a factor of 6.5 caused it to fail completely.

To correct this problem, Newell instructed Cessna to use both additonal ribs and wider cap-strips in the affected area, and production wings were modified to comply with this change.

Six automobile-type jacks were placed under each wing, three of them under each spar. As the load factor was increased with more sandbags, the jacks were carefully lowered to allow the wing to carry the weight for at least five minutes between each increment.

Finally, after a factor of 6.5 was successfully reached, load was increased in one half factor increments

An "A"-series fuselage is loaded with sandbags before undergoing drop tests from a height of 24 inches to satisfy Department of Commerce certification requirements. All load tests were observed by a government inspector who carefully documented every detail. (Bob Pickett Collection/Cessna Aircraft Company)

until 7.0 and utimately a factor of 8.0 was attained. The spars carried the load without failure, with the tips being about one-half inch off the floor.

Men stationed at each tip were instructed to alternately push down on the wingtips with vigor, quickly releasing them to spring back. Again, both spars and all ribs stood the test, with the compression ribs showing no signs of buckling or distortion.

That ended the static test because the supply of sand was exhausted and the wingtips couldn't be loaded any further without resting on the floor. When the load was removed, every inch of the wing was critically inspected for signs of failure, especially the steel straps used for internal bracing.

These straps, a very critical component in the full-cantilever wing structure, were required to provide torsional stiffness to the entire wing assembly. Also, they had to possess at least a 200% safety margin in the nose dive condition.

Newell's investigations showed that, as originally designed, the straps were inadequate, requiring a new design using cold rolled steel pieces, three-quarters of an inch wide, between rib #5 and #8, and one-half inch wide in the outer wing bays. The redesigned straps were installed on the test article wing and showed no signs of failure nor was there any evidence of elongation in the strap holes or the bolt holes in the spars where each member was anchored.

With the aforementioned changes, Cessna's wing was approved by the Department of Commerce for the Anzani, Warner, and Siemens-Halske (and later, the 130 hp "Comet") engines. With the Wright J-5 installation on the "A"-series airframe, however, Newell's initial analysis for the Model BW showed a 2 1/2% negative margin of safety for the wing spars at a point near where they attached to the fuselage. He used a design gross weight of 2,265 pounds for his revised calculations, as opposed to the original weight of 2,586 pounds on all engineering data submitted to the Department of Commerce in the summer of 1927.

However, based on results of the static tests on the "A"-series wing, Newell believed the structure was adequate to take the J-5 engine, especially since the spar chords were 1/4 inch wider on the Model BW wing than those on the other airplanes. The increased spar chord gave a margin of safety of 7.61, easily exceeding the required increase of 7.35. The spar webs and drag truss braces were also found to be satisfactory for the nine-cylinder Wright.

FUSELAGE

Chrome molybdenum steel tubing, of varying outside diameter and wall thickness was used for the fuselage assembly. The structure was adequate for the Anzani, Warner, Siemens-Halske and Comet, but with the Wright J-5 one tube of the fuselage door truss was found to be weak in the three-point landing condition. To overcome this, the tube was increased from 1 1/4 x .049 inch outside diameter and wall thickness to 1 1/4 x .058 inch and carried the load easily.

LANDING GEAR

Chrome molybdenum steel tubing was used for the gear struts, with the front strut 2 1/2 inches in diameter, .065 inch wall thickness, the rear tube being 1 3/4 inches, .049 inch wall thickness. Both tubes were formed to a streamline shape, and were slotted to accept a one-eigth inch steel gusset plate, welded in place.

The axle tube was 1 3/4 inches in diameter, ground down to 1.688 inches diameter and heat treated to 150,000 pounds per square inch (psi) ultimate tensile strength. The axle tube was removeable without disassembly of the gear struts, and was inserted into a steel sleeve with a one-half inch nickel steel bolt passing through the sleeve and the tube for retention. The bolt also carried any twisting force on the axle during a braked landing. Two 28 inch x 4 inch wheels were standard equipment.

A load factor of 6.5 was required for the level and three-point landing attitude, with a factor of 3.25 for a braked landing. Analysis was made based on a gross weight of 2,435 pounds, using the J-5 engine. Calculations showed no problem with normal landing loads, but a slight weakness was noted in a sideload condition, as could be encountered during a cross-wind landing. However, Newell pointed out that sideload stresses would be virtually impossible to ascertain, and believed the gear was sufficiently strong as originally designed for any of the five engines to be used.

Bending moments on the tripod assembly were only encountered during sideload situations, when the tubes were subjected to a direct force along their length. Only axial loads were encountered under normal landing conditions.

Shock absorber cord was three-quarter inch in diameter, with 16 loops per gear tripod assembly. The chassis was capable of absorbing the weight of the airplane, without failure, in the drop test. Each loop of cord was stretched around four welded, steel studs (two in front, two in rear) on the lower fuselage carrythrough assembly and another four studs on each tripod unit.

The tail skid was 1 3/4 inch chrome molybdenum tubing, streamlined, with a .065 inch wall thickness. Shock cord was attached at the front of the skid, with a pivot point provided at the sternpost. Newell found that the original design skid would suffice for either the Anzani, Siemens-Halske, Axelson, Warner or Wright engines, although the center of gravity shifted forward slightly (about one inch) with the J-5 installation.

EMPENNAGE AND CONTROL SYSTEMS

Static tests on the horizontal and vertical stabilizer, elevator, rudder and ailerons were made with loads 25% higher than those specified by the handbook.

The wing was inverted for the aileron tests, with 282 pounds being applied to each surface, subjecting it to compression loads. A spring balance was attached to the stick to measure forces. The torque tubes were connected to the ailerons, and suffered only slight deflections and no permanent set while under test. However, one tube of the control stick mount did bend and gussets were welded in place and the test run again. This time, the tube held and all production ships were to receive the the reinforcement plates.

One of the more serious deflections noted centered around the aileron spar; at full load the spar exhibited a definite deflection in the area where the aileron horn was attached (the horn was located between two of the hinges). Another hinge was installed adjacent to the horn and the test repeated, with no further deflection observed.

The horizontal stabilizer and elevator tests were conducted with a 25% overload applied, with the control stick connected to the elevator through torque tubes. At 125% of required design load, the torque tube on each elevator horn showed some deflection, returning to its original position when the load was removed. The horizontal stabilizers exhibited no excessive deformation during the tests, and also resumed their original position when unloaded.

Both the vertical stabilizer and rudder were loaded 25% beyond design requirements, showing no permanent deformation when the load was removed.

After all changes dictated by the long, tedious static tests were incorporated into the stress analysis, Newell sent the report to the Department of Commerce for their inspection.

SERIAL NUMBER, MODEL NUMBER AND APPROVED TYPE CERTIFICATE

When the first two prototype Cessna airplanes were built, they were known as "Cessna-Roos Number 1" and "Cessna-Roos Number 2", and after Roos' departure in December, 1927, they were called "Cessna Design No. 1" and "Cessna Design No. 2."

Cessna applied for a Department of Commerce license for both the Anzani and Wright-powered air-

Seven-ship lineup at the First Street and Glenn Avenue factory, August, 1928, prior to flying east to compete in the Transcontinental Air Derby. Right to left: Model BW, c/n 117, 5835; Model BW, c/n 135, 6623; Model AS, c/n 136, 6624 (did not compete in the derby); Model AA, c/n 124, 5335; Model AW, c/n 140, 7107; Model BW, c/n 125, 5336; Model AF, c/n 141, 7462 (did not compete in the derby) BW 5835 belonged to Owen Haugland of Buffalo, Minnesota, and was equipped with special cabin fuel tanks with 350 gallon capacity for the non-stop transcontinental speed race. Tanks are barely visible behind cockpit while fabric- covered side windows show up well. (Bob Pickett Collection/Cessna Aircraft Company)

craft, being issued the numbers 1626 and 1627 respectively. He decided to use these and future license numbers for serial numbers as well, and the first eight monoplanes, 1626 through 1633, utilized this system.

By early 1928, it was obvious that this method would not work, since the government didn't issue a single manufacturer large blocks of numbers, so Cessna reassigned all eight of the early ships new serial numbers, starting with the number 112. Exactly why Cessna elected to start with the number 112 is not known, but evidence points to his pre-1927 aircraft as the reason.

From 1911 through August, 1927, Clyde V. Cessna built or owned 10 monoplanes and one biplane. Using serial number (constructor number, c/n) 100 as a starting point, the first 12 airplanes can be accounted for as follows:

100: 1911 Queen "Silverwing"
101: 1911 monoplane with Elbridge engine
102: Rebuilt "Silverwing" (after September, 1911 crash)
103: 1913 monoplane; first Cessna-designed and built aircraft
104: 1914 monoplane; first Anzani radial engine installed
105: Remodeled 1914 monoplane (1915 exhibition season)
106: Rebuilt 1914 monoplane (after July, 1916 crash)
107: 1917 monoplane, first airplane built in Wichita
108: 1917 two-place monoplane, second airplane built in Wichita
109: Modified two-place monoplane, 70 hp Anzani engine
110: 1924 'New Swallow' biplane
111: 1926 cabin monoplane
112: 1927 "Phantom"

Cessna considered a rebuilt airplane as a 'new' model, since he frequently made changes to the airframe and engine while repairing the craft.

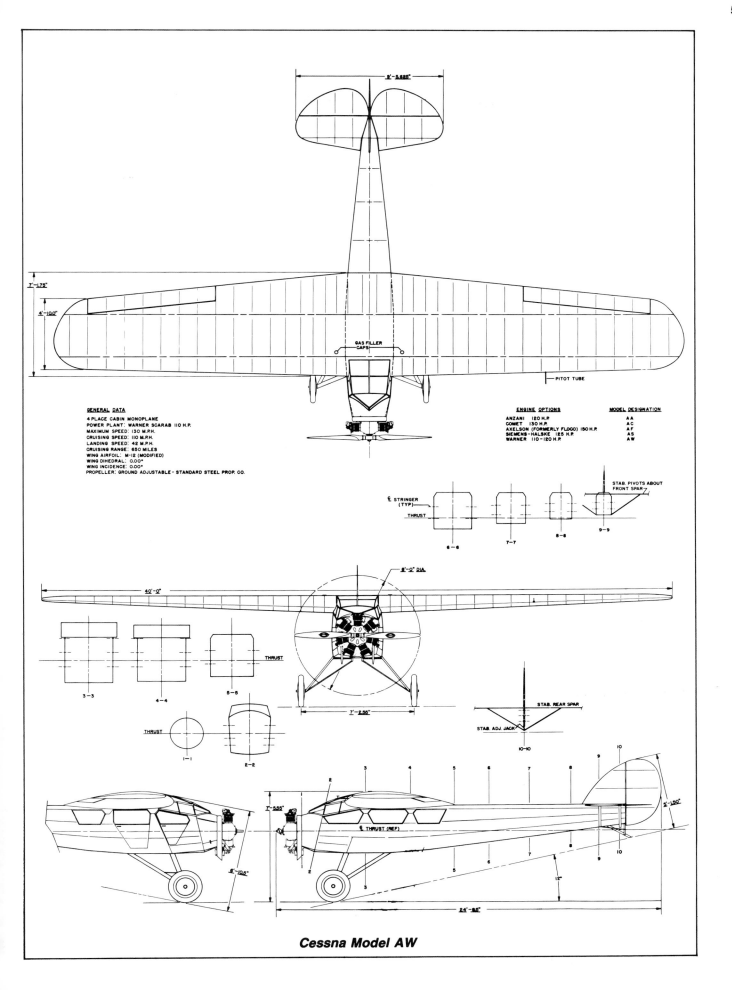

Cessna Model AW

51

Initially, company advertising for the "A" and "B"-series monoplanes and official Department of Commerce records referred to the models as "4-120" or "4-200", meaning 4 seats, 120 or 200 horsepower.

By December of 1928, all models were known by a two-letter code, indicating the airframe design and engine. The following listing is based on airplanes in production at that time (all engines were air-cooled, static radials) and includes prices with standard equipment:

Model AA: 120 hp Anzani $5,750
Model AC: 130-150 hp Comet $7,500
Model AF: 115-150 hp Floco (Axelson after August, 1928) $7,500
Model AS: 118-125 hp Siemens-Halske $7,500
Model AW: 110 hp Warner 'Scarab' $7,500
Model BW: 220, 225 hp Wright 'Whirlwind' $9,800

After December, 1926, the Department of Commerce was charged with responsibility to license all airmen and mechanics, and to ensure that all engine and airframe manufacturers received an Approved Type Certificate (ATC) for their products before they could be sold to the public or used for commercial purposes.

In 1927, the Bureau of Aeronautics Division set about the huge task of certifying almost 284 types of aircraft then being built in the United States. Among that number were Cessna monoplanes. Once the stress analysis and static tests were completed by Joseph Newell and reviewed by the government, ATC number 65 and 72 were granted to the Cessna Aircraft Company.

The initial two ATCs were awarded to the Model AA and Model AW, but the Model BW and the Model AC, AF and AS were certified under the Group Two Approval system. This method allowed, in Cessna's case, a basic airframe that used four different engines to be approved without seeking a new certificate.

Cessna intended to have the Model BW share the Model AA's ATC, however, the government refused to allow this, saying that another type certificate was required because of the higher gross weight than the "A" series was approved for. A complete stress analysis and static testing were required if Cessna wanted to sell the Wright-powered monoplane as a four-place ship. The Department of Commerce allowed Cessna to sell the Model BW with four seats, but because of the center of gravity change caused by the heavier J-5 engine, it was often flown only with three seats occupied; the pilot up front and passengers in the back.

The added weight aft helped during flight and landing to get the tail down so the skid could dig in the ground and slow the ship's speed.

The company did not want to go to the expense and delay involved with a new ATC, and decided to classify the ship under the Group Two approval system as a four-place cabin airplane. Based on aircraft in production as of December, 1928, the following list gives model, Approved Type Certificate and Group Two approval number and dates for six airplanes:

MODEL	ATC NUMBER/ DATE	GROUP TWO APPROVAL/ DATE
AA	65 8-28	N/A
AC	N/A	#2-407 5-32
AF	N/A	#2-237 7-30
AS	N/A	#2-8 1-29
AW	72 9-28	N/A
BW	N/A	#2-7 12-28

Only 13 of the Model BW were built before production was terminated. Four Model AS ships were built (but only three can be confirmed from company records as actually sold and delivered), with one Model AC and three Model AFs finding their way into customer service. The solid popularity of the Model AW thrust production of this version to 50 by 1929, while the company sold approximately 14 examples of the Model AA.

---

[1] The names "All Purpose", "Common" and "Phantom" were unofficial names, never used by Cessna for advertising or sales promotion.

[2] Joseph S. Newell was born in Springfield, Massachusetts, on August 10, 1897. He graduated from Massachusetts Institute of Technology in 1919 with a Bachelor of Science degree in Civil Engineering, which was granted jointly by MIT and Harvard University. He spent five years at McCook Field, Dayton, Ohio, from 1922 until 1927, serving as a junior and assistant engineer. It was during this period of time that he received much of his education on aircraft structures, and upon returning to MIT as an instructor in 1927, he was eventually named Executive Officer of the Department of Aeronautical Engineering in 1946. One of his greatest contributions to aeronautics was "Aircraft Structures", a standard reference text that Newell and Professor A.S. Niles co-authored in the late 1920s. Newell died on May 5, 1952, at age 54. His strong reputation as an aeronautical structures expert was well known by Clyde Cessna, who sought Newell's expertise in gaining government approval of the Model AA monoplane.

[3] George I. Myers learned to fly in the army in 1919 and flew with the Reserves out of North Platte, Nebraska. He later flew the air mail on the Omaha to Chicago run for two years. A highly skilled pilot with over 6,000 hours in the air, Cessna had no doubts about Myers' capabilities in flying the air derby.

[4] Victor H. Roos was born and raised in Omaha, Nebraska, and attended business college after high school. He was engaged in the bicycle and motorcycle business from 1907 to 1926, when he became interested in working with Clyde Cessna. Earlier, in 1920- 1923, he was a financial backer of Giuseppe Bellanca during the early days of that company and served as an instructor of motor vehicles at the Fort Omaha Balloon School in World War One. Roos was president of the Lincoln Aircraft Company, Inc., after departing Swallow in 1929. He held a private pilot license.

[5] "Chief" Bowhan flew for just about anybody who needed a pilot around the Wichita area and beyond. One of his most daring exploits occurred in Bartlesville, Oklahoma, in the late 1920s. As the story goes, Bowhan was chided by some friends that he wouldn't fly his airplane down the city's main street, so Chief quickly accepted the challenge, took off and flew below the rooftops all the way down the thoroughfare, standing up in the cockpit shouting Indian war cries.

[6] Apparently, Roos was considered an outsider by the board members, some of whom believed that Clyde Cessna should be in full charge of the company. Exactly who precipitated the firm's name change is unknown, but Roos found the proposal totally unacceptable.

[7] Swallow Airplane Company was doing a booming business when Roos became general manager in December, 1927. The company had been saved from extinction by George Bassett and other interested parties after Jake Moellendick's failure to guide the firm toward prosperity early that year. Jake's most costly error (and the final blow financially) was construction of the "Dallas Spirit" monoplane for the ill-fated Dole race from California to Hawaii, held in August. After an abortive start because of torn fuselage fabric, the airplane was withdrawn from the race, but pilot William Erwin and his navigator volunteered to search for other pilots whose ships had gone down over the Pacific. Weather was poor, and it is believed Erwin fell victim to spatial disorientation, spinning into the sea. No trace of the airplane was ever found, and the Swallow company went into receivership soon thereafter.

[8] Guy Vaughan, president of Wright Aeronautical, once stated that before Charles A. Lindbergh's epic flight across the Atlantic in May, 1927, the company had produced about 35 nine-cylinder 'Whirlwind' radials, but orders took such a drastic jump after Lindbergh's journey that production for the rest of the year was virtually sold out.

CHAPTER SIX
Rabbit, Ringers And Tailspin Bill

September 5, 1928, dawned overcast and chilly. It was the morning 47 pilots had anxiously awaited for more than 30 days; the start of the New York to Los Angeles Air Derby.

By 4 A.M., the flight line at Roosevelt Field, Long Island, was bustling with activity. With $57,500 in total prize money up for grabs, pilots and sponsors double-checked their airplanes, mechanics ran up engines, changed spark plugs and adjusted carburetors for peak performance. Fuel trucks scurried from ship to ship, pumping in gasoline and topping off oil tanks.

Clyde Cessna gathered his airmen together for a final pre-race skull session, discussing fuel loads and consumption, throttle settings and the 16 control points (stopover locations) where each pilot had exactly 30 minutes to refuel, make any necessary repairs and takeoff again (five of these locations were designated as overnight stops).

Both Class A and Class B divisions would fly the same route and share the same control points, so Cessna knew it would be easy to keep track of the progress and problems encountered by his pilots along the course. Of all the Cessna ships entered, Clyde was especially confident of a Class A victory by Earl Rowland in a Model AW (c/n 140, Warner #26, C7107). The airplane's cruising speed of 105-110 mph, coupled with its fuel-thrifty engine made it a top contender in that group.[1]

Among the 35 Class A entrants, Rowland would face tough, seasoned opponents in Travel Air, Kreider-Reisner and Waco, but he respected the Scarab-powered American Moth monoplane, piloted by Robert Dake, as his most serious competition.

As takeoff time approached, a hotly-contested debate was still raging between the Class B entrants and the race committee. According to the rules, only stock airplanes, of which at least two examples had

been built before August 1, 1928, were eligible to enter the race.

Cessna, along with virtually all the other pilots in Class B, howled about the Waco CTO and two Laird LC-RJ-200 biplanes, objecting to their non-stock modifications. The taperwing Waco ship, flown by Johnny Livingston, was almost a standard production model except for the special, small-size landing gear designed for racing. The Lairds, flown by Charles "Speed" Holman and E.E. "Eddie" Ballough, featured 'speedwing' airfoils that gave them a decided aerodynamic advantage in reduced drag (both ships were actually Laird LC-B models in their basic form, but after being altered with the new wings were known as LC-RJ-200 versions by the factory).

Many of the entrants threatened to withdraw from the event, including Clyde Cessna, who labeled the modified airplanes 'ringers'...a term echoing back to horse racing days when a fast horse was entered under a new name.

The Richfield Oil Company of California, suppliers of fuel to all contestants, offered to add a whopping $7,000 to the jackpot in a vain attempt to appease the rebellious aviators, but the money was refused by the race committee. The whole incident threatened to spoil the competitive spirit of the event. Stephen Day, chairman of the Starting Committee, was forced to play diplomat and managed to soothe quick tempers, talking respectfully with the Class B pilots. He informed them that the committee's decision had

Seven-ship lineup at the Cessna factory affords a good view of Model AF, 7462 (c/n 141), with the First Street and Glenn Avenue facility in the background. Note protective tape wrapped around AF's landing gear struts; the tape was used for paint masking and was removed prior to delivery. (Bob Pickett Collection/Cessna Aircraft Company)

54

Race #98 was assigned to Model BW C6623 (c/n 135) for the 1928 air derby. Pilot Francis "Chief" Bowhan (left) withdrew the ship at Roosevelt Field after learning of the Laird and Waco "ringers" entered in the race. The two people with Bowhan are believed to be his wife, Charlotte (center) and airplane owner F.J. Grace, associated with the Pioneer Tire Company of Omaha, Nebraska, owner of the monoplane. Big 220 hp Wright J-5 radial seriously blocked forward visibility from cockpit. (Smithsonian Institution Photo #A2231)

been made: anyone not happy about the questionable entries could withdraw, but the race would go on as scheduled.

The Waco and Laird ships took their position in the starting lineup, despite a constant grumble from irritated competitors. However, their presence exacted a toll: Chief Bowhan refused to compete, withdrawing his Model BW from the race. Cessna, although disappointed at this turn of events, respected Bowhan's decision and almost joined him on the sidelines, but decided to compete because it was "good sportsmanship to do so." When Clyde asked his other Class B pilots what they intended to do, all agreed to carry on with the race as planned.

At exactly 5:43:45 A.M. on Wednesday, September 5th, George H. Townsend, official starter for the Air Derby, dropped his red flag and Albert R. Jacobs pushed the throttle forward on his Waco 10, the first ship off on the great aerial marathon.

26 airplanes followed, with Earl Rowland and Cessna #99 in 13th spot. Launching simultaneously with the Class A ships, 20 Class B airplanes were quickly winging their way west, including the four remaining Cessna monoplanes.

In the B division, virtually all of the aircraft were powered by the mighty Wright "Whirlwind" radial, except for the Model AA flown by Clyde and his pilot, Curtis Quick. Waiting their turn for takeoff, the duo watched a succession of thundering Whirlwind ships blast out of Roosevelt Field. Finally, it was their turn to depart and the Anzani rattled its way skyward, a tortoise among the hares. Unfortunately, there was little hope that Cessna #97 would enjoy a fairy-tale ending to this race.

Rowland, like many contestants, was carrying a passenger along, but his sidekick was also a mechanic named William "Tailspin Bill" Kowalski; an ace wrench-man with the Warner engine company.

Kowalski (and another technician who never showed up for the race) was assigned the awesome task of caring for the six 'Scarab'-powered entrants during their trek across the continent.

The baggage compartment of #99 was stuffed full of spare engine parts that might be needed during the long, arduous journey. Cylinders, pistons, valves, springs, spark plugs galore and a tool box stood ready if they were needed. Other pilots, not having such providence, would regret their error as the race progressed.[2]

The two men were cramped in the tiny cockpit as the monoplane headed west toward the first control point, Columbus, Ohio. Earl kept the Warner firewalled most of the way, conserving power only when necessary for descent.

Rowland, who hailed from Valley Springs, Arkansas, had been working for the Stearman Aircraft Company in the summer of 1928 when he became very interested in flying Cessna's Model AW in the Air Derby. He approached his boss, Lloyd Stearman, with the idea and encountered no opposition there, so the next step was to go see Clyde Cessna, who quickly signed Rowland as pilot.

"Rabbit", as Earl was known by close friends, learned to fly in the army during World War One, but the Armistice precluded his finishing the course. After attending college in Chicago, where he studied aeronautical engineering and radio electronics, he bought a war-surplus Curtiss JN-4 "Jenny" and flew to Little Rock, Arkansas, to live with his family.

Jake Moellendick hired Rowland in 1925 as a pilot and flight instructor for Swallow. That year, Earl and Jake flew a New Swallow biplane in the first Ford Reliability Tour, finishing among 11 other pilots who obtained a perfect score.[3]

Genial, quiet and well-liked by all who knew him, Rowland was blessed with a talent for flying airplanes. Clyde Cessna had no qualms about Earl flying in the Air Derby...he knew Rowland would give his all to win.

And he was doing just that as the Cessna neared Columbus, haunted all the way by Dake in the Moth. Time was as precious as gold; the pilot who kept his enroute times the lowest would be the leader, and if he did that all the way to Mines Field in Los Angeles, he would be rich.

Cessna #99 built up a nine-minute lead the first

day, and Earl was very tired from the noise of seven-cylinders banging away in his ears for hours on end. Kolwalski, despite being just as fatigued as Earl, spent more time on the flight line tending to his engines. There were always spark plugs to change, valve and carburetor adjustments to make. Working solo, it wasn't long before Tailspin Bill was exhausted, but he always got the job done.

Next stop, Kansas City, where #99 was still in the lead and threatening to widen the margin against its adversaries. Robert Dake cornered Rowland while the ships were on the ground and discussed how well the race was going for everyone, especially Earl. Dake was not far behind in the battle against the clock, and his American Moth monoplane was performing flawlessly.

Even by this early stage of the contest, everyone knew it would be a head-to-head fight between the Cessna and the Moth. William H. Emery, Travel Air distributor from Pennsylvania, was a worthy competitor in his specially-built, speedwing-equipped and Warner- powered DW-4000 biplane, and was giving Rowland and Dake a run for the money. As expected, Theodore Kenyon in the Kreider- Reisner was never far behind the leaders, battling Emery every step of the way.

For the next leg, Travel Air Field at Wichita, Kansas was slated as the stopover point. Rowland wanted to be first into his home town, and asked his fellow airmen to allow him that honor. To make such a request in a highly competitive event like an air race, where everyone was out to win, may seem foolhardy, but Rowland's peers gladly granted his wish.

In return, Earl explained to his friends how to locate Travel Air Field and where the best area of the grass landing field would be that time of year.

Just in case Mr. Dake did get the jump on #99 on departure from Kansas City, Earl made his exit through an area of heavy smoke, thereby veiling his true path as he aimed the monoplane southwest along a course intimately familiar to him.

Bending the Warner's throttle, Rowland kept an eye out for the speedy Moth and its pilot, but they were nowhere to be seen. Emporia, Kansas, fell prey to the Cessna's speed in less than one hour's flying time, and minutes later the destination lay dead ahead.

Model BW "Miss Marietta" was flown to eigth place by Jay Sadowski. Ship was owned by Paul Allen of Marietta, Georgia. Registration number was C5336, c/n 125. (Photo by Wayne Sheldon via Truman C. Weaver Collection and Bob Pickett)

Rowland planted his airplane solidly on Travel Air Field and rolled to the assigned parking area. He peered out of his side window as the engine came to a stop, and there was Dake, only one minute behind. It had been a close race after all, and Earl's covert departure from Kansas City had been a wise decision.

After 10 hours of flying time since leaving New York City, Earl Rowland was nearly 28 minutes ahead of Dake. The Model AW's clean design was slipping through the air with the greatest of ease, to the glee of its crew. Some other Cessna pilots were having engine trouble, however, and during the 30-minute stay at Wichita, Rowland opened up his aerial parts department and gave them what they needed to get back in the air. Kolwalski, who "worked like a dog" according to Earl, helped make most of the repairs and adjustments required.

J. Warren Smith, one of Cessna's Class B entrants, was forced out of the race at Travel Air Field with

Edward G. Schultz flew #96, a Model BW (c/n 121) to fourth spot in the derby, capturing $1,000 in prize money. The airplane was owned by Mayer Aircraft of Bridgeville, Pennsylvania. Note the inscription "My Name is Red Wing" under cockpit window. Wing on this ship was painted Cessna Red. The cabin windows have been covered with fabric to decrease drag, and small fairings cover the mechanical brake levers on each landing gear. (Photo by Wayne Sheldon via Truman C. Weaver Collection and Bob Pickett)

56

#52 is believed to be a Model BW flown by J. Warren Smith, Cessna dealer in New York City. Men standing in cockpit and on the stepladder are fueling the wing tanks through chamois-covered funnels. Smith withdrew from the race at Wichita because of mechanical problems. (Photo by Wayne Sheldon via Truman C. Weaver Collection and Bob Pickett)

unspecified technical problems, leaving Cessna and Quick, Jay Sadowsky and Edward G. Schultz to continue the contest in that division.

Prior to taking off for Fort Worth, Texas, Rowland was teased about his big time lead, as pilots shook his hand, telling him what a great job of flying he was doing, then mumbling "I hope you get lost" as they walked away, a wry smile on their faces.

They had good reason to be envious of the 30-year old aviator. He was flying a tough, disciplined race, calculating every step before he took it and being eminently successful at navigating. Upon landing at the Fort Worth airport, Earl had an elapsed time of 14 hours and 14 minutes, increasing his time cushion over Robert Dake to more than half an hour.

Texas, and the southwestern desert, proved to be nothing but trouble for pilots and airplanes of the Air Derby. Mercury readings in the high 90s and low 100s caused cylinder head and oil temperatures to soar above design limits and landing fields were infested with cactus thorns. Many tires and tubes burst on takeoff, touchdown or while taxiing. Then physical aggravations came along to make matters worse for everyone. Chapped lips and facial blisters plagued the airmen, with the usual skin balms giving little relief to cracked, burning flesh. Eating was a painful ordeal, suffered only because of its necessity.

Things had been easy until now; with more than half of the country behind them, the racers faced a challenging odyssey to the west coast. Trouble for Rowland set in at after leaving Fort Worth. The Warner began to run rough, and nothing Earl did or Kowalski suggested improved the situation.[4]

They could hardly expect to make El Paso without risking a forced landing, and that possibility loomed greater with every passing minute as the radial's ailment got worse. Facing a choice between returning to Fort Worth for repairs that would cause him to lose some of his hard-won time advantage, or risking an engine failure in the bleakness of the desert, Rowland decided to throw caution to the wind and kept on flying, nursing the 'Scarab' as best he could.

Holding altitude was difficult. Convection currents from the hot ground sent fists of turbulence high into the sky, knocking the little monoplane around like a toy. The engine's distinct lack of power only made

matters worse, with Rowland having to fly at full throttle just to combat the rough air.

What seemed like a flight of eternal torment finally ended when the Cessna plopped onto El Paso's field. Eight precious minutes of elapsed time had been lost on the trip, and Earl, assisted by the ever-helpful Kowalski, tore into the Warner as soon as he shut it down.

After a short time of troubleshooting, Tailspin Bill found the trouble: the ignition system needed overhauling, and this task was promptly accomplished by use of the back seat parts department. With one crisis solved, another one appeared: the left main landing gear tire was dying a slow death, hissing its last breath as it settled to the ground, flat as a pancake. There, in the tire's carcass, was the culprit; another of the seemingly ubiquitous cactus thorns.

Rowland shook his head, then declared war on the Texas thistles that caused him and the other pilots so much grief. He bought six spare inner tubes and a compressed air bottle from a repair shop on the field to combat the pesky thorns, and the tire was soon good as new. Earl's purchase of the air bottle proved to be a real time saver, since the 30-minute limit at control points was strictly enforced, and any clock violations were computed against the pilot's elapsed time. After a good night's sleep at El Paso, everyone would be ready for the final dash to Mines Field.

Earl was up at his customary time of 3 A.M., just as he was every day of the race. He was at the field an hour later and ready for takeoff at 5 A.M., as the rules required.

Dawn was just breaking over the desert southwest as the starter's flag dropped, signalling the start of the final leg of the Air Derby. Sand, dirt and dust were kicked high in the air as each flyer took off. The ground trembled as Whirlwinds, Warners, one Curtiss C-6 and one Anzani roared away into the blue. The hopes of two men were at stake; Earl Rowland and Robert Dake. Rowland held more than a one hour advantage over Dake...the only thing between Earl and glory was nine hours of hard flying.

Following the 'iron compass', Rowland was flying solo; Kowalski had boarded another Warner-powered

Earl Rowland takes a rest with the winning AW, C7107, after the New York-Los Angeles Air Derby, September, 1928. Filler neck on engine boot cowl was used to replenish the Warner's oil tank. (Les Forden)

ship for the last leg of the race. There was little chance of anything going wrong with the Cessna's powerplant in the next half a day, so Earl felt confident as his monoplane winged its way toward Los Angeles.

The next control point was Yuma, Arizona. Earl climbed the monoplane higher to find cool air, the Warner again sang its old, familiar song of power.

Rowland, determined to regain the earlier time lost to ignition problems, had no mercy on the little radial enroute to Yuma. He shoved the throttle full forward and kept it there all the way. Despite this valiant effort, the American Moth was first to land at Yuma, with the Cessna right behind it. Still, Earl had regained seven minutes, 50 seconds of the eight minutes he lost previously, and still had a firm grip on the lead.

In the Class B race, the Waco CTO flown by Johnny Livingston was, as feared by the other contenders, racking up a sizeable lead, with E.E. Ballough in the non-stock Laird a close second. These two ships, while magnificent performers, were unfair competition for the stock airplanes.

Of Cessna's group of entrants, only Edward G. Schultz had any chance of staying up with the 'ringers'. He was in fourth place as the racers landed at Yuma, with almost two hours elapsed time separating him from the front-runners.

Only if Livingston, Ballough and John P. Wood (flying another Waco with special racing gear) encountered a mishap could Schultz hope to cross the finish line in first place. Jay Sadowsky was a distant eigth, with Clyde Cessna and Curtis Quick bringing up the rear in 14th place.

Clyde was very pleased with Rowland's achievement thus far, and encouraged him to take it easy across the desert and to conserve the engine.

At 2:34 P.M. on Monday, September 10th, #99 landed on the grass at Mines Field, capturing first honors in the Class A division. Only one minute later, Robert Dake put the American Moth down for second place. William Emery was third with Theodore Kenyon and Tex Rankin placing fourth and fifth repectively. 23 of the 27 starters finished the race, but only the first five claimed any cash reward for their efforts.

When Earl taxied in to the parking area, swarms of people, many of whom were reporters lugging cameras, charged the AW. Earl quickly shut down the Warner and slowly climbed out of the cockpit he had called 'home' for the last five days.

Amidst the screams of excited spectators, torrents of unintelligable questions from reporters and the seemingly endless sea of humanity pressing around his ship, Rowland spotted the familiar and welcome faces of Arch Merriam, Colonel H.G. O'Dell, Roscoe Vaughan and Marcellus Murdock, all representing Wichita's National Aeronautic Association chapter at the races. The four men embraced Rowland, shaking hands enthusiastically while praising him for a tremendous win, not only for himself and Cessna, but for Wichita, too.

Minutes later, Rowland was congratulated by Dudley M. Steele, head of the aviation department of Richfield Oil Company and serving on the contest committee for the National Air Races.

Earl Rowland had won $5,000, Dake $2,500 with Emery, Kenyon and Rankin earning $700, $500 and

Interior view of a factory-fresh Model AW shows thickly upholstered bench seat, control sticks, stabilizer trim handle on left sidewall, throttle lever on the instrument panel with altimeter and tachometer mounted below it. Aileron push-pull tube extends from left window sill up to wing bellcrank. Note padded spar carrythrough which doubled as a headrest. (Bob Pickett Collection/Cessna Aircraft Company)

$300 respectively. Later that day Rowland was handed checks for $2,000 each from the Richfield Oil Company and Kendall Oil Company. Including lap prizes for lowest elapsed times between certain con-

Earl Rowland and his Model AW NC9091 (c/n 151) show off dependable 110 hp Warner "Scarab" radial and openable cockpit hatch that was standard on all Cessna cabin monoplanes. Note magnetic compass mounted on front face of spar carrythrough. (Bob Pickett Collection/Cessna Aircraft Company)

trol points of $1,910, Earl corralled $10,910 for himself and the Cessna Aircraft Company in the 1928 Air Derby.

In the Class B division, Johnny Livingston took first place and $7,000, while Ballough and Wood came in second and third, collecting $3,500 and $2,500 in prize money; there was no doubt about it, the outlaws had robbed the bank, but not before Edward G. Schultz lassoed $1,000 for the Cessna gang by taking fourth spot.

Jay Sadowski finished a disappointing eigth while Clyde, Curtis Quick and their Model AA came in 14th and last. The following list gives the official results of the Cessna racers entered in the Class A and Class B divisions:

PILOT	CLASS	AIRPLANE	TIME
Earl Rowland	A	Model AW #99	27:00:31
Edward G. Schultz	B	Model BW #96	24:55:08
Jay Sadowsky	B	Model BW #100	26:57:53
Curtis Quick	B	Model AA #97	40:14:22

Owen Haugland, the sole Cessna entry in the non-stop Transcontinental Speed Dash, took off on September 12th as scheduled along with seven other contestants, but was forced down at St. Louis later in the day and the landing gear collapsed from the weight of fuel, putting Haugland out of the race.

Art Goebel, flying his famous Lockheed Vega "Yankee Doodle" was the only one to cross the finish line at Los Angeles. He was disqualified, however, because he landed for fuel. Nobody won the $12,500 purse for first place out of a total of $22,500 offered,

Candid view of Rowland taken at Mines Field, Los Angeles, after the race. Earl and #99 flew just over 27 hours to clinch victory in one of the toughest, competitive aerial events held in 1928. Note the weathered, worn appearance of the airplane. (Smithsonian Institution Photo #77-10313)

and the event was the only failure of the successful 1928 National Air races.

Earl Rowland, flushed with success in the Air Derby, entered his ship in the 75-mile, civilian Free-For-All, closed-course event held during the week. It was open to all airplanes with engines not exceeding 510 cid, and Earl flew the now-famous #99 to first place money of $1,200, with a speed of 111.74 mph in just over 26 minutes, 50 seconds.

The outcome of the air derby vindicated Cessna's beliefs in his full-cantilever wing, and the volume of letters being received daily at the factory bore testimony to the Model AW's impact on the commercial airplane market.

Within three days of Rowland's achievement, 60 written inquiries had been received, with more continuing to come in for days afterward. Meade Hargiss, an official with the Cessna company, announced that a large quantity of Warner 'Scarab' engines would soon be ordered, as the popularity of the Model AW was expected to skyrocket.

With the busiest and most successful week of his life behind him, Rowland pointed the Warner east toward Kansas, arriving at Wichita on September 20th. He was, to put it mildly, hailed as a true hero by his fellow citizens.

Gala celebrations were held to honor his victory, including a 550-seat banquet at the Hotel Lassen. Never feeling comfortable before a crowd, Earl gave a general, but accurate, narrative of the cross-country marathon. Everyone loved it.

As the dinner affair ended, Rowland was presented with a very expensive leather, fur-lined flying suit, complete with mocassins, gloves and helmet. He was overwhelmed with appreciation for his gift, always displaying that unique modesty he was known for all his life.

It was expected that he would travel back to Long

Another closeup view of the seven-cylinder Warner engine. Bonnet cowl behind propeller had cooling shutters that could be opened or closed from cockpit. Note bayonet exhaust stacks that collected gases from five cylinders, while bottom two cylinders had their gases routed through special tube arrangement on carburetor housing to warm intake air and protect against carburetor icing before being exhausted. (Bob Pickett Collection/Cessna Aircraft Company)

Island to allow the public there to view his winning Cessna, and within a few days of his triumphant return to the Plains he was answering more questions posed by New York City reporters.

Both pilot and airplane were put on display on Long Island, and later they attended various airport dedications as guests, giving brief flights for the crowds. In LeRoy, New York, Rowland pushed C7107 to a first place win in one closed-course race, although he was

barred from the remaining races by local officials who believed other airplanes had little chance against the silver Cessna speedster. Rowland graciously accepted their verdict, wishing no ill will to befall himself or the Cessna company.

Back in New York City, he signed up the Atlantic Air Service Corporation as the newest Cessna distributor on the east coast, based in Newark, New Jersey. Meanwhile, back in Wichita, it was Clyde V. Cessna's turn to be feted for the Air Derby Win.

Employees of the company gave a rousing dinner for the air pioneer at the Green Parrot Inn, with 120 people attending. On display was the two-foot high, silver trophy awarded to Earl Rowland for his Class A victory.

The sterling performance given by the Model AW and BW monoplanes was a clear testimony to their performance and efficiency, telling the world what Clyde Cessna already knew, that his airplanes were truly "A Master's Expression."

Another view of famous #99 shows placement of race and registration numbers, red trim around vertical stabilizer and fuselage longerons. Stains on top of the wing center section were caused by fuel streaming back from filler tubes. The derby win gave Cessna tremendous publicity that increased the popularity and sales of the Model AW almost overnight. (Truman C. Weaver Collection via Bob Pickett)

---

[1] Clyde Cessna knew that the Model AW could compete very favorably in the Class C division. Compared to the biplanes and semi-cantilever wing monoplanes it faced, (most of which had more drag and burned more fuel for a given power setting) the AW was capable of 21 miles per gallon of gasoline while averaging over 110 mph. It's interesting to note that it was Clyde Cessna who picked Rowland's number 13 starting position at a meeting on Roosevelt Field, since Rowland was asleep in a hotel at the time.

[2] Rowland helped other pilots who had minor breakdowns along the route, by giving some of his parts away in a true gesture of sportmanship. Many of the participants carried their own parts, but the Cessna team, and particularly #99, were well stocked and ready to deal with just about any possible engine problem. Earl also flew #99 at low altitude for part of the race to minimize the adverse effects of headwinds.

[3] The Ford Reliability Tour was conceived and implemented by the Detroit Board of Commerce in 1925, to encourage civil aviation by demonstrating to the public the dependability and safety of airplanes. Edsel Ford donated a gold and silver trophy, four feet high, as the grand prize. Pilots entering the tour promised that they did not take alcohol in any form and stated that they were in good health. The Swallow company was awarded $350 for their "perfect score" in the first tour, with Rowland's name being included among those engraved on the trophy.

[4] William Kowalski proved to be a source of good humor and friendship for Rowland and the other pilots. Never favoring any one pilot or airplane over another, 'Tailspin Bill' kept the engines humming along throughout the grueling race. He apparently knew the 'Scarab' radial intimately, as he always seemed to be able to fix whatever ailed the engine quickly and efficiently. All of the pilots flying Warner-powered ships were indebted to Kowalski for his tireless efforts. Rowland said that Kolwalski held his foot against the Warner's throttle for much of the race, so it wouldn't creep back. Tailspin Bill also devised a unique (but somewhat risky) method of dealing with the thorns and flat tires they caused. He and Rowland quickly learned that it was better to leave the thistles in the tire since air leaked out at a slower rate. At El Paso, one tire was practically flat when Rowland lined up #99 for takeoff. Ten seconds before the starter dropped his flag, Kolwalski took the compressed air bottle and shot a burst of air into the tire. This stop-gap procedure gave the tire enough inflation for the takeoff roll and Kolwalski had just enough time to scurry back into the cabin before the ship was airborne. Landings at the next control point (Yuma, Arizona) were made very gently and the damaged tire repaired or replaced before departure.

CHAPTER SEVEN
A Year To Remember

Hundreds of people cheered as Earl Rowland racked Cessna #99 around the home pylon, diving to get every sliver of speed from his famous monoplane. He flashed across the finish line, victor in the 20-mile Free-For-All race at the dedication of Skyline Airport in Pratt, Kansas.

The little ship was quickly on the ground, taxiing toward the grandstands and the winner's circle. As the Warner radial clanked to a stop, Rowland stepped from the cockpit amidst a rousing ovation from the spectators.

In the past five weeks, this team of man and machine had thrust the name Cessna into the forefront of American aviation. Letters and inquiries

Cessna capped off 1928 by introducing the Model CW-6 six-place cabin monoplane, shown here suspended from the ceiling at the Wichita Automobile Show in early 1929. Note mannequins in cabin and 225 hp Wright J-5 engine. (Bob Pickett Collection/Cessna Aircraft Company)

flooded the small factory in Wichita, with orders quickly piling up in the front office.

As expected, the majority of customers wanted the Model AW with its spunky, 110 hp 'Scarab' engine, whose new-found notoriety assured its appeal. Rowland, employed by the company as a traveling representative, continued to fly promotional tours within Kansas in C7107 well into October.

For Clyde Cessna, fame and fortune had dealt the company both a blessing and a curse: demand for his airplanes was up, but productivity was down. Without sufficient means to produce monoplanes there was little hope of cashing in on the sales bonanza just beginning to occur.[1]

The only remedy was to refinance the firm, build a much larger plant and design a next-generation series of airplanes to broaden the company's product line. By October, the board of directors were hard at work discussing refinancing and laying plans for a

new facility, while the engineering department spared no effort with the design of new airplanes.[2]

The Wichita newspapers, however, were giving top billing to rumors of a merger between Cessna and Swallow, which was flatly denied by both companies. Talk of refinancing for Clyde's company had fueled the local rumor mill for weeks, until Cessna finally disclosed to the Wichita Eagle that expansion plans were being discussed with an unnamed eastern business concern.

Many of the city's citizen's objected to outside financial aid, especially when it came from eastern sources, but the fact was that nobody in the 'Peerless Princess of the Prairie' could foot the bill for necessary expansion of the Cessna Aircraft Company.

Financiers from Chicago tried to cash in on Cessna's fame by offering $2,000,000 to the company in early October, in return for rights to build Cessna monoplanes in the windy city as well as set up and operate a chain of flight schools. The offer was refused, however, and plans to refinance the company continued unabated with the east coast parties.

Cessna stock, being traded in New York City, had over-the-counter quotations of $150 per share, with preferred stock selling at $111 per share in mid-November, while prior to the September Air Derby win, the same stocks were offered at $20 and $10 per share respectively.

On November 28, 1928, Clyde Cessna announced that capitalization had been increased to $500,000 (original amount was $200,000), and that a new factory, built on a new site, would be a reality sometime in early 1929. Concurrently with Cessna's proclamation in Wichita, the business firm of E.H. Holmes in New York City released offers of Cessna common stock at $17.50 per share, sales of the stock issue to be used in building the new factory.

Meanwhile, company engineers were completing drawings and blueprints for new airplane models. A six-seat cabin monoplane, powered with a Wright 'Whirlwind' engine of 300 hp, was approaching final drafting and blueprint status, while a 12- 14-seat ship, carrying a 420 hp Pratt & Whitney 'Wasp' radial on it nose, was still in the planning phase.[3]

The six-seat job was given top priority and the designation CW- 6 ("C" for the third series of Cessna designs, "W" for the Wright powerplant and "-6" for the number of seats). Bearing license number 6446 (c/n 146), it was first flown in November, 1928, using a Wright J-5 engine of 225 hp since the 300 hp J-6-9 could not be obtained in time (the J-6-9 engine had just recently been introduced on the market and initial deliveries were slow).

A 44-foot wing graced the CW-6's fuselage with its three entry doors on the right side, giving easy access to the pilot and his five passengers. Length of the ship was 32 feet, with a totally new landing gear arrangement featuring a vertical "oildraulic" strut connected to the front spar and each tripod gear assembly. A non-steerable tailwheel replaced the conventional skid, possibly by order of Cessna himself, who often commented that tailskids were obsolete by 1928 standards and should be discarded.[4]

Jay Sadowski made the initial flights on the CW-6, because Francis Bowhan had left the company in November to become chief pilot for the Pioneer Tire concern in Omaha, Nebraska, flying their Model BW

In March, 1929, Earl Rowland and W. C. Vail flew the CW-6 to Mexico on a demonstration tour. The ship was seized by the Federales and reportedly used for reconnaissance and offensive bombing missions. (Bob Pickett Collection)

(c/n 135, NC6623). One reason Bowhan left Cessna was reportedly linked to an aerial offense he committed and which Clyde Cessna wouldn't tolerate.

The Chief had apparently run afoul of the law back in October when he was cited by city police for flying below the 2,000-foot altitude limit over Wichita. Hauled into court, Bowhan defended himself, saying that he was coming in to land at the company's field when he hit an "air pocket", causing his ship to descend into the treetops on final approach. The Model BW collected a few limbs, causing the controls to jam, and Bowhan proceded to the huge California Section (in southeast Wichita), landing without any problems.[5]

Both Earl Rowland and Curtis Quick testified that they had encountered the same downdrafts many times, but it was not enough to persuade the judge, who levied a $35 fine on Bowhan. Clyde Cessna didn't take the incident well at all, suspecting that other factors (unknown) were involved. The two men had experienced minor disagreements in the past year, and this fact, coupled with the treetop transgression,

Atlantic Air Service of Newark, New Jersey, bought the only known factory-built, Comet-powered Cessna (c/n 150) in January, 1929. Seven-cylinder radial produced 130 hp. (Bob Pickett Collection/Cessna Aircraft Company)

Hot on the heels of the CW-6 came the DC-6 series cabin monoplanes. The prototype (c/n 157) is shown here in April, 1929, soon after it was built at the First Street and Glenn Avenue factory. Cessna's agreement with Curtiss Flying Service basically obligated him to use the six-cylinder, 170 hp Curtiss "Challenger" radial. High vibration levels and lack of power limited Challenger-equipped production models to only five and four were later converted to Wright J-6-7 engines. Note two cabin doors, attachment of landing gear strut to fuselage longeron, regression to tailskid instead of CW-6's tailwheel. (Bob Pickett Collection/Cessna Aircraft Company)

forced Cessna to find another chief test pilot.

Although Bowhan was missed by the company, Sadowski and Earl Rowland performed flight test duties without difficulty, flying the CW-6 almost daily to define its performance capabilities. Maximum speed observed was 135 mph, with landing characteristics being very docile. Small air lines, who were always on the lookout for an airplane with room, comfort and speed, quickly learned of the new Cessna's existence and wanted a closer look.

Robertson Aircraft Corporation, of St. Louis, Missouri, was very interested in the new craft, sending Bud Gurney to the Cessna factory to wring out the ship. He did just that, doing barrel rolls and loops while Clyde Cessna watched from the ground. After landing, Gurney was very impressed with handling and flying qualities, but Cessna refused to disclose to the public details about the airplane or Robertson's intentions.[6]

Clyde put the lid on information about the monoplane because of the upcoming Chicago International Aeronautics Show scheduled for early December. He planned to exhibit the ship along with a Model AW, giving the CW-6 maximum publicity during the event.

Earl Rowland, accompanied by Clyde and Eldon Cessna, flew the first and only CW-6 to Chicago in five hours and 52 minutes, with the J-5 purring along at 1600 rpm all the way. Carrying a payload of 1,150 pounds, average speed was a respectable 121 mph for the 730-mile trip.

Clyde Cessna had more to do than just display his wares at the show, as 44 other aircraft manufacturers and W.P. MacCracken of the Department of Commerce met to discuss trends and innovations developing in airplane design.

Among the topics were seat belts and anchoring of seats to the cabin floor, with some participants expressing their belief that belts should be standard equipment, while other men felt they were unimportant. On the subject of anchoring chairs, Cessna believed they should be secured to the floor, but

Company officials and friends pose before a Model AF in 1929. Left to right: George R. Bassett, Clyde Cessna, unknown, Jack Turner and McGinnis Moore. Bassett, Turner and Moore all contributed financially to Wichita's aircraft industry. (Bob Pickett Collection)

easily removeable. He also commented that transports of the future would need to move chairs so that dancing could occur on board the airplane in flight. This statement drew considerable laughter from the crowd, but Mr. Cessna meant every word he said.[7]

During the exhibition, thousands of people viewed hundreds of aircraft on display, with the CW-6 getting favorable comments from everyone who saw it. R.V. McIntosh, sales manager for the company, believed the sales picture looked very rosy for the new monoplane model, and he intended to establish a small airline owned by the Cessna company, using the first 10 production examples of the airplane.[8]

The Chicago show was a distinct success for the Cessna Aircraft Company. When it came time to head for home, Art Goebel was in command of the CW-6. Goebel still had dreams of a non-stop transcontinental speed dash, but had no airplane capable of making such a trip. He had abandoned the Travel Air monoplane "Woolaroc" earlier that month, after modifying it with a 400 hp Pratt & Whitney 'Wasp' engine.[9]

The "Woolaroc" was too slow for a record attempt, making only 130 mph in cruise and 160 mph at full throttle, despite the overall drag reduction effort which included moving the cockpit back to the passenger compartment and completely fairing in the original forward cockpit location. This change, while it lowered frontal drag, made the "Woolaroc" almost totally blind for takeoff and landing.

Despite warnings from Herb Rawdon and other Travel Air engineers that forward visibility over the big wing would be virtually zero from the new pilot's position, Art ordered the changes, test-flying the ship himself in November, 1928. The mild-mannered monoplane he once knew had become a tiger, veering from side to side on takeoff, but shooting into the sky like a bullet behind the sting of its Wasp radial.[10]

Walter Beech warned his friend that the airplane was never designed to be a speedster, and with its deplorable visibility from the cockpit it just might kill Goebel. Undaunted, the California pilot took off for St. Louis later that day, arriving at night. He hit hard on landing, never being able to see the unlighted runway clearly (the airplane was not equipped with landing lights of any kind), damaging one landing gear.

After makeshift repairs, Art climbed back into his potential flying coffin and headed toward Wichita. Cruising in haze and fog with very poor visibility, Goebel strained to see ahead from the side windows next to his seat. Suddenly, a water tower flashed by the wing, startling the pilot who got only a glimpse of the obstruction. That near disaster was the last straw.

Arriving at Travel Air Field, he grounded the "Woolaroc", informed Frank Phillips that the airplane was unfit for any record attempts and ordered the ship restored to its Dole race configuration.

Frank Phillips still backed Goebel in his plans for a cross-country record, and Cessna's new ship offered good potential for renewed attempts. It had lots of room in the cabin for fuel tanks, and the forward cockpit location was a must after the "Woolaroc" fiasco.

After landing at Kansas City, Clyde and Eldon Cessna, along with James P. Verts and R.V. McIntosh, deplaned and took the train back to Wichita due to inclement weather. Goebel, who occasionally resided in Kansas City, remained behind and flew the airplane to Cessna Field when the weather improved. He continued to evaluate the CW-6 as a racer, and seemed pleased with all aspects of the craft's basic performance.

Cessna, although interested in helping Goebel with an airplane in his quest for fame, couldn't do much at the moment with the frenzied activity of refinancing the company, planning a new factory and finishing the details of capitalization. The factory would be tied up for months building planes for customer delivery, and it seemed unlikely that room or time would be found to construct Goebel's racer in the near future [although no firm plans for a Goebel plane were announced publicly, there would be a future association between Goebel and Cessna in the coming year that had its roots in the CW-6].

Further discussions between the two men were held during Goebel's brief visit in Wichita, then he flew out to California in a Model AW (c/n 145, NC6445) destined for Cessna's west coast distributor Morrison Morrison, of Hollywood.

January, 1929, saw a fresh start for the Cessna Aircraft Company. Clyde Cessna kicked off the new year with a bang by announcing that plans to expand the firm were about to be made public, a factory site was being negotiated with the Wichita Park Board and that order books were bursting at the seams.

The eastern financial firm that Cessna had been working with to complete expansion plans was The Shawmut Corporation of Boston and New York, one of many enterprising conglomerates flourishing in the ripe business climate of 1929. Shawmut officials took a long, hard look at the Cessna Aircraft Company, liked what they saw and offered to throw in over $300,000 cash for the firm's much-needed expansion program.

Hugo A. Kenyon, well known in Wichita business circles, was appointed representative of the Shawmut Corporation to oversee their interest in the Cessna company. Kenyon was elected to the Cessna Board of Directors, joining president Clyde V. Cessna, Vice President Henry J. Allen, Secretary James P. Verts

Interior of a DC-6B shows thickly-padded front seat, tall control sticks, stabilizer trim crank at right. Two of the 16 wing-to-fuselage bolts are visible at each end of the spar carrythrough. (Bob Pickett Collection/Cessna Aircraft Company)

Instrument panel of a DC-6-series monoplane. Flight and engine instruments, throttle and magneto switch are in center, with engine primer at left and mixture control at right. Rudder pedals at bottom show up well, with foot-operated mechanical brake levers on left pedals only. Note how the bolts extend through canopy side frame. (Bob Pickett Collection/Cessna Aircraft Company)

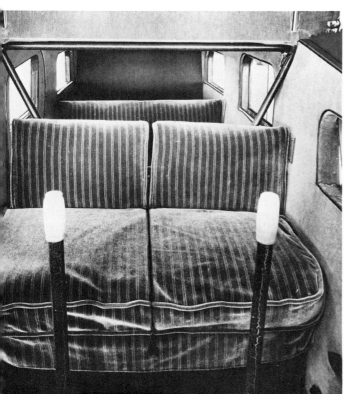

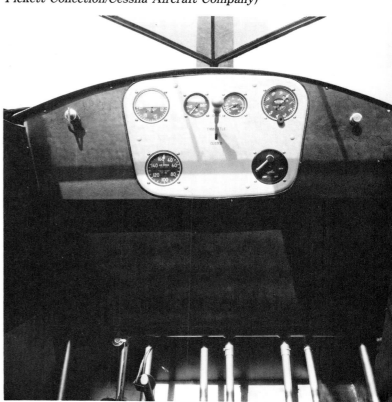

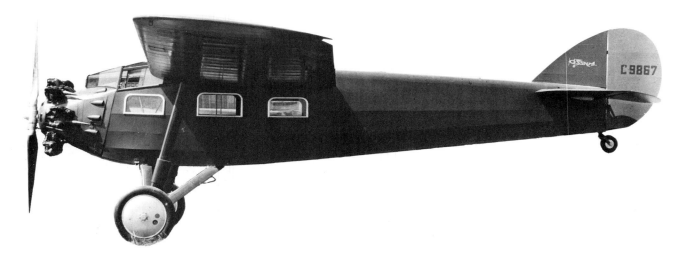

Production DC-6 (c/n 202) with Challenger radial went to Curtiss Flying Service of New York in August, 1929. DC-6 airframe was a good design but lacked a satisfactory powerplant until installation of the Wright J-6-7. (Bob Pickett Collection/Cessna Aircraft Company)

and Treasurer W.B. Harrison. W.H. Barnes, of Pratt, Kansas, was also elected to the board and rounded out the group of executives who were destined to lead the company to its pinnacle of success.

Cessna faced a transition from small-time to big-time aircraft manufacturer, and such a quick, complete change of status required professional help, especially when it came to managing the company. Clyde, already burdened with minute details of the business, needed a right-hand man he could depend on to take the reins and control the firm's day to day affairs without his constant supervision.

Howard F. Wehrle was just such a man. Born in Charleston, West Virginia, on January 20, 1890, Wehrle received his management education at Alexander Hamilton Institute of Modern Business and the University of Wisconsin. He served in the National Guard from 1908, earning the rank of captain by 1917, later rising to major and giving him his well-known nickname, "Major Wehrle". He was a very competent pilot as well as an ace manager. Cessna engaged Wehrle's services under contract for a period of one year, commencing December 31, 1928. Wehrle had been working for a hangar manufacturing concern before joining the Cessna team.

The second man hired on was Stanley T. Stanton, filling the chief pilot position vacated by Chief Bowhan. He was quickly put to work flying the CW-6 and other factory ships, testing them as fast as they came off the production line before delivery to anxiously-awaiting customers.

During the first week of January, Stanton took a Model BW down to sunny Florida to compete in the Miami All American Air Races, beating two Lockheed Vegas in one event, then defeating a Bellanca and two Ryans in events for 200 hp-class cabin ships for a total of three first-place victories.

Other personnel changes occurring in January, 1929, included Jay Sadowski, who moved over to Swallow as their chief pilot and engineer A.E. Riggs, who left Cessna to design and build a semi-cantilever wing, parasol-type monoplane for the Excelsior-Henderson Cycle Company of Wichita, powered by a 32 hp engine of original design.

Curtis Quick, perhaps having tired of rebuilding Anzani engines, hired on with Sam Watkins of El Paso, Texas, Cessna dealer for the Lone Star State, flying charter trips and selling airplanes.

With people coming and going, the first few weeks of 1929 were hectic ones around the factory. Space was at a premium, and the heating units, removed the previous summer so more production space was available, had been reinstalled in November, 1928, further reducing workspace.

To remedy this, Wehrle worked his managerial magic by adding an upper level of balconies. Upholstering and some welding was accomplished in the suspended areas, giving the wing and fuselage departments some breathing room. Major Wehrle also rebuilt the entire front section of the main building, eliminating the visitor's area, relocating some offices and instituted a pass key system for all employees to gain entry to the factory floor.

These were merely stopgap measures taken to hold the line until a new factory could be built, since the weekly production rate of 2 1/4 airplanes in January was a drop in the bucket compared to the rate of 25 ships per week that was actually anticipated once the new factory was available.

Atlantic Air Service had 16 airplanes on order that month, one of them (c/n 150, N6450) mounted a "Comet" radial engine in its first appearance on a Cessna airframe. The ship was delivered January 31st to pilot Philip Boyer, who flew it back east for display at the New York Aeronautic Show in February.[11]

Cessna dealers nationwide were experiencing a sales boom unheard of prior to 1929. They sent the factory orders for 57 monoplanes by the end of January, and the real blockbuster came on Tuesday, February 19, 1929, when the huge Curtiss Flying Service of New York state signed a contract with Cessna for exclusive rights to sell his airplanes in the United States and Canada. Cessna would deliver planes to dealers who had already placed orders, but after February Curtiss Flying Service would be the company's sole distributor.

Curtiss placed firm orders for 39 monoplanes, inflating the production backlog to 96 aircraft. The manufacturing situation was critical, and pleas went out for workers to augment a labor force already taxed to their limits by overtime. Draftsmen and engineers were also needed, and the only requirement for employment, according to Major Wehrle, was getting past the interview with Clyde Cessna. More than 90 people contacted the company on February 20th alone, and within a few weeks the factory workforce was building up.

The export market was still virtually untapped by 1929, the most convenient and promising territory being Mexico. Travel Air and Swallow had already penetrated that country with sales, and the Mexicans were very enthusiastic about seeing more Wichita-made airplanes in their country.

Clyde Cessna was not about to let such a potential market go untouched, and sent Earl Rowland and the CW-6 to Mexico City in March. Accompanying Rowland was W.C. Vail, sales representative for the company, who intended to whip up some interest for Cessna south of the border.

Also flying down to Mexico City was Howard Jones, pilot for the new Knoll Aircraft Company in Wichita, builder of the Knoll KN-1 cabin biplane, powered with a Wright Whirlwind engine. The KN-1 was the design of Felix Knoll, German aeronautical engineer who migrated to America intent on producing aircraft. Setting up shop at 471 West First Street in downtown Wichita, the company's first airplane flew very well, carrying five people (including pilot) at just over 100 mph cruising speed.

Mr. J.S. Joffre, representing a Mr. Castelan in Mexico City, reportedly ordered 35 Knoll biplanes to serve as airliners flying between southern California and the west coast of Mexico. Joffre was traveling with Jones to demonstrate the KN-1's abilities to other officials of the upstart airline.[12]

The local papers tried to make a race out of the trip, the Eagle and Beacon trading guesses at whether the CW-6 could beat the KN-1 to Valbuena Field in Mexico City. All this journalistic sensationalism offended both Clyde Cessna and Felix Knoll, each man stating that there was no race of any kind. Major Wehrle, handling the press with his usual effective tact and diplomacy, told reporters that the CW-6 had been consigned to the Bank of Mexico with U.S. Ambassador Dwight L. Morrow assisting the Cessna company in its contacts with Mexican government officials.

Enroute to Mexico, both Rowland and Jones intended to stop at Laredo, Texas, prior to crossing the border. Jones, who arrived in Laredo first, had engine trouble and was forced to wait for a mechanic from the Knoll factory to fix the ailing J-5.

Rowland and Vail landed, fueled up the Cessna and, upon hearing of Jones' plight, offered Joffre room in the CW-6 to continue his journey and he gladly accepted.

In addition to receiving a new passenger at Laredo, Rowland also received warnings about the rebellion then in full swing in Mexico, being advised that Americans would be killed by the rebels if captured.

Thanking their informers for their concern, Rowland gathered his companions and launched for Mexico City, with a fuel stop at San Luis Potosi. Using crude navigation charts and his skills in dead reckoning (a method of navigating based on time and speed estimates), Rowland found the little town and cautiously set the CW-6 down on the improvised field used for aircraft operations.

The rough ground broke a wheel, disabling the monoplane but not causing any serious damage, although it put its passengers and pilot in a somewhat precarious position: there was no telegraph service to wire the factory about what had happened, no repair facilities existed in San Luis Potosi, and within hours the rebels knew there were three Americans and an airplane in town. The welcoming committee, however, was not quite what Earl had expected.

He was met by an armed guard, placed under arrest by the governor of the area, and given free run of the town. Their only restriction was a mandatory check-in every morning with officials. For almost a week the three men had one of the grandest times of their lives, being treated like heroes by the local population.

Finally, Federales arrived and repairs were made to the landing gear, using an improvised wooden wheel (without brakes). An officer named Colonel Fierro then demanded that Rowland fly him to Mexico City, which he did, along with Vail and Joffre.

One of the most popular and best-selling Cessna airplanes in 1929 was the Model AW. This example (c/n 151) was originally sold to R.P. Shannon of Ponca City, Oklahoma, in February, 1929. (Bob Pickett Collection/Cessna Aircraft Company)

Refined and reengined with the 225 hp Wright J-6-7, the Model DC-6B was Cessna's best design yet when it was certified in September, 1929. The bigger, more comfortable cabin of the DC-6- series was a welcome improvement over the cramped quarters of the "A"-series ships. This is c/n 211, sold to Curtiss Flying Service of Texas. (Bob Pickett Collection/Cessna Aircraft Company)

66

Upon arrival, the colonel wanted Rowland to land at a military field, but Earl flatly refused and put the ship down on the commercial airport, Valbuena Field, knowing that to do so would constitute surrender of the ship.

The Wright J-5 had barely cooled off from its exciting adventure before Rowland was informed that the CW-6 was being impressed into military service for the government. There was nothing Earl could do to stop the confiscation, and Ambassador Morrow concurred. Fierro had the CW-6 towed to the military airport and within 30 minutes gave Earl a receipt for the monoplane and told him the government would pay for it later.

Confiscation was a quick and easy method employed by the Mexicans to boost their small and pitifully inadequate air force, and Rowland wasn't alone in losing his airplane. Other Yankee entrepreneurs who happened to be in Mexico City soon found themselves without wings.

At least two monoplane Stinsons, two Dehavilland Moth biplanes, a Consolidated Fleet trainer, one Ryan monoplane and a Swallow biplane were already serving the Federales. 21 aircraft were reported to have been used to assist the government in its fight against the rebels, mostly for reconnaissance missions.

The CW-6, being one of the largest ships on Valbuena Field, was snapped up by the army and studied for possible use as a bomber. Charles A. Lindbergh, who had flown to Mexico City in a Travel Air Model 6000B (c/n 962, C8139) to visit the ambassador's daughter Anne, was asked to accompany Colonel Lazama on a test flight to determine the CW-6's military potential. Lindbergh agreed to the proposal, and the two men took the ship up within the next

few days, evaluating its adaptability for offensive missions.

Apparently, the craft showed considerable potential, as all seats were removed and a large hole cut in the bottom fuselage to enable 70-pound bombs to be hand-dropped from the cabin. The only known sortie ever flown by the CW-6 was a reconnaissance flight over the town of Torreon, to confirm that it had been evacuated, but it is highly probable that it dropped its bombs in anger at some time during the rebellion.

W.C. Vail, who based his sales efforts out of a swank hotel in downtown Mexico City, sent Mr. Cessna a telegram talking about how much the Mexican military pilots liked flying the CW-6. Every morning the aviators would gather around the ship and argue over who would fly it first that day.

To the Federales airmen, the CW-6 was the greatest flying machine they had ever flown, but suddenly their favorite airplane was taken from them by General Calles, one of the top commanders in the war, who impressed it into service for his headquarters.

Earl Rowland flew with Lindbergh in the Travel Air during inauguration of the Pan American route between Mexico City and Brownsville, Texas, while a Ford Trimotor transport full of Mexican officials accompanied them. Rowland left Mexico soon after his flight with Lindbergh, traveling to Vera Cruz by rail where he booked passage on the Honduran steamer "Morazan". He arrived in Wichita near the end of March, telling everyone that he had been through an exciting time in the last few weeks, and couldn't wait for another chance to visit Mexico City.

As for the CW-6, it was used by the Federales and General Calles throughout the war, and was reported as "washed out" by 1930. The Mexican government did pay full price (amount unknown) for the ship

Closeup of J-6-7 radial shows the exhaust collector ring that reduced noise and improved powerplant appearance. High quality of fit and finish on boot and engine cowls is evident in this view. (Bob Pickett Collection/Cessna Aircraft Company)

300 hp Wright J-6-9 as installed on a DC-6A. Heat-resistant finish on exhaust collector ring is wearing off; a common occurrence after only a few hours of flying time. (Bob Pickett Collection/Cessna Aircraft Company)

about the time Calles obtained it.

Clyde Cessna was grateful to have been paid for his airplane. Under the circumstances of war, there would have been nothing he could have done to force payment. He offered two Model BWs to the Mexicans in March after sale of the CW-6, but there was no sale of those ships for the war effort.

Production of the Model BW had already ceased by this time, as the airplane was not granted an approved type certificate and the company was about to introduce the follow-on series to the CW-6, called the DC-6, making the "B" design obsolete.

Closely resembling the CW-6, the DC-6 design was the fourth major airframe development by the company, and was slated to be powered with the 170 hp Curtiss "Challenger" static radial engine then being produced in quantity by the New York firm (although the designation "DC-6" implies six seats, the airplane was strictly a four-place cabin airplane, and use of the Challenger powerplant was part of the agreement between Cessna and the Curtiss company).

First flown in February, the prototype (c/n 157, 8142, later changed to C9867) retained the M-12 airfoil section for its 40-foot, eight-inch wingspan, with a fuselage length of 27 feet, 11 inches and a overall height of seven feet, 8 inches.

Empty weight was 1,767 pounds, a useful load of 1,221 pounds and fuel capacity of 66 gallons. Gross weight was 2,988 pounds with a maximum speed observed on flight test of 130 mph, rate of climb nearly 780 feet per minute and a service ceiling of 16,000 feet. Landing gear design still featured the tripod arrangement, but the oildraulic struts were attached to the upper fuselage longeron instead of the front wing spar (c/n 157 only).

On March 23, 1929, Major Wehrle announced the long-awaited news about a new factory. An 80 acre tract of land, actually a part of the California Section known as the Herman P. Jacobs place, would be the new home of The Cessna Aircraft Company.

Director Kenyon said that 19 airplane manufacturing facilities were inspected before the Cessna factory plans were finalized, including production methods. He wanted the construction and assembly of the monoplanes to be as fast and efficient as possible, and he firmly believed the new plant would be capable of doing just that.

Six units were planned, totaling 55,000 square feet of space, compared with 18,000 square feet at the First Street and Glenn Avenue site. Two of the buildings would be 75′ × 180′, the other three units being 75′ × 100′. A two-story office building, 48′ × 52′ was also to be erected, and a 100,000 gallon water tank would be located adjacent to the complex. Estimated cost of the entire plant was $200,000.

All of the buildings would be of brick and steel construction, with unit "A" designated for experimental use; "B" would house the metalworking department; the woodworking area was placed in unit "C". Building "D" was slated to house all dope and painting operations, and featured a completely automatic sprinkler system in case of fire. Unit "E" housed final assembly.

Ground breaking ceremonies were held March 25th, with Hugo A. Kenyon turning the first spade of dirt as local dignitaries and fellow board members looked on. The cornerstone was carefully laid in place, everyone shook hands and smiled for the cameras and

Air racing! Cessnas won their share of prize money in the high speed, ground-hugging races so popular in the late 1920's. Barely 15 feet off the deck, this Model AW (c/n 176, C8791) banks hard around a pylon with its Warner screaming at redline rpm. (Smithsonian Institution Photo #75-16019)

then it was back to work as usual.

Edward Forsblom was selected as architect, and the W.S. Henrion Construction Company was chosen as contractor for the project. Since the stockholders had given the board of directors complete power to get the factory built and meet the ever-growing demand for Cessna products, time was of the essence.

Within days of the ground breaking, heavy equipment moved in and started leveling the ground. Back at the original factory, 50 employees were going full speed to build Model AWs for Curtiss Flying Service,

A Cessna mechanic stands with an early DC-6, showing good detail on the Challenger engine. The Curtiss radial was America's only six-cylinder design. Attachment of landing gear vertical strut was moved back to front spar location on production DC-6-series airplanes. Note brake cable routing along leading edge of gear V-brace. (Bob Pickett Collection/Cessna Aircraft Company)

Parker "Shorty" Cramer stands beside AW NC7107 after his marathon flight to Alaska and Siberia in April, 1929. During the 13,000-mile trip, 7107's Warner needed only valve adjustments and one spark plug. Note map on fuselage, fabric repairs on outboard right wing and left, aft lower longeron. (Smithsonian Institution Photo #77-10214)

as well as getting ready to begin initial production of the DC-6.

Cessna planned to exhibit the DC-6 at the Detroit show coming up in April, and the first and largest order for the type came from Curtiss Flying Service that month, totaling 20 aircraft. A further order of 49 Model AWs was also received from Curtiss at the same time, completely selling out production for the first six months of the year.

On April 5th, Stanley Stanton flew the prototype DC-6 to the Detroit Aeronautical Exposition along with Parker Cramer, who was a new pilot for the Cessna company, flying a Model AW. Stanton and his passenger, Meade Hargiss, made the trip in five hours, 40 minutes, while it took Cramer six hours, 10 minutes to reach the same destination.

As expected, a lot of interest was shown in the DC-6, but the lack of horsepower seemed to quell some enthusiasm. Realizing this would likely happen, Cessna already had his engineers working on a program to re-engine the monoplane with the 225 hp J-6-7 and 300 hp J-6-9 Wright radials.

Only five airplanes were built and originally powered with the R-600 "Challenger" engine, and sold for $9,250. They are listed here by constructor number, Department of Commerce license number and Curtiss engine serial number. Except for c/n 157, the other airplanes were re-engined with the Wright J-6-7 at a later date and received DC-6B designations.

1. c/n 157, 8142/C9867, Challenger serial #18
2. c/n 200, NC9865, Challenger serial #187
3. c/n 202, NC9867, Challenger serial #179
4. c/n 203, NC9868, Challenger serial #198
5. c/n 213, C634K, Challenger serial #82

The DC-6 was granted Approved Type Certificate #207 on August 19, 1929, but the company was hard at work pursuing two new ATCs for the J-6-9 and J-6-7 versions to be called the "Chief" and "Scout" respectively.

To get the new approvals, Cessna once again turned to Joseph S. Newell for the stress analysis that would dictate what structural changes would be required to mount the bigger powerplants.

A weight difference of 251 pounds between the Curtiss and Wright engines resulted in a new design gross weight of 3,350 pounds, with an overall increase in the load factor for high incidence, nose dive and

three-point landing conditions of 1.21. Therefore, any structural members affected critically by inflight and landing stresses on the DC-6 needed to exhibit a minimum margin of safety of 21% for the J-6-9, DC-6A installation and 11% for the J-6-7, DC-6B version.

Some weakness was found in the wings between the fuselage longeron centerline and rib #12 on each panel for the DC-6A analysis, and rib #4 and #8 on the DC-6B. These areas were strengthened with wood members to meet the positive margins of safety for both airplanes.

The landing gear, however, posed a more serious problem. Analysis showed that one member of the original-design DC-6 landing gear tripod had a negative margin of safety and was weak when subjected to bending and torsion loads required for the Wright engine installations.

Newell suggested that a drop test of the landing gear be made in its original form to check its strength, instead of designing a new tripod [the Department of Commerce allowed such tests in lieu of imposing the burden of redesign on the manufacturer, and Newell already believed the gear was basically adequate to handle the heavier engines despite the calculated negative margin of safety]. Lester Orcutt and Oliver Rosto, government inspectors for the Wichita area, witnessed the tests.

A complete landing gear assembly was mounted on a prototype fuselage and subjected to two different drop tests. The first series consisted of drops from three, nine, 18 and 23.6 inch heights with 2,470 pounds of bagged sand added to the 632-pound fuselage/gear assembly, the actual load being 3,102 pounds. No failure or distortion occurred, but the Department of Commerce requested that another drop test, made in the three-point condition, be conducted at 3,350 pounds.

The first drop was made at 3,100 pounds from 24 inches high, the second at 3,350 pounds from the same height with no failures or distortions being observed. Because of a typographical error in a message sent by the Washington office to Inspector Orcutt, the final drop was made from 34 inches, but no failure of any kind or the slightest distortion in any member was detected. These tests clearly supported Newell's opinion that the gear, as designed for the DC-6, was stout and rugged enough to handle the mighty Whirlwinds. Therefore, no changes to the landing gear were required by the government.

Another static test was carried out on the door truss of the fuselage simultaneously with the landing gear tests. The truss was under greatest loading in the three-point landing condition, and the test fuselage did not have the specified 1 1/4 inch diameter, .058 inch wall thickness tubes called out by Newell's analysis as necessary to carry the higher loads (tubes in the static test fuselage were 1 1/8 inch x .049 inch).

The first two drops made from a height of 24 inches showed no problem with the structure, but on the third drop, done at a height of 34 inches instead of 24, caused a failure in one tube that connected to the door truss (the truss itself withstood the loads). Newell was consulted, and he pointed out that the test fuselage did not have the proper diameter and wall thickness tubing, nor a 0.065 inch steel gusset plate that was welded over the truss assembly as called out by the stress analysis. A revision was made to the drawing used to build the door truss section so that production airplanes would feature the change.

Analysis of aileron, elevator and rudder controls and their actuating mechanisms showed more than adequate strength for both the DC-6A and DC6-B versions. Static tests were completed on the entire airframe structure in accordance with Department of Commerce Aeronautics Bulletin 7A, with no problems encountered.

With the stress analysis and static testing completed, Cessna submitted the paperwork to the Department of Commerce for approval while the factory finished building the necessary jigs, tooling and fixtures for the "Chief" and "Scout". Throughout the spring and summer of 1929, the company continued to experience good sales on the Model AW, and Parker Cramer set out in early April on a cross-country flight that would further enhance the little monoplane's sterling reputation for speed and dependability.

Flying C7107, Earl Rowland's famous ship from the 1928 air derby, Cramer took off from Cessna Field and flew to Detroit, where he made final preparations for a flight to Nome, Alaska, and eastern Siberia. The purpose of the trip was to survey possible air routes between the United States and Alaska's territories for future air service (Cramer also entertained the desire to circle the globe, and may have been checking the northern route from Siberia to the U.S. at the same time).

"Shorty" Cramer, as he was called, was accompanied by Willard S. Gamble on the flight. The duo hopped through North Dakota and the western provinces of Canada enroute to Fairbanks, Alaska, then on to Nome, using skis instead of wheels for landing gear. They flew to East Cape, Siberia, to climax their aerial odyssey, then returned to Detroit after a thrilling 30-day journey.

In 127 hours of flying, Cramer and Gamble covered 13,085 miles, a distance of more than halfway around the globe. The Cessna performed admirably, averaging over 95 mph to Nome, and 100 mph on the return journey. The Warner 'Scarab' radial required only routine valve adjustments and spark plug cleaning.

The Alaska flight in April was only a prelude to the summer's activity for Cessna. Progress on the new factory was rapid, and by the end of May the complex was nearing completion. Some equipment was already moved in, the water tank was up and Mr. Cessna expected the production lines to be humming along by June 15th.

Warm weather always meant the dawn of another racing season, and the first event that caught Cessna's attention was the Gardner Trophy Race, sponsored by Russell E. and Fred W. Gardner. 1929 was the first year for the event, and was somewhat different from other races in its format.

Efficiency, load carried and time were of no importance in the Gardner race; it was a sheer speed dash, with throttles to the firewall all the way. The competition consisted of two phases: a qualifying run from five widely separated points in the nation, and the actual speed event from St. Louis to Indianpolis and return. The winners of the qualifying heats would earn $750 and the first and second-place pilots of each heat would earn the right to fly in the grand finale event.

Clyde Cessna had every intention of entering and winning that $5,500. Stanley Stanton would fly the prototype DC-6 (c/n 157, 8142, bearing race #9) from Denver, Colorado; Marvin T. O'Dell would launch from Buffalo, New York and Earl Rowland would take off from San Antonio in a sleek, new Cessna creation called the CM-1.

Licensed X9860 (c/n 195), this ship was radically different from production Cessnas. It was a mid-wing design, with a span of 36 feet (two feet were chopped off each stock wing panel) and a length of 20 feet, 10 inches for the fuselage, which was steel tubing covered with laminated plywood instead of fabric, giving a smooth, rounded appearance. The open cockpit sat far back behind the wing, and a large mail pit was located in the forward section of the fuselage, designed to hold 500-800 pounds of express.[13]

The landing gear assembly was basically a stock production unit, supporting a 225 hp Wright J-5 engine nestled snuggly within is tight-fitting NACA cowling. There was very little time for exhaustive flight testing before the Gardner race, so Rowland and the factory crew worked out as many bugs as possible before he left for San Antonio, Texas. Maximum speed was expected to be around 180 mph.

Built by Cessna as a racer, the CM-1 used an "A"-series landing gear and empennage, but featured a clipped wing and plywood-covered fuselage. Powered by a 225 hp Wright J-5 under a NACA-type cowling. Earl Rowland flew the ship in the May, 1929 Gardner race. (Truman C. Weaver Collection via Bob Pickett)

Registered X9860 (c/n 195), the CM-1 had a maximum speed of around 160-170 mph, but was plagued with engine fuel problems throughout the event, finishing fifth. Smooth contour of fuselage shows up well in this view taken at Parks Air College, St. Louis, Missouri, during the race competition. (Bob Pickett Collection)

Owen Haugland's Model AF (c/n 137, 6625) was used for unsuccessful 1929 endurance attempts. "Miss Minneapolis" was the first Model AF built, delivered to Haugland in July, 1928. (Bob Lemm Collection via Noel Allard)

On May 28th, Rowland flew unopposed to St. Louis and easily won his division, while Stanton and O'Dell clinched victory in their divisions, too. The big race was scheduled for Memorial Day to coincide with the Indianpolis 500 classic. 468 air miles lay between the five contestants and a lot of money.

Things just didn't go well for the Cessna team. First, O'Dell's ship lost a sheet of fuselage fabric, forcing him down, the CM-1 suffered throughout the battle from a lack of full power (caused by a section of fuel line that was too small and didn't feed the Wright engine enough gasoline at full throttle) and Stanton found the Challenger-powered DC-6 just too slow to be competitive.

When it was all over, Charles "Speed" Holman flew his Laird LC-RJ-200 biplane to victory in two hours, 58 minutes, 40 seconds, averaging 156 mph. Sydnor Hall placed second, Art Davis third, John Wood fourth, Earl Rowland a distant fifth and Stanton sixth.

In June, the CM-1 was damaged beyond repair when a severe windstorm struck the Wichita municipal airport without warning. According to Rowland, the ship was tied down outside when the winds swept across the field.

The one and only CM-1 wasn't the only victim,

Art Goebel's CPW-6 (c/n 190, R9855) as it appeared soon after rollout from the factory, August, 1929. Designed to compete in the Los Angeles-Cleveland non-stop race, over 600 gallons of fuel could be carried in fuselage. (Bob Pickett Collection/Cessna Aircraft Company)

however. Standard Oil's "Stanolind II" Ford Trimotor and a Fokker trimotor were the two largest aircraft destroyed, being nothing more than devastated hulks after the 125 mph gale swept them aside. Only the cockpit instruments and engines were salvageable.

Deed Levy, chief test pilot for the Stearman Aircraft Company, had just landed following a short hop in one of the company's new LT-1 cabin biplanes, earmarked for delivery the next day to an airline operator. He quickly shut down the 525 hp Pratt & Whitney "Hornet" radial engine, jumped from the cockpit and tried in vain to tie down the aircraft, as he could see the wall of wind and dust approaching at a very fast speed. He was too late and dove for cover nearby the helpless aircraft.

With unbelievable force, gusts ripped the frail machine from its moorings and in a matter of moments thrashed it to pieces, tumbling the big ship end over end across the Kansas sod. Lloyd Stearman and J. Earl Schaefer, who had rushed outside to aid Levy, were forced to embrace the only stationary object nearby; a telephone pole. As quickly as it had come the storm was gone, and the three men picked themselves up from the ground, staring in disbelief at the tangled, twisted wreckage that only minutes before was a flying machine worth over $15,000.

Among the 20 aircraft destroyed or damaged by the savage wind was Edgar B. Smith's beloved old Standard J-1 biplane, crushed inside its collapsed hangar. $300,000 in losses occurred during the brief but furious storm. Fortunately, the new Cessna factory was spared any damage, and work continued to put finishing touches on the six buildings.

Cessna's Minnesota dealer, Owen J. Haugland, who had flown a Model BW in an unsuccessful transcontinental attempt during the 1928 Air Derby, found new challenges in 1929 in the form of endurance flights, then the rage among aviators and the public.

Such flights were big news, and it seemed that somebody, somewhere, was trying to stay up in an airplane longer than anybody else. Haugland had teamed with Eugene Shank, another well-known Minnesota flyer who had already set two unrefueled records for OX-5-powered aircraft in 1928, flying a Waco 10. The third member of the trio was Verne Nelson, another native of the northern state who would fly Haugland's rebuilt Model BW (c/n 117, N5835) as the refueling and supply airplane, using a hose 42 feet long to transfer the gasoline.

Haugland used his Model AF (c/n 137, 6625), modified to carry 100 gallons of fuel in a cabin tank to feed the 150 hp, seven-cylinder Floco (the word "FLOCO" actually stood for "Floyd L. Odebreit Co."). A makeshift bed was laid out atop the tank so that the off-duty pilot could get some rest.

On May 25th at 8:58 A.M., the all-red Cessna named "Miss Minnesota" took off from the Braley School of Flying, just east of the new Cessna complex, and headed north. The pilots planned to fly to Robbinsdale, near Minneapolis, and then follow a route running to the Canadian border and back to Robbinsdale.

Arriving over Minneapolis later that day, the first refueling transfer went well until the hose snagged one of the AF's navigation lights. Shank, working the controls carefully, was able to free the hose but

First production DC-6A was c/n 199, shown here with its 300 hp Wright J-6-9 radial engine and polished Standard steel propeller. Solid as a rock in cruise trim, the DC-6-series ships flew well but were difficult to three-point, especially with a forward center of gravity loading. This airplane is under restoration by Forrest Lovley in Lydia, Minnesota, as of 1985. (Bob Pickett Collection)

it couldn't be reeled back into the refueling ship, so pilot O.P. Harrah landed with it trailing behind.

After 52 hours, the record attempt was cut short by a faulty fuel gauge that indicated lots of fuel when there was actually none remaining, as the two pilots discovered upon seeing the propeller saluting them through the windshield. A forced landing was made near Robbinsdale, Minnesota. The airplane was renamed "Miss Minneapolis" and readied for the next flight.

The second attempt was made on June 19th, but only lasted 13 hours when oil was discovered siphoning out of reserve cans into the black of night. To make matters worse, thunderstorms and turbulence threatened the little monoplane's safety, so the craft landed and was quickly prepared for another assault on the sky.

Taking off again on June 21st, an engine failure put them back on the ground the same day, but on the 23rd, the ship was up in the air once more. Shank was not aboard, however, as he decided to fly the BW supply ship, turning his seat in the AF over to Thorwald "Thunder" Johnson.

This time things seemed to go right. One day, then two passed by, the airplane and its pilots battling inclement weather and fatigue all the way. By the end of the fifth day, the airmen were getting lots of attention from the press as they passed the 6,000-mile mark. A sticking valve on the Floco caused the fourth attempt to cease with only 23 hours left to break the existing record. The northern airmen were not alone in their quest for the endurance record. As the Cessna was readied for its fifth try, four other teams of high flyers took off, each one dedicated to wearing out themselves and their airplanes if that's what it took to lay hold of glory.

Haugland was not about to give up now. He installed a new engine and took off with Preston L. Crichton, an official of the National Aeronautics Association, as relief pilot on July 22nd. All went well for two days, then four. Soon six days had passed

and the duo were finally starting to attract national attention as they continued their monotonous circuit above Minneapolis. On the seventh day they were getting very weary, but both men kept up their spirits and were determined to hold out as long as it took to establish a record.

On July 29th, Crichton was flying at 150 feet over Minneapolis' Wold-Chamberlain Airport, throttling the engine back to slow down while feeding in back pressure on the stick to hold altitude. He dropped a note to the ground crew, and moments later the Cessna stalled and spun in, killing Crichton immediately. Haugland received serious injuries and was rushed to the Fort Snelling hospital, but died the next day.

The fifth endurance attempt had logged 11,000 miles and stayed aloft 154 hours, 45 minutes, refueling 18 times. It was a valiant effort by Haugland, his fellow pilots and the Cessna monoplane, but Forrest O'Brine and Dale "Red" Jackson, who were still in the air when "Miss Minneapolis" crashed, kept their Curtiss 'Robin' airborne for over 420 hours, clinching a spot in the record books of 1929.

Back in Wichita, a mass exodus of equipment and personnel was underway at the old Cessna facility. Everything was being moved as fast as possible to the new factory. Major Wehrle announced that the production rate at the original plant had reached an all-time high of five airplanes per week, 47 being built in the last 90 days. He expected production to be two ships per day at the new site, accelerating to four per day and then 25 per week by the end of the summer months. If necessary to meet demand from Curtiss Flying Service (who had a total of 545 airplanes on order from Cessna, as of June 15th, worth more than $5,540,000), Wehrle was ready to implement a night shift that would boost production all the way to 40 ships per week.

By June 25th, Model AWs and a few DC-6 models with Challenger engines were under construction in the Franklin Road plant (Franklin Road was a thoroughfare immediately north of the factory. Its name was often used to designate the new facility).

Hugo A. Kenyon and Clyde Cessna discussed what raw materials were needed to build almost 550 airplanes in the next seven months, in particular the DC-6A and DC-6B models that were on the threshold of full scale production.

72

Servicing the engine oil tank required lifting up the bottom seat cushion, as demonstrated here by a Cessna mechanic. Late production DC-6 airplanes had the oil tank relocated in the aft cabin area for improved weight and balance. (Bob Pickett Collection/Cessna Aircraft Company)

Orders were already in hand for the two new monoplane models, and the Model AW continued to be held in high demand by the Curtiss Flying Service, who couldn't get the handsome airplanes in sufficient numbers to satisfy customer demand.[13]

Like the A-series monoplanes, the DC-6 ships were fueled by opening the upper hatch and standing on the front seat. It was tough on upholstery but did eliminate the need for a stepladder. (Bob Pickett Collection/Cessna Aircraft Company)

They were such a good selling craft that Wehrle was always under pressure to get them out the door at a faster and faster rate. But the move from the old facility to the Franklin Road site forced a production slowdown, and almost three months were required to catch up on the backlog.[14]

Eldon Cessna, who had worked with the company engineers on the design and certification of the DC-6 series, was also very interested in the new sport of gliding. He was elected president of the Wichita Glider Club on July 3rd. The newly-formed organization ordered one of the powerless aircraft from Glider's Inc. of Orion, Michigan, and by the second week of July, flights were being made from Cessna Field (Eldon was not a licensed airplane pilot, but was taking instruction toward his private pilot certificate).

While gliders were certainly not the rage in the summer of 1929, the light, portable aircraft were gaining popularity as an inexpensive way of flying. Towed behind automobiles, the single-seat ships could stay close to the ground while being pulled by a tow cable or the pilot could gain some altitude and cut loose from the tow car, sailing along in silence for a short distance.

The company had no plans to build gliders commercially at that time, but Cessna saw gliders as a useful promotional tool leading to potential airplane sales. If someone could earn their wings in a glider, then perhaps they could make the transition to airplanes more easily.

Amidst the blistering heat of a Kansas August, Clyde Cessna laid plans for the upcoming Miami-Miami Beach to Cleveland dash that would precede the spectacular 1929 National Air Races, to be held in Cleveland during the first week in September.

Earl Rowland was the only factory pilot entered in the event, and he won his division, but had to argue with officials after landing at Cleveland when he was listed as being in fourth place. Rowland protested, insisting that a time zone error had been made by someone. A careful study was made of all elapsed times and the race committee discovered a one hour discrepancy, making Rowland the winner with an elapsed time of twelve hours, 30 minutes over a distance of 1,483 miles and a little bit richer with the $1,500 victory check. He flew his 1928 Model AW, bearing race number 903 and sporting a newly-installed NACA cowl around its Warner engine.

A non-stop race, flown between Los Angeles and Cleveland, was another event of the Ohio-based extravaganza, and Art Goebel had his eye on the $5,000 first prize.

After discussing his needs for a racer with Clyde Cessna back in the early summer, Goebel placed an order for a special airplane, designed to carry over 600 gallons of fuel at a speed of more than 160 mph.

The ship's existence was kept quiet, as Goebel didn't want pre-race publicity. Work on the airplane proceeded quickly, with the major departure from stock Cessnas being the fairing of the fuselage into a barrel-like shape for streamlining the bulky, 420 hp Pratt & Whitney nine-cylinder radial, reportedly taken from the retired Travel Air "Woolaroc".[15]

The entire cabin space was consumed by fuel tanks, equipped with dump valves for emergency jettison of gasoline, if required. The landing gear was strengthened and so were the ailerons, to handle the

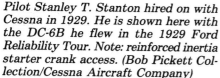

Pilot Stanley T. Stanton hired on with Cessna in 1929. He is shown here with the DC-6B he flew in the 1929 Ford Reliability Tour. Note: reinforced inertia starter crank access. (Bob Pickett Collection/Cessna Aircraft Company)

A.J. "Steve" Lacey gives an airman's pose with a DC-6B. Lacey reportedly worked for the Air King company before joining Cessna in 1929. He was killed in a DC-6A crash in April, 1930. (Bob Pickett Collection/Cessna Company)

The winning combination of Earl Rowland and his Model AW won the Miami-Miami Beach to Cleveland race in 1929, giving the Wichita pilot and his machine back-to-back victories for two years in the National Air Races.

expected in-flight stresses. In addition to the standard complement of flight instruments, a clock, rate of climb and turn and bank indicator were also installed.

Goebel was in Wichita on August 27th to take delivery, but problems with last minute construction details prevented the first flight from taking place until the 30th, when newly-hired Cessna pilot Steve Lacey flew the all-silver ship.

Maximum speed was not disclosed to the press, but optimistic company officials estimated the monoplane could hit 180 mph (this speed was unlikely even when the airplane was light, but with 3,600 pounds of fuel on board such speeds were highly improbable).

Only rudimentary flight testing was done. There was no time to work out any problems with the big monoplane. Goebel had to be in Los Angeles to prepare for the race, so he was very anxious to be on his way. Taking off on August 31st from Cessna Field, the CPW-6 climbed very slowly after a prolonged ground roll.

Only 400 gallons of fuel were in the tanks, and climb performance continued to be marginal as the R-985 radial strained to lift its load higher and higher on the way west. Art wondered about that other 200 gallons that were not aboard; he feared that another 1,200 pounds might wipe out what climb capability the ship had.[16]

After a nine hour, 40 minute non-stop flight to the west coast, the seasoned racing veteran reluctantly decided to withdraw from competition, claiming that although the Cessna could carry a lot of gasoline, there was serious doubt that it could ever climb over the Sierra Nevada and Rocky Mountains enroute to Cleveland. Fuel leaks, possibly caused by vibration-induced cracks in the tanks, were rumored to be another reason for Goebel's decision.

Since there was a race from the west coast to Cleveland, officials decided to hold one from

Philadelphia to the host airport, too. Tragedy struck, however, when a Cessna (model unknown) flown by E.J. "Red" Devereaux, accompanied by his wife and his mechanic, Edward Reiss, were killed when the ship crashed during the event.[17]

What caused the accident was not determined for certain, but aileron flutter or separation of the surfaces from the wing were listed as possibilities. The Cessna company made a public announcement very soon after the mishap, advising all pilots of Cessna monoplanes not to enter any races until a thorough investigation was conducted on the wreckage. The only exception to this ban was Goebel's CPW-6 with its reinforced ailerons.

Curtiss Flying Service then contacted Cessna, requesting that demonstration flight tests of the DC-6 and Model AW be performed at the company's Long Island, New York, headquarters to prove the flight control system's airworthiness.

The Cessna company didn't feel there was any need for the tests, but complied with the Curtiss request. Steve Lacey, Clyde Cessna and Major Wehrle flew back east to witness the flights. After a thorough wringing out of both airplanes by Curtiss test pilots, no faults could be found in either model.

Lacey, who was sent aloft to really put on a show for the eastern boys, threw a DC-6 around the sky with reckless abandon, doing mild aerobatics with the ship as Curtiss officials watched. Only one challenge remained: a power dive designed to prove once and for all if the airplane would stay together at a rate of speed far above its design envelope. Again Steve Lacey rose to the occasion, climbing a new DC-6 high into the azure sky above Long Island.

The dive was made at full throttle from a starting altitude of 5,000 feet down to 2,000 feet, with the airspeed indicator reportedly nudging 350 mph on the scale (such a high velocity is questionable for an aircraft of the DC-6 class, but Cessna claimed the speed was attained), followed by a pull-up maneuver

The new Cessna factory on Franklin Road as it appeared in the summer of 1929. DC-6 ships are in the foreground with engine engine covers installed, while the CM-1 is visible next to the building at far left. Note arrow on building at right that pointed toward north. Such arrows were common at many airports and helped orient pilots to true north. (Bob Pickett Collection/Cessna Aircraft Company)

into a zooming climb.[18]

After landing, Lacey stepped from the airplane with a smile, indicating that no problems were encountered during the unorthodox test. Curtiss technicians inspected the airplane for signs of excessive stress, particularly the aileron attach fittings.

Nothing was amiss, and Curtiss was fully satisfied that Cessna airplanes were completely airworthy in every respect, proving the point by placing an order for another $300,000 worth of cabin ships only days after the demonstrations were held.

Clyde Cessna and Howard Wehrle returned to Wichita with renewed confidence in the future, a huge order in their hands and increased pressures to deliver their product on time. The assembly lines were already turning out more than four ships per day, but it would take six times that rate to fill the Curtiss contract by the specified date of October 1, 1930 (the factory was still working on the order for 545 ships placed in April and June of 1929).

September continued to be a month of success for the company when the Department of Commerce granted approved type certificates for the DC-6A and

Model DC-6 fuselages under construction in the welding department of the Cessna factory, September, 1929. Note the pre- welded fuselage side assemblies hanging on T-racks at right, awaiting their turn in the welding jig. (Bob Pickett Collection/Cessna Aircraft Company)

DC-6B models. The 300 hp "Chief" was given ATC #243 on the 30th of the month while its 225 hp brother, the "Scout", was alotted #244 on the 29th.

The first DC-6B (c/n 198, N9863) and DC-6A (c/n 199, NC9864) had been built in June, with N9863 being sold to Curtiss Flying Service of the South, Memphis, Tennessee, and NC9864 to H.B. and G.H. Rudd of New York City, later that summer. The government permitted Cessna to build and sell the DC-6A and DC-6B models prior to issuance of an ATC (as was commonly done for any aircraft manufacturer) since the Department of Commerce had approved engineering data on file in Washington and the type certificate was pending issuance.

On September 30th, Steve Lacey flew a DC-6B to an official altitude of 18,100 feet with H. G. O'Dell (National Aeronautics Association representative responsible for the sealed barograph) Marcellus M. Murdock of the Wichita Eagle newspaper and Cessna engineer Frank Dobbe. Nearly 120 miles were consumed in the one hour, 10 minute climb, and Lacey was able to fly hands off much of the time, while Dobbe recorded engine instrument readings and made an overall evaluation of the aircraft's performance.

To publicize the two airplanes, Cessna entered one of each model in the 1929 Ford Reliability Tour along with 'ol reliable, C7107, flown by her famous master, Earl Rowland (Joseph A. Meehan and Harry Poindexter also flew the ship). Stanley T. Stanton was piloting the DC-6B (c/n 214, NC632K) with his new bride riding shotgun for the whole tour which doubled as their honeymoon. Steve Lacey commanded the company's DC-6A in the tour.

Twenty-nine airplanes started the tour, flying a 5,017-mile route stretching from Dearborn, Michigan, through eastern Canada, down to Florida then back to Dearborn via the deep South and the midwest states, including a stop at Wichita.

Rowland became ill at the Richmond, Virginia, stopover point and relinquished the stick to Harry Poindexter, a Curtiss Flying Service representative. Poindexter did well until bending the propeller on landing at Jacksonville, Florida, but got back in the air and finished the tour in 13th place, with Stanton completing the event in 12th position and Lacey in 14th spot. All three airmen won $200, but first place

Five Model DC-6 fuselages await primary assembly in this September, 1929 photograph. Ailerons, stabilizers, elevators and rudders can also be seen. (Bob Pickett Collection/Cessna Aircraft Company)

and $2,500 was taken by none other than Johnny Livingston, flying a Wright J-6-7-powered Waco CSO biplane.

America's growing aircraft industry had enjoyed phenomenal growth since 1927, when a young, shy airmail pilot flew his Ryan monoplane across the Atlantic Ocean and propelled aeronautics into the big leagues of the business world.

Throughout 1928 and part of 1929, the nation's aircraft manufacturers built and sold airplanes like hotcakes. Wichita's builders were no exception, with Travel Air leading the way in June of 1929, expecting to build 50 ships per week, mostly cabin monoplanes.

The Stearman company was very busy constructing mail planes and some custom-built sportsman models, and Swallow was turning out biplanes for training and pleasure flying at a feverish pace. Five aeronautical investment firms were located in the prairie city, three airport engineering companies and one export corporation.[19]

In all, sixteen aircraft factories were designing, building and selling their products, with six engine companies doing the same. Investors had poured over $10,000,000 into the city's most famous industry, and by the fall of 1929, Wichita was known by another name: The Air Capital of the World.

On a national scale, sales of aircraft climbed at an ever-increasing rate, and the stock market found prospective buyers eager to spend their money on aeronautical ventures. Travel Air was absorbed by the gigantic Curtiss-Wright conglomerate in August, and Stearman became a member of the United Aircraft and Transport Corporation the same month.

Throughout the summer and early fall of 1929, buying and selling of stocks wavered, and Wall Street was in the throws of a potential selling spree. On Thursday, October 24th, a massive sellout of stocks caused the market to take a nosedive, and the following Tuesday another wave of panic selling caused a total collapse in prices, ushering in the Great Depression.

Every business in the nation was immediately affected, and that included aircraft builders like the Cessna Aircraft Company. Just when the airplane business seemed about to takeoff for Clyde Cessna, the economy clipped his wings.

The board of directors met to decide on strategy that would hopefully cope with a new and very uncertain marketplace. One of the first actions taken by

View of wing jig shows a nearly completed front spar with its tapered design. (Bob Pickett Collection/Cessna Aircraft Company)

The factory wood shop produced component parts for the wing structure as well as assembling the entire unit. Note completed spars on rack in background at right, wings in various stages of construction. (Bob Pickett Collection/Cessna Aircraft Company)

Cessna was cancelling the contract it had with Curtiss Flying Service, who also sought to sever the agreement in light of the shaky financial situation faced by the big eastern firm and its national network of dealers. However, both parties agreed to honor the contract until January 1, 1930.

By November 1, 1929, Cessna had delivered about 37 Model AWs, four DC-6 and three DC-6A monoplanes to Curtiss. According to Cessna company records, 16 of the total of 22 DC-6B and 15 of the total of 22 DC-6A models built were delivered to the flying service by January, 1930.

Without Curtiss as a customer, the Cessna company had to totally rebuild its dealer/distributor force, and Howard Wehrle set out on an east coast tour to sign up new sales agencies in November. He and company pilot Jack Sinclair were successful in persuading eight men to sign the dotted line as franchise owners.

In the November 23, 1929, issue of "Aviation", Cessna printed its "most important message of the year", saying the company was strong financially, led by men with vast experience in the aviation industry and was armed with a new sales organization ready to do more business than ever before.

It sounded good, but the financial base, strong though it was in October, was beginning to crumble 30 days later. Stock costing over $100 per share after the 1928 air derby victory had an over-the-counter quote of $18 per share 12 months later, and fell to $12 by December.

To bring in more cash, the company sold the First Street and Glenn Avenue factory to the Burgan Corporation of Iowa for approximately $50,000. The firm intended to manufacture camping equipment and found the factory ideal in size and layout for their needs[20].

The Franklin Road factory was still turning out airplanes at a rate of nearly four per day as December began, and there was reason to believe that things might just get better because of newspaper reports of a stock market recovery. But as soon as a little upward movement on Wall Street started, it failed to gain momentum and prices sank to new depths.

The export market, however, seemed to be promising, and Cessna sent Stanley T. Stanton, Hugo Kenyon and James P. Verts south of the border the first week of December, attending an aeronautical exposition in Mexico City. They flew a DC-6A outfitted with special upholstery and reclining seats.

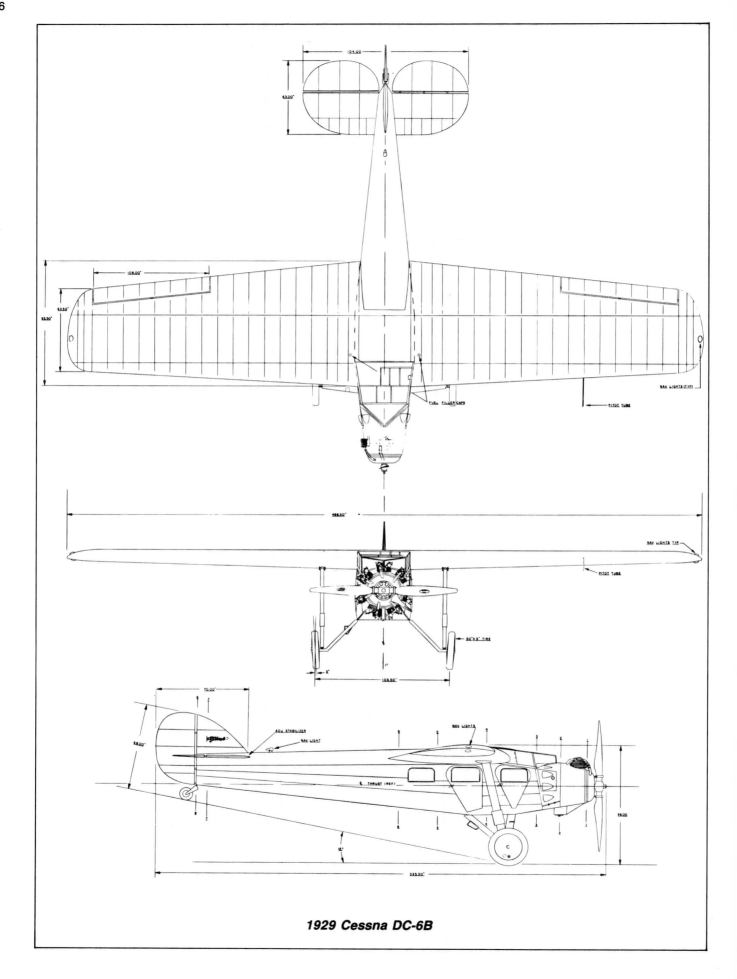

1929 Cessna DC-6B

Sales interest was high, but the trio returned home without any firm orders.[21]

Despite the gloomy business climate, there was cause for celebration around the plant one day in December when young Eldon Cessna soloed a Model AW. He had been taking flying lessons from Stanton and Rowland, logging six hours, 15 minutes before winging his way into the sky alone.

Eldon, who had remained actively involved with the Wichita Glider Club, was busy at the factory designing a production prototype glider for the company. He had been a full-time employee since the spring of 1928, when his father had called him home from Kansas State Agricultural College to help out in the engineering department.[22]

Known as the CG-1 ("Cessna Glider, Model 1"), two examples had been built by Christmas, and Gilbert C. Budwig, well-known official with the Washington office of the Department of Commerce, was in Wichita that month and took his turn at the stick of the one and only CG-1 (c/n 1, 649K), being towed aloft by automobile for a short but enjoyable flight.

As it became more and more evident that airplanes sales were heading for an all-time low, Clyde Cessna was faced with the task of keeping the company solvent and the production lines busy.

One way to accomplish that was building and selling gliders, coupled with a campaign to encourage formation of clubs throughout the mid-western United States. As 1929 drew to a close, plans were already well underway to mass produce the CG-series craft, design new, low-cost airplanes and continue to win as many air races as possible (always a ready-made source of publicity and quick cash).

It had been a year to remember, with record profits, a high volume of business and continued prosperity. Just what the future held for Clyde Cessna and his company was uncertain, but he was sure of one thing; the new year would bring with it an uphill battle to survive.

---

[1] In September, 1928, the little factory at First Street and Glenn Avenue was producing less than two airplanes per week. Because of the very limited space available, there was little hope of building five or ten ships per week in answer to the boom in Cessna sales generated by Earl Rowland and #99.

[2]. Clyde Cessna was listed as Chief Engineer at this time. F.H. Dobbe, who joined the company early in its existence, was also in the engineering department along with several draftsmen. Cessna knew that the "A"-series airplanes were good designs, but recognized that they offered too little cabin space and comfort. The CW-6 and DC-6 cabin ships then in planning phases were the right airplanes at the right time. They would have sold in far greater numbers than a mere 44 machines if the Great Depression had not intervened.

[3] Cessna had big plans for a small airline-oriented ship, but the Pratt & Whitney version never materialized due to its uncertain sales appeal and expensive ($7,000) engine.

[4] In 1928, Clyde Cessna told the Wichita Eagle that tailskids were damaging the sod of landing fields so bad that some airports could become useable. He encouraged all aircraft manufacturers to equip all new models with tailwheels. However, tailskids continued to be standard equipment on Cessna airplanes until the advent of the CW-6/DC-6 series.

[5] According to one eyewitness of this event, a large limb had lodged in the Model BW's landing gear, and as Bowhan flew over the field it fell to the ground. The observer, who heard the engine noise and had run outside to see what was happening, retrieved the limb and retained it for Clyde Cessna to see. What other mitigating circumstances were involved in Bowhan's eventual dismissal are not known.

[6] Robertson did not order any CW-6 airplanes, but did buy a Model BW for its St. Louis operation. This was one of the last BWs built (c/n 138, NC 6442) before the type was phased out.

[7] One has only to fly aboard a Boeing 747 with its spacious upper deck, featuring enough room for dancing, to realize that Clyde Cessna knew what he was talking about. His statements before his 1928 peers are just another example of the air pioneer's foresight.

[8] The airline never got off the ground. It was conceived by McIntosh, who was from California, when he saw an opportunity to establish air service in the west coast state. Only one CW-6 was built, and the Cessna company wasn't interested in backing McIntosh's entrepreneurial plans. The proposed air service never materialized.

[9] Art Goebel and William V. Davis flew the "Woolaroc" from California to Hawaii on August 16-17, 1927, to win the $25,000 first prize in the Dole race. After Goebel's abortive attempts to turn the docile ship into a racer, it was restored to its Dole race configuration by the Winstead brothers in Wichita, flown on a short farewell tour by Goebel in 1929, then placed in a special stone building on Frank Phillips' estate "Woolaroc," for which the plane was named (Woolaroc meant-"Woods, Lakes and Rocks"). In 1984, complete restoration began on the famous monoplane, and it will rest in a special building when completed (1985) for future generations to see.

[10]. Witnesses at the first takeoff of the rebuilt Woolaroc said that Goebel barely controlled the ship's direction from his blind cockpit. Fortunately, the powerful radial engine got the craft airborne quickly.

[11] According to factory records, c/n 150, N6450 is the only known company-built, Comet-powered Cessna.

[12] Wichita newspapers said that the CW-6 was actually destined for Joffre's airline operation, purchased for him by M. Castelan and his brother, who owned hotel interests in Mexico City and were part of the financial power supporting Joffre.

[13] Cessna was far behind in meeting their contract for 545 airplanes. Curtiss Flying Service was selling the Model AWs at a faster rate than the factory could produce them.

[14] By August, 1929, the new factory was just beginning to catch up with some of the tremendous backlog of orders from Curtiss-Wright Flying Service. Major Wehrle was trying to get production up to at least 25-30 ships per-week in the new factory, but that number was never attained.

[15] The Wichita papers reported that Goebel had taken the 'Wasp' from the Woolaroc. He apparently owned this powerplant since there is no known evidence to the contrary.

[16] There seems little doubt that Goebel's choice was the right one. Heavily loaded with 3,600 pounds of fuel, it seems unlikely that the CPW-6 could have cleared the 14,000 foot peaks it would have faced not long after takeoff.

[17] The airplane involved in the crash is believed to have been a Model AW. Newspaper reports described the Cessna as hitting the ground "at 200 mph", but this is sheer speculation. In any case, aileron problems were the center of attention by the Department of Commerce, Curtiss Flying Service and the Cessna company.

[18] The DC-6-series, based on a general evaluation of their design performance envelope, probably had a never exceed speed (Vne) of about 200-225 mph. If Lacey truly did hit 350 mph in his 3,000-foot power dive, then the Cessna's were stout ships, indeed. Some structural problems should have surfaced, not to mention aerodynamic controllability, at such a high airspeed followed by the so-called "quick pull-up" described by the newspaper reports of the tests. There is very serious doubt that the airplane ever reached 350 mph in the power dive.

[19] Wichita was very proud of being one of the largest aircraft manufacturing cities in the world. It boasted more factories and ancillary aeronautical endeavors than any other town by 1929, the height of its early day glory. In 1985, only Beech, Cessna and Gates LearJet are based in the city, with Cessna being the only fully autonomous company until it was acquired by General Dynamics in September, 1985.

[20] Cessna had been using the old plant buildings for storage and possibly some experimental work, according to Howard Wehrle's comments in June, 1929. Camping equipment is still made in Wichita as of 1985, being the worldwide headquarters for the Coleman Company.

[21] Early Model DC-6A and DC-6B airplanes had the engine oil tank located under the front seat, contributing to a forward center of gravity that resulted in a nose heavy condition which was very apparent when flying at low speed and when landing. However, the same situation made the airplanes very stable at cruise once they were trimmed up. To alleviate the nose heavy problem, Cessna sought and received approval from the Department of Commerce to relocate the tank behind the cabin area in Engineering Memorandum #244, dated September 29, 1930. Constructor number 200, 201, 202, 205 and up were eligible for this change. A new placard was placed in the baggage compartment after the modification was completed, limiting the load to 75 pounds. Earl Rowland reported that the monoplanes landed much easier after the tank relocation without sacrificing cruise stability.

[22] Eldon Wayne Cessna enrolled at the college in September, 1925, in the mechanical engineering program. In his junior year, (May, 1928) he left the campus to work at the Cessna factory. Two other Wichita airmen also attended Kansas State Agricultural College, back in 1917-18; Lloyd Carlton Stearman and Mac Short.

CHAPTER EIGHT
Cessna's Last Stand

Christmas, 1929, wasn't much of a holiday for the aircraft industry of the Air Capital. The town's big four in aviation, Travel Air, Cessna, Swallow and Stearman were still recoiling after the disastrous financial events of October.

Airplane sales went slowly but steadily downward. Walter Beech and Clyde Cessna had little to look forward to in the next year, although both men exhorted their sales agencies to be aggressive and sell, sell, sell! Beech had been forced to lay off several hundred employees at the Travel Air plant, and Bob Phelps, who was a foreman at the Cessna factory, did the same unpleasant task for the Cessna company. Swallow was also forced to cut their work force nearly in half or more by the end of the year, and Stearman struggled along under the able leadership of J. Earl Schaefer.

Prices of new aircraft were falling almost as fast as the value of company stock, with Curtiss-Wright Flying Service (as it was known by 1930 after the Curtiss and Wright companies merged in the summer of 1929) asking $3,430 for a Model AW with ferry time only, almost $3,700 under the normal price of $7,200. Even the DC-6A and DC-6B models were being sold at drastically reduced prices of $9,800 and $8,000 respectively, on airplanes that normally sold for $11,500 and $10,500.[1]

Money meant survival, and Clyde Cessna intended to gather as much of the ever-scarce green stuff by building and selling airplanes and gliders as well as winning air races. He started off the new year by sending company pilot Jack Bridges to sunny Florida.

The purpose of the trip was strictly to race and win

Eldon Cessna flies a CG-2 (304M) on a silent flight in early 1930. The CG-2 was an improved CG-1 glider that was intended for mass production. It sold for $395 complete with launching mechanism. Maximum gliding speed was about 25-30 mph. (Bob Pickett Collection/Cessna Aircraft Company)

money, as much money as possible, at the second annual Miami All-American Air Meet held on the 13th, 14th and 15th of the month. Bridges flew a DC-6B to the meet, with orders to enter every event for airplanes equipped with engines of not more than 800 cubic inch displacement.

Cessna knew that the DC-6B was very tough to beat in that class, with its 225 hp Wright R-760 pulling it along at nearly 150 mph. Dale "Red" Jackson, who had set an endurance record of more than 450 hours in a Curtiss "Robin" with Forrest O'Brine in 1929, was also at the races with a DC-6A belonging to the Curtiss-Wright Flying Service, for whom Jackson was employed.

Bridges won first place in both 15-mile races for 800 cid class cabin ships, and Jackson cleaned up in his Chief by winning two 15-mile events for 300 hp planes, with Bridges nipping at his tail all the way to the finish line in both races.

The Miami competition was very successful and financially rewarding, with Bridges bringing home hundreds of dollars in prize money to keep the bank account from hitting bottom.

Probably one of the biggest setbacks to the company was the departure of General Manager Howard Wehrle on January 1, 1930, whose one year contract had expired on December 31, 1929. Wehrle left to perform consulting work for the military services and would be sorely missed by the company. He had done a magnificent job of marshalling the firm's resources to produce airplanes, and was a key factor in the company's success story in 1929. Wehrle did retain an undisclosed amount of Cessna stock after his departure.[2]

Clyde Cessna took over the general manager's spot from Wehrle, and immediately faced a threat he had never encountered before; receivership. F.M. Munoz, stockholder and engineer for Cessna, filed a petition in Wichita District Court early that month asking that a reciever be appointed to handle the affairs of

the company. He charged that mismanagement was the primary reason the firm had finished 1929 nearly $100,000 in the red, after selling $750,000 worth of airplanes and over $300,000 worth of stock.

Munoz further stated that Clyde V. Cessna had exerted too much influence on the company's affairs, and contributed to the overall mismanagement and lack of profits. Judge I.N. Williams, who heard the charges, claimed that Clyde Cessna had every right to exert influence in his own company, and the matter should be settled by the stockholders and not a court of law.[3]

Clyde had won the battle but could still lose the war unless he and the board took immediate action to quell the growing tide of opposition from within and without the company. Cessna's hopes for financial relief were at least partially pinned on son Eldon's CG-2 gliders that would have to be sold in very large quantities to bring in enough cash to help the company.[4]

Cessna also realized that the sport of gliding would have to be sold to a public that knew little or nothing about flying or the aviation industry itself, so he arranged an open house on January 4th and invited all of Wichita to come.

Hundreds of people did just that, touring the factory and seeing Eldon Cessna fly one of the long-winged CG-2s, although the wind was gusty that day and made towing the ship aloft by automobile somewhat difficult. Many of the spectators took rides in two monoplanes stationed on the field for that purpose. The open house was definitely successful, and encouraged Cessna even more that gliders could be sold in a time of economic depression.

The company formally announced its commitment to build and market gliders that month, with advertising placed in both "Aviation" and "Aero Digest". The ads claimed that Cessna recognized the importance of gliding and developed its version of the craft so "that man might fly first, without power, in safety." Eldon Cessna and Frank A. Dobbe, also an engineer with the company, spearheaded the factory's efforts to sell the powerless ships and establish clubs throughout the mid-west states.[5]

Walter Beech took his turn at the stick of a Cessna CG-2 and did very well, saying that he thought all pilots should familiarize themselves with gliders, as did Charles A. Lindbergh, who didn't fly one of the craft but believed in their importance as vehicles to teach the fundamentals of flight to prospective airmen.

Each glider was shipped in a crate, ready for assembly and flight, and also included an assembly and instruction manual, shock cord and rings for launching, a seat belt, automatic release for hand launching (pulled by people who ran as fast as they could) and a release for use in cutting loose from a tow aircraft. Selling price was $398, F.O.B. at Wichita, and the first production CG-2 went to the Norwich, Kansas, glider club in February, and the second example was sold to a club just forming in Oklahoma City, Oklahoma. Specifications for a standard production CG-2 were:

Span: 35 feet
Chord: 54 inches
Area: 157 square feet
Wing Loading: 1.82 pounds per square foot
Empty Weight: 120 pounds

Constructor number 18 in the CG-2 glider sequence was assigned to the CS-1. It first flew in March, 1930, and was apparently an experimental craft as no other CS-1s are known to have been built. (Bob Pickett Collection)

Flying Speed: 25 mph (typical)
Landing Speed: 15 mph

As of January, 1930, Clyde Cessna had not been pilot-in-command of any aircraft since late in 1927, (according to an article published in the Wichita Eagle). However, if Mr. Cessna was going to ballyhoo how great gliding was, then he decided that it would be prudent if he learned to pilot one himself.

On January 24th, the Kansas air pioneer was ready to fly, being launched by a ground crew using shock cord. Clyde and the CG-2 sped through the sky as he made small corrections to the ship's attitude with the stick, just as he had 19 years earlier with the frail "Silverwing" on the Salt Plains. Only a minute after the flight began, Clyde eased the glider down to a safe landing.

A broad grin graced Cessna's face as he climbed from the small seat. He liked gliding just fine, and openly harbored the belief that individuals, and even whole families, could participate in the sport without danger.

Eldon, who was already very proficient at piloting powerless aircraft, followed his father's Friday performance by earning his private pilot's license in a Model AW on Saturday, January 25th, after accumulating 17 1/2 hours of flight time.

As the sale of DC-6 and Model AW models fell lower and lower, there was less and less for the company pilots to do. Stanley Stanton and Jack Sinclair left the company in January to fly for oil firms needing their expertise in the cockpit. Clyde Cessna didn't like losing two of his best pilots, but he also knew they were better off flying oilmen around the country than sticking it out with the Cessna company, whose financial future seemed very uncertain as January passed into history.

Cessna stock fell to a new low in February, with the asking price per share falling to $10; a two dollar decrease since the first of the year. Just when Cessna needed a boost in his bank account, he almost got one. A man claiming to be Lloyd Waner, famous outfielder with the Pittsburgh Pirates, strolled into the factory office one day in February saying he wanted to buy the latest Cessna monoplane model.

Clyde met the gentleman and eagerly showed him the DC-6A, giving him a sales pitch that had been honed to perfection over the years. Producing a checkbook, the man said he'd take the airplane, and wrote out a personal check for almost $12,000.

Then, in what must have seemed an odd request to Cessna, the buyer asked if he could borrow 50 cents to buy a pair of socks. Clyde responded by handing the man not 50 cents but a five dollar bill, thinking there was nothing to worry about since the gentleman had just bought a very expensive airplane.

Clyde was happy about the sale he had just made to one of the most well-known ball players in the nation. The buyer left a telegram to be sent to his brother and also informed Clyde that he was staying at the Hotel Lassen and would return the next day for delivery of his all-red monoplane.

Unfortunately for Clyde, the customer was nowhere to be seen the next day, and Cessna began checking up on him fast. The Hotel Lassen never heard of Lloyd Waner, there was no brother at the non-existant telegraph address and the real Lloyd Waner was sick in a Pittsburgh hospital. Having been thoroughly taken by the smooth-talking con-man for a mere five dollars, Clyde Cessna summed up the situation as only he could: "as far as (he) was concerned, the man displayed a distinct lack of drive and self-motivation in asking for only 50 cents to buy a pair of socks when he could have asked for a ten dollar bill."

The company's annual stockholder's meeting was held at the factory on February 5th to discuss the current state of the airplane market and to formulate plans for the coming year. 25 stockholders attended with enough proxy votes to constitute a quorum (three weeks earlier, the meeting had to be cancelled for lack of a quorum).

Five men were elected to the 1930 board of directors: Clyde V. Cessna, Eldon Cessna, William B. Harrison, William Priest and L.B. Rogers. The next day, elections were held for company officers, with Clyde Cessna retaining the presidency, Hugo Kenyon in the vice presidential slot, Eldon Cessna was elected secretary while William B. Harrison became treasurer and James P. Verts took on the job of assistant secretary and treasurer.

Cessna reported to the stockholders that 25 gliders were under construction and that sales were expected to be good, especially since the warm season was approaching. He also told the group that clubs were being formed in Kansas and the latest formation had been in Oklahoma City, with more requests for information being received every week from other towns and individuals desiring to get in on the gliding craze.

To gear up for mass production of the CG-2 as well as keep the factory busy building as many DC-6A and DC-6B airplanes to fill orders already in hand, the stockholders decided that more money was needed to compensate for losses that were being incurred almost daily. The company needed a large infusion of cash and it needed it right away.

On February 26th, the stockholders and board of directors voted to completely reorganize the Cessna Aircraft Company. Two men, Charles Yankey and M.L. Arnold, both well-known Wichitans, now entered the scene. Yankey was a respected lawyer and Arnold was known for his shrewd business acumen which he used in operating the Arnold Motor Company in Wichita.

They promised Clyde Cessna $50,000 for capitalization, and the company's 50,000 shares of no par value stock was doubled. Along with this change, elections were called for to select officers for the next year. Clyde V. Cessna was again elected president; M.L. Arnold, vice president and treasurer; Eldon Cessna, secretary and James P. Verts, assistant secretary and treasurer. Other men elected to the board were Carl Evans, longtime friend of the Cessna family, Will G. Price and William B. Harrison.

Hugo Kenyon and the Shawmut Corporation withdrew from the Cessna organization at this time, realizing that there were no profits to be made in aviation until the nation's economy was strong again. The eastern firm also had enough troubles holding on to its own cash and could ill afford to support a Kansas airplane builder, too.

Immediately after the reorganization, Arnold told the press that "sweeping cuts" were to be made in the prices of production airplanes, with the DC-6A

Left: Art Goebel took his turn at the stick of a CG-2 and found the gliding experience fun and exciting. Goebel ran a flight school in Kansas City, Missouri and often visited Wichita. (Bob Pickett Collection)

Middle: Eldon Cessna took a CG-2 glider, added a two-cylinder, 10 hp Cleone engine, fuel tank and simple landing gear to create the CPG-1. It flew in the spring of 1930. Eldon Cessna (far left) observes some fellow airmen as they fuel up the little airplane for another flight. Only one CPG-1

was built, N344M, c/n 39 in the CG-2 number sequence. (Bob Pickett Collection)

Right: Continuing to experiment with his light airplane concepts, Eldon Cessna (seated) revamped the CPG-1 by moving the engine forward and added a fairing and Pyrolin windshield for streamlining. This ship was a familiar sight around the Cessna factory in the summer of 1930, buzzing across the sky at nearly 30 mph. (Bob Pickett Collection/Cessna Aircraft Company)

Eldon took the powered glider concept one step further in 1930 by modifying CG-2 c/n 77 into the prototype Cessna EC-1, shown here soon after construction. Power came from a 25 hp Cleone engine. Continuing development produced the improved EC-1 and EC-2 airplanes. Note rough similarity to early Aeronca C-2 series lightplane. (Bob Pickett Collection/Cessna Aircraft Company)

N403W was the first production EC-1, built in the summer of 1930. Still using Aeronca power, the single-seat EC-1 was promising but there was little interest from customers. (Bob Pickett Collection/Cessna Aircraft Company)

being reduced to $11,000 and the DC-6B to $9,750. New and improved interiors were planned for all models and a small, open cockpit, two-place monoplane was to be designed that would sell for less than $2,000.

Arnold and Cessna wanted to get the CG-2 out in the open where it could be displayed at a national show, and the St. Louis aeronautical exposition held in March afforded just such an opportunity. A Chief, a Scout, and a CG-2 were exhibited, with the glider getting the lion's share of attention.

That spring, a strange-looking Cessna creation was seen at the flying field. It was the CS-1 ("Cessna Sailplane - Model 1"), designed by factory engineers to have a glide ratio of one foot down for every 30 feet forward. Wingspan was reported as 47 feet, with an empty weight of 150 pounds. It could be launched by hand or from towing by automobile, and had remained in the air for over three minutes by March [Although such a short time in the air does not sound impressive when compared to the sailplanes of today, one must remember that the CS-1 was launched with only a few hundred feet of altitude at the most, leaving very little time to glide].

Art Goebel, who had never flown a sailplane before, flew the ship and quickly became an advocate of sky sailing. Only one CS-1 was built (c/n 18 in the CG-2 sequence, N322M) strictly as an experimental aircraft.

Goebel also piloted a CG-2, and Dwane Wallace got some time in the air in gliders as well. Young Dwane had always been interested in airplanes and his affiliation with his famous uncle soon led him to enroll at Wichita University in the aeronautical engineering program.

March was the first month of quantity production and sales of the CG-2, with one glider per day being produced and over ten were sold that month, including five that were shipped to the Equipment and Supply Company of New York City.

M.L. Arnold went to Winnipeg, Canada to encourage formation of glider clubs in that country, and planned to attend the Detroit aero show on the way. There was much interest in gliding in the north country, and two CG-2 gliders were sold as a result

of his trip. At the Detroit exposition, gliders from other companies were on display, but Cessna didn't send any of its products to the show, primarily because of the costs involved.

Clyde Cessna had suffered his share of trouble since the new year began, but a tragedy occurred on April 16th that hit him very hard: A.J. "Steve" Lacey, who had been flying for the company since 1929, was killed when the DC-6A demonstrator he was flying (c/n 236, NC648K) crashed about nine miles southwest of Hays, Kansas.

Lacey had been giving demonstration flights to Dr. H.C. Hill of Holyoke, California, and was taking him back home, accompanied by Lacey's 20-year old wife Omiria and Russell Guild, who was a friend of Dr. Hill.

After taking off from Cessna Field, the flight progressed nicely, with Hill and Guild very confortable in the back seats, and Mrs. Lacey up front with her husband of 14 months. Nearing Hays, they encountered a lowering cloud layer and the 27-year old airman tried in vain to find a hole to descend through.

Knowing that he needed to get below the clouds in order to navigate by pilotage on the trip, Lacey elected to penetrate the layer, hoping to break out before hitting the ground. He had little or no instrument flight training, and the DC-6A was equipped with absolutely no gyroscopic instruments to help keep the ship in a level attitude (without a natural horizon to guide the pilot, and no instruments to display an artificial horizon that would help keep the wings level, it was almost impossible for a 1930-era pilot to fly an airplane in the clouds without becoming disoriented as to which way was up, down, left or right. Lacey knew of this danger, but decided to take the risk anyway).

He managed to keep the big Cessna under control for a short time, but gradually fell victim to spatial disorientation, or vertigo. He couldn't tell if his wings were level or not...his brain told him one thing while his body told him something else. Struggling to fly the airplane, Lacey's control inputs only aggravated his vertigo condition. He watched the altimeter slowly unwind, hoping he'd see the ground any second and level off to continue the trip.

Down and down the ship came. The ground was still not in sight. The young, but experienced pilot must have thought about levelling off and climbing back on top of the clouds. Perhaps his one moment

82

of hesitation made the difference.

The monoplane smashed into the earth at over 100 mph, tearing the engine from its mounts and heaving it like a pebble 200 feet from the twisted wreckage. Lacey was killed instantly. His wife died later that day of massive injuries and Guild was hospitalized with a fractured spine. Hill received only a broken nose and cracked ribs.

Word of the accident was sent as quickly as possible to the factory. Cessna, Earl Rowland and a Department of Commerce inspector took off for Hays in a DC-6A. They were forced to turn back not far from Hays because of the clouds, but were able to reach the location the next day. A formal investigation was conducted, and no fault in the airplane was found. It was determined to be a case of a non-instrument trained pilot entering instrument conditions, succumbing to vertigo and crashing.[6]

Dr. Hill, however, recovered quickly from his injuries and returned to Wichita on April 22nd to select another cabin Cessna. Hill's nerves were steady and he wasn't going to let a crash stop him from flying. He bought a DC-6B (c/n 240, NC303M) and had another pilot fly him home to Holyoke.

Although it had been a year since Earl Rowland's exciting escapade in Mexico with the CW-6, he was glad to see a group of aviators from Mexico City who were in town to take delivery of a new DC-6A (c/n 234, NC646K). They also told Rowland and Cessna that a very early model Cessna plane, with six seats, was still flying out of Valbuena Field, giving rise to speculation that the venerable CW-6 was still airworthy.[7]

While the sale of airplanes was still far behind 1929 figures, glider production increased to more than one per day. A new version of the Cessna CG-2, equipped with small floats and called the "Hydro-glider", was aimed at training pilots to fly off water instead of land.[8]

Test flights were conducted on the Little Arkansas River and in a very small, man-made lake near the burned-out Braley Flying School campus in May. Eldon Cessna conducted most of the flights, and found takeoffs and landings to be easy and smooth with the CG-2's good handling characteristics being unaffected by the float installation.

Eldon then took the next logical step with the CG-2 design by installing a two-cylinder, 10 hp Cleone engine on CG-2 344M, c/n 39, in a mid-fuselage position, adding a five-quart fuel tank to the upper pylon and bolting a welded steel tube landing gear to the fuselage uprights.

This creation was called the CPG-1 ("Cessna Powered Glider - Model 1") and made many successful test flights in May and early June. Weight and balance was not the best with the aft engine installation, so Eldon reconfigured the aircraft that summer by installing the Cleone up front on a tube/truss assembly, then adding a piece of clear Pyrolin to protect the pilot from the propeller's blast. The final touch was a simple aluminum fairing that supported the windshield and covered the pilot's feet. Everybody who saw the little ship buzzing through the sky was quite impressed by its performance, with observers estimating its speed at 25-30 mph.

Based on his success with the powered glider, Eldon took the CPG-1 design to its zenith of development by covering the fuselage with fabric, adding a door on the right side plus a windshield in front of the pilot, who sat in an semi-enclosed cockpit. Power was supplied by a 25 hp Cleone, two-cylinder opposed engine. The only one built was c/n 77 (in the CG-2 number sequence) and licensed as 133V. This airplane was a prototype for the EC-1 series and is considered to be the first of the type built. It was successful in proving the concept of a very light aircraft to Cessna management, and further development was authorized.

Two other EC-1s were built during the summer of 1930, c/n 71, 199V (in the CG-2 number sequence) and c/n 251, N403W. Cessna records indicate that 403W was converted into the first EC-2, but no evidence exists to substantiate the documents. In 1935, it was a single place ship. At least one EC-2 was built, N405W (c/n 253), in March, 1931, using an Aeronca 30 hp engine. It was the last product of the original Cessna Aircraft Company.[9]

In September, Guy P. Poyer, an engine designer, was trying to set up a company in Wichita to build his three-cylinder, 30 hp radial engine, known unofficially as the "Poyer-Tres". One of the powerplants was reportedly installed in a Cessna light airplane

Good view of 405W with Eldon and Clyde Cessna aboard. Although a good design with acceptable performance, sales never materialized. The EC-2 was Clyde Cessna's last stand against the Great Depression and became the last airplane built by the company before closing the doors for three years. (Bob Pickett Collection/Cessna Aircraft Company)

and flown by Eldon on September 10th. Poyer claimed fuel consumption was only 1.5 gallons per hour. Another feature of the engine was its adjustable compression ratio.

Initial testing seemed to be encouraging. Eldon was slated to make a flight of the Cessna/Poyer combination before the public on September 14th, but it was cancelled due to bad weather.

Ten days later, a pilot named Nicholas Evancho was reported to have flown the Cessna/Poyer airplane at the Wichita Municipal Airport. The purpose of the flight was to demonstrate the monoplane to the Ford Reliability Tour entrants, who were making an overnight stop in the prairie city.

By December, 1930, Poyer's engine had been further developed and now produced 45 hp and weighed 85 pounds. Five of the powerplants were under construction in a factory at 840 North Main Street, and the name was changed to "Tri-Clone", a clever, but unsuccessful attempt by Mr. Poyer to cash in on the notoriety of Curtiss-Wright's "Cyclone" radial engine.

Apparently, nothing ever came of the marriage between Poyer's three-cylinder powerplant and Cessna's light airplane. According to the Wichita Eagle, Poyer found financing for his company in Kansas City and disappeared from the scene by January 1, 1931.

In addition to the EC-1 and EC-2 models, Cessna engineers also designed a two-place, high-wing monoplane using a Cirrus inline engine. Known as the FC-1, it featured a full-cantilever wing of 33 feet, and a length of 21 feet. Gross weight was approximately 1,458 pounds. A 95 hp, four-cylinder, inverted, inline engine powered the airplane. The one and only FC-1 was sold in June, 1930.

W.C. "Penny" Rogers, who had been flying for Cessna on a part-time basis since 1929, was officially added to the employee list that summer, and George Harte, another well-known member of the Wichita flying fraternity, was also doing some pilot work for Cessna but was not directly employed.

Jack Bridges, who had done such a good job rounding the pylons for Cessna, packed up and left in early June but bought a DC-6B (c/n 244, NC305M) before he departed, and planned to team up with George Harte who also owned a DC-6B (c/n 214, NC632K) to operate as the "Harte and Bridges Transportation Company", offering charter flights to virtually anywhere in the United States.

As the mid-point of 1930 arrived, Cessna officials took a hard look at how well the company was doing. Statistics showed that while less than 10 DC-6-series ships were built, at least 25 CG-2 gliders were sold. Other Wichita aircraft firms were doing better with Travel Air licensing 119 ships, Stearman 28 and Swallow 32.

Clyde and his fellow executives didn't like the numbers staring them in the face, but Cessna still believed that a fast comeback in the economy was not likely, and held fast to his conviction that only a conservative, hard-line approach to the aviation business would see the company through the sales doldrums.

Cessna's involvement with American Cirrus Engines, Inc. of Marysville, Michigan, had begun with the FC-1, but a special racing airplane was designed in the summer of 1930 that also used the powerplant.

Another airplane built in 1930 was the two-place Model FC-1 (far left), powered by a four-cylinder, 95 hp Cirrus engine. Only one was built, N138V, c/n 248.

The Cirrus engine company, which was a subsidiary of Allied Motor Industries, Inc., organized and sponsored a 5,541-mile aerial trek to demonstrate long distance flying by light airplanes. All entrants were required to use a Cirrus engine in their aircraft. Total prize money was a whopping $25,000, guaranteeing that some of the biggest aircraft manufacturers in the country would compete in what was popularly known as the "Cirrus Derby."

Stanley Stanton, who had left the Cessna firm to fly for the Harris and Haun company of Blackwell, Oklahoma, earlier in the year, came up with the idea to have Cessna design and build a pure-bred racer for the Cirrus competition.

Stanton convinced his boss, Carl B. Haun, that he had a good chance of winning the race if the right airplane was available. Mr. Haun and his associates agreed to the proposal and paid out $3,500 to Cessna for construction of the GC-1 ("G" for the seventh Cessna design, "C" for the Cirrus engine and "1" for the first example) and named the ship "Miss Blackwell". Company engineers, including Eldon Cessna, worked on the GC-1 hard and fast, working out the stress analysis, building the airplane and delivering the all-red speedster (c/n 249, NR144V) to Stanton by July 9th.

Wingspan of the GC-1 was 27 feet, length 21 feet and gross weight 1,450 pounds. Two, 30-gallon fuel tanks gave the red GC-1 an eight-hour endurance with the 90 hp engine throttled back to cruise power. The American Cirrus "Ensign" (serial number 307) featured a supercharger designed by the famous race car driver Ralph De Palma. It was claimed to boost horsepower by up to 30% while reducing fuel consumption but proved to be the most troublesome component on the monoplane. Eleven other entries also used a supercharger on their Cirrus engines. Stanton had only a few days to test-fly the ship, and found maximum speed to be about 160 mph.

On July 15th, the GC-1 departed Cessna Field for Detroit, the starting point for the derby. Eighteen airplanes took off from the Motor City, heading east, then south and west across the vast expanse of America. It was the longest air race held up to that date, and was plagued by bad weather. Stanton's problems began soon after the start of the event when the supercharger began to rebel on the leg to Buffalo, New York. It wasn't pumping in enough air for the Cirrus to breathe and produce full power, and never improved for the remainder of the competition.

The little Ensign also had its share of troubles. It

ran rough much of the time, the intake manifold cracked, all of the pushrod seals leaked oil, exhaust stacks broke and fell off and then Stanton damaged a wheel in a rough landing along the route. Perhaps he remembered Earl Rowland's fix for such a problem with the CW-6, as Stan rigged up a wooden replacement until repairs could be made at a stopover point.

The GC-1 was first into Detroit at the end of the race, but finished out of the money. "Miss Blackwell" was dubbed the "winged torpedo" by the press because of her smooth curves and graceful shape, but she only averaged 72.50 mph overall and took seventh spot in the final standings. Lee Gelbach won first place in the low-wing, open cockpit Command-Aire monoplane with an average speed of 127.11 mph. Stanton believed the GC-1 could have given Gelbach a good run for the money had it not been for all the mechanical problems encountered.

After the All American Flying Derby, the GC-1 was modified by removing the temperamental supercharger, but retained its NR144V restricted racing license. Earl Bunker Smith, an associate of Mr. Haun, groomed the GC-1 for battle at the National Air Races in Chicago, placing fourth in the 1,000 cubic inch displacement (cid) class race for open cockpit ships. That wasn't a bad showing, considering the fact that Smith was up against the likes of Jimmy Haizlip in the Travel Air/Shell "Mystery Ship" and Charles "Speed" Holman in his dashing Laird, both equipped with fire-breathing 300 hp Wright radials. Bearing race number 89, the sleek Cessna was also entered in the Thompson Trophy event, but was withdrawn before the race with engine trouble.[10]

In June, 1931, Earl Smith, then president of Skyways, Inc. of Blackwell, Oklahoma, bought the ship and used it for pleasure flying and advertising until March, 1932, when it was completely destroyed in a hangar fire at Blackwell along with the DC-6B owned by the firm of Harris and Haun and flown by Stanton.

Hot on the heels of the GC-1 was the GC-2, almost a carbon copy of the first ship except for a Warner Scarab radial engine of 110 hp nestled beneath an NACA cowl. It was completed on August 16th and intended for racing only. Earl Rowland was listed as owner and pilot of the monoplane, and Walt Ander-

son's White Castle hamburger business in Wichita sponsored the racer for the season.[11]

The GC-2 (c/n 252, NR404W) featured a mid-wing layout like the GC-1, with a 24-foot wingspan and a length of 20 feet, five inches. Fuel capacity was 45 gallons, and eight gallons of oil were carried.

Rowland was very optimistic about the airplane's potential, and when he made the first flight on August 19th, speeds approaching 170 mph were obtained with full throttle. Three more days were spent working out minor discrepancies, then Earl blasted off for the National Air Races at Chicago. Clyde and Eldon Cessna also left town to attend the races and see first-hand how well the GC-2 performed.

Earl Rowland entered several events but didn't place in the money despite a good showing. The GC-2 was also flown by William Ong and Mary Haizlip, with Ong placing second in the men's 450 cubic inch Free-For-All race at a speed of 145.49 mph, winning $300, then striking paydirt in the 650 cubic inch event by grabbing second place again, earning $360 at a speed of 147.83 mph. The third race entered by Ong was the 800 cubic inch Free-For-All, where he placed third at 148.25 mph and collected $300.

Mary Haizlip took second place in the Mrs. R. McCormick Trophy Race with a speed of 148.42 mph and gathered $750 for her efforts. The little red racer had done well for its baptism of fire, and over the next 14 months Rowland continued to fly the ship, entering it in the 1931 Miami All American Air Races where he placed second to Johnny Livingston in the Hialeah Trophy Race.

Earl flew the GC-2 to his home in Harrison, Arkansas, after the Miami races, where he used it at airshows held to raise money for the needy. In 1931, the ship's license expired and a ferry permit was issued granting permission to fly the machine to Dallas, Texas, where the nearest Department of Commerce inspector could issue an airworthiness certificate.

The actual inspection, however, took place in Waco, Texas, and a new restricted racing license was issued on March 28th, 1931. The airplane's license was canceled by the Department of Commerce on August

Stan Stanton poses with his Cessna GC-1, NR144V (c/n 249), before the Cirrus Derby race in July, 1930. The engine featured a DePalma supercharger which caused trouble throughout the competition and caused Stanton to finish seventh. The airplane was later lost in a hangar fire in 1932. (Bob Pickett Collection/Cessna Aircraft Company)

A sister ship to the GC-1 was the Warner-powered GC-2 racer, built in August, 1930 and flown by Earl Rowland, Mary Haizlip and William Ong at the National Air Races in Chicago. 110 hp Scarab pulled the ship along at nearly 170 mph. William Ong runs up the Warner in this view taken at Chicago. Note dirigible flying in distant background, autogyro parked at left. (Bob Pickett Collection/Cessna Aircraft Company)

15, 1931, as Rowland had placed the ship, less engine, in storage. According to Earl, the GC-2 was destroyed in a crash at Brownsville, Texas, during a familiarization flight by a prospective buyer sometime later that year.

1930 also saw the younger pilots of the nation getting into their own brand of competition. Stanley C. Boynton, 18-year old pilot from Lexington, Massachusetts, claimed the junior transcontinental record in both directions in October. Flying a DC-6A, he flew from Rockland, Maine, to Los Angeles in 24 hours, 2 minutes, making a short stop at the Cessna factory to have the ship checked over by engineers and company technicians. George Harte took the ship up for a quick test hop and pronounced it fit to continue the flight.

After getting some good advice about navigating cross-country from none other than the old master himself, Clyde Cessna, Boynton climbed in the monoplane and sped on to Los Angeles. He made the return trip east in just 20 hours, 29 minutes, breaking the previous record set by Bob Buck earlier that year, who had in turn taken the title away from Eddie Schneider who flew a Model AW coast to coast in record time back in August.

At the board of directors meeting held on October 2nd, William B. Harrison had some bad news for Clyde Cessna and his fellow directors; the Fourth National Bank in Wichita was calling in some of the debt owed to it by the company, and a proposal was made that M.L. Arnold, vice president of Cessna, buy four airplanes and some of the land still available at the old First Street and Glenn Avenue factory.

Since the company had no cash on hand to pay the bank, Arnold's gracious gesture was fortuitous and timely, amounting to $22,000. He bought a DC6-A (c/n 237, NC300M), a DC-6B (c/n 246, NC145V) and two Model AWs, c/n 243 (NC337M) and c/n 140 (NC7107) known as the "Warner racing job." Cessna had licensed the craft NR7107 in August, 1929, for racing purposes, but the commercial license had been reinstated by December of that year. Arnold paid $1,000 for the airplane on October 2, 1930, and then sold it back to Clyde Cessna on October 8th for an unknown amount. Apparently, the two men agreed to this action so that Cessna would have the aging monoplane in his possession since it was of little value to Arnold.

The Cessna Aircraft Company ended 1930 with little improvement from the first of the year. Sales had been agonizingly slow, and the CG-2 sales, while helpful, didn't add much to the bankroll because of their low price. Less than 20 airplanes had been sold, all of them DC-6-series ships.

In January, 1931, another crisis arose for Clyde Cessna, who was now feeling the heat of the stockholders more than ever before to produce a profit or shut down the plant. One year before, Mr. Cessna was fighting only to save the company, but now he was fighting a losing battle to save his presidency as well as the company's existence.

On the 22nd of the month, Thad C. Carver, president of the People's Bank of Pratt, Kansas, was elected president of the Cessna Aircraft Company. Clyde V. Cessna was now vice president and factory manager, Andrew S. Swenson, secretary and A.B. Sanders, treasurer. These men were also on the board of directors, along with Roscoe Vaughan, who was

George Harte flew this DC-6A with drag cleanup on the cockpit and landing gear as well as an NACA-type cowl that was removed when this photograph was taken. Harte squeezed more than 150 mph out of NC6441 (c/n 226) on the race course, and top money often went to the big Cessna whenever it stood on the starting line. (Bob Pickett Collection)

associated with the Mercantile Bank and Trust Company of St. Louis, Missouri.

All of the directors thought that the business climate would improve in 1931, and announced that new models of cabin planes would be introduced during the year.

On top of the problems Clyde Cessna had with the company, its stockholders and directors, his father died in March at age 74 at the family homestead near Norwich, Kansas. James W. Cessna had prepared his children for this time in previous months, telling them exactly how and where he wanted to be buried, including a simple service presided over by his offspring.

His children did as he wished, handling all the arrangements themselves and directing the burial procedures. Clyde, Roy, Noel and Bert Cessna prepared the body for interment, dug the grave, acted as pallbearers and directed the service. Pearl Cessna, one of the younger brothers, did not attend the funeral. He had left home years before to live in Canada and never returned to Kansas.

In March, the Cessna Aircraft Company calculated its assets at $289,363, while accounts payable and mortgage notes totaled less than $33,000. The first of the new planes announced in January flew in early March with Eldon Cessna piloting the rejuvenated EC-2, hailed as the latest of the "Baby Cessna" line that began with the EC-1, for the benefit of the board of directors.[12]

It had a wingspan of 34 feet, and still had the 30 hp Aeronca powerplant, although company plans called for a 40-50 hp Continental engine to be used on production models. Other new designs announced that day were a four-place, low-wing cabin monoplane featuring retractable landing gear, another four-place airplane designed specifically for long range and high cruising speed and a ship aimed specifically at the mail/express market, with a capacity of 800-1,000 pounds and the pilot seated well aft of the full-cantilever wing.[13]

March also saw a fateful meeting of the board of directors, with Clyde Cessna, Thad Carver, Roscoe Vaughan, A.B. Sanders and Andrew Swenson attending. Business was conducted regarding sale of the CPW-6, which had been returned to the company and was in the process of being converted into a six-place cabin plane by George Harte. The directors ques-

Young Eddie Schneider shakes hands with a local dignitary after establishing a transcontinental record in August, 1930. Schneider flew a Model AW (c/n 152, C9092) east to west in 29 hours, 55 minutes, then returned to Newark, New Jersey in 27 hours, 19 minutes. Long range tank can be seen through rear door window. (John W. Underwood Collection)

tioned the value of spending further funds to complete the transformation, and decided to take action to dispose of the airplane as soon as possible and bring some sorely-needed cash into the company coffers.

Next came discussion of a most serious subject. A motion was made by A.B. Sanders that, in view of the very low sales of the firm, and the fact that no profits could hope to be made under the current economic conditions, the Cessna factory be closed and locked immediately and everyone, including Clyde Cessna, be eliminated from the payroll with only a watchman being retained to patrol the facility day and night.

Mr. Cessna strongly objected, but found himself a minority of one as Swenson, Carver and Vaughan concurred, with Carver appointing the three men a committee to arrange the closedown as soon as possible.

All inventory on hand was to be sold at a 20% commission, and the CPW-6 price tag was set at $1,500. Clyde Cessna's DC-6A, which he had been using for improvements to the type and was stored in the experimental department, was to be left alone since Cessna had stood bond on the ship. He agreed to pay all outstanding bills against the airplane before taking it out of storage.[14]

Cessna was saddened by the turn of events that day. He had worked so hard to keep the doors open, but it just wasn't enough. He was at the mercy of the stockholders and the board of directors. Although they didn't enjoy closing the factory, something had to be done soon or the only recourse would be to declare bankruptcy. Not even Clyde Cessna wanted to see that happen, so he was forced to accept his peer's decision.

Despite the meeting's decision to close the plant,

it remained open for a short time that spring since the board of directors, in an apparent reversal of their gloom and doom attitude, decreed that a "Baby Cessna" would be exhibited at the National Aircraft Show held in Detroit, Michigan, in April. Unfortunately, there were no buyers to be found for the little ship and the Cessna Aircraft Company essentially ceased to exist, except on paper, by that summer.

Since the company began business operations in September, 1927, approximately 240 airplanes had been built and delivered, with the Curtiss Flying Service taking 75 of that number during its contract period with Cessna and was their biggest single customer.

Clyde Cessna had made his last stand during 1931, with the CG-2, EC-1 and EC-2 designs showing promise but falling far short of sales expectations. The DC-6-series aircraft were among the best airplanes in the nation, yet they couldn't be sold, even at half their original retail price.

Surrounded by the Great Depression, attacked from all sides by grumbling stockholders and outgunned by his fellow board members, Cessna fought back with all the sincere hard work and sweat he could muster in a gallant attempt to make a profit.

While lesser men might have thrown up their hands in defeat, Clyde chose to fall back and regroup his efforts. He and Eldon waged their own war against the tough times in aviation by modifying and racing the most famous Cessna airplane of them all: NC7107, which they owned.

The father and son team had big plans for the Model AW and intended to capitalize on its virtues of speed and agility to make the ship a racer in its own right in the next two years.

The last big event in the 1931 racing season took place from Santa Monica to Cleveland, host city for the 1931 National Air races. Known as the Transcontinental Handicap Air Derby, both Eldon Cessna and Earl Rowland were planning to enter the event, which paid $3,000 to the first-place winner and was one of the "On To" events being held as part of the National Air Races.

Rowland would also be flying an AW that was undergoing final pre-race detailing, and was sponsored by the Wichita Flying Club. By August 5th, the airplane was almost completed and flight testing was done within the next 10 days.

Meanwhile, Eldon won a 25-mile race at Shenan-

Clyde Cessna intended to design and develop a new breed of cabin monoplanes in 1930-31, perhaps feeling the pressure of potential competition from new, modern ships like this Swallow low wing designed by Dan Lake and the Alexander Eaglerock "Bullet", created by Al Mooney. (Ben Bitler)

doah, Iowa on August 15th, and George Harte was there, too, taking his powerful DC-6A to first place in the Free-For-All event. It was a good warm-up for the National Air Races. Soon, Eldon was back in town ready to join his teammate Rowland for the journey to California.

A total of 63 pilots were registered for the race, and both Eldon and Earl were ready to go when the starter's flag dropped at Santa Monica. Eldon was leading the derby as the contenders crossed into Arizona, but Rowland was forced out of the race when the normally reliable Warner quit cold, forcing him to land about 20 miles east of Douglas, Arizona, causing damage to the airplane that could not be repaired in the field. Rowland was not hurt at all in the landing. He planned to dismantle the monoplane and ship it back to Wichita by rail.

Eldon Cessna continued to lead the pack, but when they arrived at Bartlesville, Oklahoma, he had slipped to third place. On August 30th, the derby racers landed at Cleveland, with Cessna NC7107 completing the race still in third spot, winning $1,200. Eldon also won Event #36-A, a speed and efficiency race for single-engine ships only, winning $750 plus a seven-foot high grandfather clock with a built-in radio. He also clinched top honors in the dead-stick landing contest held on September 1st.

The 1931 air racing season was over. Eldon Cessna had distinguished himself as a tough competitor on a national scale, and had also gained invaluable experience in the air. In December, Eldon won a prize of a different sort when he married Helen Parcells of Hiawatha, Missouri.

After the races of September, Clyde and Eldon formed the C.V. Cessna Aircraft Company and took up residence in a small factory at 3301 South Oliver Street, just north of the new Stearman Aircraft Company factory.[15]

Within its brick walls a new breed of Cessna airplane was born in the closing months of the year. It would bring new-found fame and fortune to the name Cessna, exploding on the American air racing scene just as the sport was entering its golden age.

---

[1] By July of 1930, prices had fallen to unbelievable lows, even for that era. Model AWs were available for as little as $3,625 with less than 100 hours of flying time in the logbooks. A DC-6B with a mere 13 hours total time could be bought for $6,435.

[2] Howard F. Wehrle worked as a consultant to Admiral Tower and General Hap Arnold and by 1939 was employed by the Fairchild Airplane and Engine Corporation. During World War Two, he was chief quality control manager and inspector for Higgins Aircraft, Inc. He was a partner in the Howard F. & D.M. Wehrle brokerage firm after 1947. He died on December 14, 1964.

[3] Munoz was a minority stockholder, retaining only seven shares. After the judge agreed to hear the petition, Munoz agreed to withdraw it later in January.

[4] 300 CG-2s were reported to have been built between December, 1929, and September, 1931. However, only 84 can be confirmed by identification cards in the Cessna archive files. At $398 each, the company would have had to sell over 30 CG-2 gliders to equal the retail price of a single DC-6A. Also, Cessna was not the only firm in the glider business. Waco, Alexander Eaglerock and the Detroit Aircraft Company all had good, high-quality gliders on the market by early or mid-1930.

[5] Dobbe was an early employee of the company and worked with Eldon on the design and construction details of the CG-2, EC-1 and EC-2 ships. The two men made numerous trips to nearby states giving gliding demonstrations throughout 1930.

[6] A.J. "Steve" Lacey started his flying career in the dust bin of a Marine Corps biplane in the early 1920s, serving with fellow Cessna pilot Jack Bridges at Quantico, Virginia, as an observer/gunner. He was reported as being an employee of the Air King company, who built an airplane for the ill-fated Dole derby of August, 1927, but it was disqualified by the race committee because flight tests proved it could not reach Hawaii and still have a 15% fuel reserve required by the rules. Lacey flew for a doctor in Peoria, Illinois, prior to his arrival in Wichita in 1929, where he was hired as a test pilot for the Swift Aircraft Corporation (which went into receivership after the stock market crash). He then flew for the Cessna company and had accumulated about 3,000 hours of flying time when he was killed.

[7] Since the CW-6 was not reported as "washed out" until sometime in 1930, some possibility exists, albeit small, that the airplane referred to by the Mexicans was Cessna 6446. Undoubtedly, the monoplane received hard use and little care during its tenure with the military.

[8] No records exist that indicate if any hydro-gliders were built in addition to c/n 2, NC304M.

[9] According to Eldon Cessna, only one EC-2 was constructed, c/n 253, N405W, but company records indicate that two ships were built, c/n 253 and c/n 251, N403W, which was sold to a Mr. Kay Jackson of Winfield, Kansas, in March, 1931. It changed owners six more times by June, 1939, when it was owned by DeWitt Ross, Jr., of Tulsa, Oklahoma. EC-2, N405W was totally destroyed in a crash on January 2, 1933. Wayne Dalrymple, an engineer for the Stearman company and a licensed pilot, bought the ship in June of 1932 and had been flying it regularly, but it was reported to have been out of license when the accident occurred. He had been giving flying lessons to Forrest Mangan, who was intensely interested in aeronautics and idolized Charles Lindbergh. The 25 year-old service station attendant told his parents he was going off to the dentist that day, but beat a path to the Buckley Aircraft Company flying field on East Central Avenue, where the EC-2 was hangered. Witnesses said the two men took off on a short flight, and when approaching to land, the craft suddenly entered a tailspin from about 200 feet altitude. Whoever was at the controls (probably Dalrymple) almost succeeded in recovering from the spin before impact, but a wingtip caught the ground and the little monoplane was smashed badly, killing Mangan and putting Dalrymple in the hospital with serious injuries. The EC-2 was a total loss.

[10] Entering the little GC-1 in a race dominated by modified airplanes with mega-horsepower engines may seem illogical, but despite its 307 cubic inch displacement powerplant, the all-red racer might have stood a chance at clinching fourth or fifth spot. All-out races like the Thompson were not won on speed alone but also on precision flying, especially around the pylons marking the course. If the pilot of a small, low-horsepower ship could hug the pylons consistently, while the more powerful airplanes were forced to fly a bigger radius of turn because of their higher airspeed, it was possible to compete effectively with the speed kings of the day.

[11] To promote White Castle hamburgers and the Cessna racer, the company offered a large photograph of Earl Rowland and the GC-2 as first prize in an essay contest. Whoever wrote the best story about the famous racing pilot and his airplane would receive the picture.

[12] The name "Baby Cessna" was another company tag for the EC-2. Officials stressed that the airplane was "not a toy", but a genuine, low-cost flying machine built for two.

[13] Except for the EC-2, no evidence exists that any of the other proposed designs ever progressed beyond the paper stage. The mail plane, with its aft-seated pilot and forward mail pits, was reminiscent of the 1929 CM-1. As for the retractable gear ship, Cessna may have been feeling some pressure from Alexander Eaglerock of Colorado, who had flown the Eaglerock "Bullet" monoplane designed by Al Mooney which featured a retractable landing gear system.

[14] According to Cessna company records, the board of directors secured a release from George Harte and his associates stating they would not file a mechanic's lien against the company for the rebuilding of the CPW-6 by Harte. This occurred on March 7, 1931. In September of that year, records indicate that a motion was made by A.B. Sanders that Eldon Cessna buy the airplane for $200. He apparently did not, as Jack Kremel, a Wichita aeronautical engineer and aircraft broker, had the ship in 1932, finishing its conversion into a six-place airplane. He did not have an engine, and sought Deed Levy's help to obtain a Pratt & Whitney 'Wasp' radial. Whether or not this powerplant was received and installed on the monoplane cannot be confirmed. Government records show the registration as cancelled by 1936.

[15] The building used by Clyde and Eldon Cessna was first erected for use by Quick Air Motors, but was never occupied by that firm. It was then used by the Swift Aircraft Corporation until the stock market crash forced it into receivership. Al Mooney was the next occupant, building his promising A-1 design that reflected his earlier experience at Alexander Eaglerock with the Model C-5 "Bullet" monoplane.

CHAPTER NINE
The Silver Bullet

In January, 1932, the Air Capital of the World had been brought to its knees by the Great Depression. In the previous two years, at least 14 aircraft or would-be aircraft manufacturers in Wichita ceased to exist. Many promising designs were wiped out before they ever flew. Stocks that were sure-fire money-makers had become worthless scraps of paper and the nation's love affair with flying had hit the rocks.[1]

The once-mighty Travel Air Company, which produced almost 50 airplanes per week at the height of success in 1929, had been silenced by Curtiss-Wright in 1931. Swallow was no more, and the Stearman Aircraft Company was keeping its doors open by testing and selling Northrop all-metal monoplanes under the Stearman name.[2]

At 5800 Franklin Road, the Cessna Aircraft Company factory was still padlocked and impotent, with a small part of its 55,000 square feet of floorspace being rented out for aircraft storage.

The Wichita Eagle and Beacon newspapers had very little to say about the city's aeronautical activity, since there really wasn't anything to report except how many passengers came and went on TWA's Ford Trimotor, and by 1932 even airline ser-

Flight tests on the CR-1 were unsatisfactory. The little ship was rebuilt by Eldon and his father into the CR-2 shown here after rollout from the shop in May, 1932, for initial engine runs. NOTE: There are no known photographs of the CR-1. (Bob Pickett Collection/Cessna Aircraft Company)

vice to the prairie town was threatened with extinction.

There was, however, no lack of news about starving Americans on the streets, businessmen committing suicide as their empires crumbled and the daily reports on the roller coaster status of Wall Street.

What the local press really needed was something to shout about, and Clyde Cessna gave them exactly that on January 4th when he announced the presence of a new airplane, a ship that was designed to do one thing: win races.

Reporters were glad to see Mr. Cessna back in the spotlight again, and they eagerly wrote down his every word as he talked about the C.V. Cessna Aircraft Company's first product. Known unofficially as the CR-1 ("Cessna Racer - Number 1"), it was a tiny monoplane, barely 12 feet in length, with a full cantilever wing mounted on the top fuselage longeron spanning only 16 feet. Welded steel tubing was used for the fuselage structure, covered by fabric except for sheet metal employed in the front section behind the firewall. The wings were of conventional wood construction, covered by thin plywood to carry in-flight loads on the full-cantilever wing as well as minimizing the torsional (twisting) forces encountered during high-G pylon turns.

The most prominent feature of the ship was its fully retractable, manually-operated landing gear located in the lower, forward fuselage. It was designed to pull up flush with the airplane's exterior, imitating the action of a bird (according to Cessna)

Designed by Clyde and Eldon Cessna with help from Garland Peed, Jr., the CR-2 possessed speed and maneuverability as well as advanced technology such as the manually-retracted landing gear. The little racer was a tough competitor around the pylons and won instant respect from the likes of Benny Howard, S.J. Wittman and Johnny Livingston. (Bob Picket Collection/Cessna Aircraft Company)

Roy Liggett runs up the 110 hp Warner prior to the ship's first flight in May, 1932. Clyde Cessna (standing with coat on) watches intently. (Bob Pickett Collection/ Cessna Aircraft Company)

tucking its legs into its breast for flight. To operate the gear, two controls were used. One was a lever that connected cables to steel downlock pins that had to be inserted by the pilot prior to landing (to prevent the gear from collapsing), but were removed after takeoff when the lever was pulled. Then a crank was turned that retracted the gear. Turning the crank in the opposite direction extended the gear, and the downlocks were pushed into place by the pilot. A large spring was positioned between the upper members of the gear's tubing for shock absorption allowing for a fairly soft ride. Bendix wheels and brakes (cable operated from the cockpit) were also fitted to the landing gear. A fixed tailskid supported the rear fuselage.

Clyde believed the gear's configuration was "the only way to arrange it", since he didn't believe that the wings, being the strongest part of the craft, should "have holes in them" to stow the gear.[3]

Not surprisingly, the CR-1 was powered with what seemed to be Cessna's favorite powerplant; a 110 hp Warner "Scarab" seven-cylinder, static radial engine, wrapped in a full NACA-type cowl. Actually, the Warner was the only practical engine for the ship since it was relatively lightweight and possessed a small frontal area; an important drag-reducing consideration for a racing airplane, since the engine's diameter largely determined the fuselage width.

While the racer's conception is credited to Clyde and Eldon Cessna, some of the design, engineering and drafting was accomplished by Garland Peed, a local aeronautical engineer hired to help transform the Cessna's brainchild into reality. Peed's talents were necessary because Eldon, although having studied mechanical engineering while attending 3 1/2 years of college, apparently could not perform all of the complex aerodynamic and mathematical calculations required to design a competitive racing craft.[4]

Clyde claimed the CR-1 was capable of 220 mph (at least on paper) stating that minor finishing details were being made on the ship prior to its first flight, scheduled for Tuesday, January 5th. If all went well, Cessna intended to speed Eldon and the CR-1 on their way to the Miami All-American Air Races to be held later that week. Unfortunately, delays in completing the airplane and bad weather kept the craft ground-

ed, and by January 7th Clyde had abandoned all hope of entering the racer in the Florida competition.

By January 18th, the airplane was ready to fly and Cessna invited only a selected group of friends to witness the occasion. Peed, who was originally to fly the monoplane, had departed the project after an alleged dispute with Clyde Cessna, leaving Eldon to man the tiny cockpit for the first time despite some apprehension by his father.[5]

Hauled out to the California Section, Eldon donned his parachute and squeezed into the open cockpit. The Scarab was fired up, engine parameters checked and then it was time to go.

The Warner roared as Eldon fed in full throttle and the ship accelerated quickly, bouncing across the rough ground as full right rudder was applied to counter the Scarab's torque. Airspeed increased rapidly to almost 80 mph, but the ship was still ground-bound as its short, semi-elliptical wings strained to produce enough lift for flight.

Back pressure on the stick produced no reaction, and the grass field's perimeter was getting closer every second. Back pressure on the stick at 100 mph went unrewarded. Then the airplane struck a small dirt mound and finally bounced into the air.

Eldon, who thought the takeoff roll was enough ex-

Al Mooney had already designed the Alexander Eaglerock "Bullet" monoplane in 1929 when he came to Wichita and set up shop, building the Mooney A-1 cabin monoplane. Only one example was built before Mooney left Wichita. The airplane is shown here after it was sold to Wichita tire dealer Woody Hockaday who reengined the ship with a Packard Diesel radial. (Wayne Dodd via Walt House and Bob Pickett)

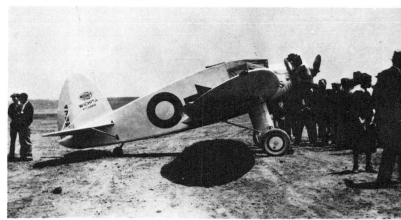

Pilot Roy Liggett strikes a casual pose with the CR-2 in this photograph taken at the Miami air races in January, 1933. A new 145 hp Super Scarab radial, installed in December, 1932, rests under the enlarged cowling. "Miss Wanda" won her greatest victory at Miami by placing first in the Col. Green Trophy Race at 195.74 mph. Note carburetor air intake scoop under cowl. (Truman C. Weaver)

citement for one day, now faced an even more serious challenge from his mount as he fought to keep the racer in a straight and level attitude. Longitudinal control was extremely sensitive, with the least stick movement provoking a nasty reaction that was immediately reversed when a correction was applied.

Realizing that the airplane was marginally controllable, Eldon elected to set the beast down as soon as possible, carefully making a turn around the field while keeping the airspeed high. Coming in at what was estimated to be 130 mph on final approach, the CR-1 landed and rolled to a stop.

He was helped from the cockpit and felt a little shaky for a minute or two, but Clyde Cessna was greatly relieved to have his son and his airplane back in one piece. So ended the one and only known flight of the CR1.[6]

NC7107 in 1932 with new windshield contour changes for reduced drag, NACA cowl over 125 hp Super Scarab radial, tight-fitting wheel fairings and regression back to a tailskid. After modifications were complete, the ship was clocked at 150 mph using a six-foot diameter propeller with the Warner screaming at 2500 rpm. Eldon won many races in his speedster and gained national recognition in 1932 by placing second in the Western Division Cord Cup Challenge Race. (Eldon Cessna via Bob Pickett)

In Eldon's opinion, the monoplane definitely needed revamping aimed at taming some of its bad habits, particularly control sensitivity in pitch and the very high takeoff and landing speed. During the next three and one-half months the ship was rebuilt into the CR-2.

Wingspan was increased to 18 feet, 4 inches, and length to 14 feet, 10 inches. Gross weight was 1,002 pounds, with an empty weight of 677 pounds. The horizontal and vertical stabilizer area were increased followed by an overall streamlining of the entire airplane to reduce drag. A useful load of 325 pounds permitted a pilot weighing up to 200 pounds plus 21 gallons of fuel (maximum tank capacity) to be carried.

On May 18th, the reborn airplane was taken to the municipal airport for its first flight, piloted this time by Roy Liggett, friend of Clyde Cessna who hailed from Omaha, Nebraska. Liggett reportedly owned and raced a Model AW, gaining victories at many local and regional air races since 1931 and picking up valuable experience in rounding the pylons.

To witness the second maiden flight of his speedster, Clyde again invited only a select audience, including some personalities that may have been backing the C.V. Cessna Aircraft Company financially such as Walt Anderson, who owned a chain of White Castle hamburger stands in town, and Marcellus Murdock of the Eagle newspaper. Also attending were Clyde's wife, Europa, Eldon and Wanda Cessna along with cousins Dwane and Dean Wallace.

The Warner was started and growled contentedly as Liggett donned his parachute, cinching the straps up tight in case he needed to hit the silk. The CR-2 wore only its outer coat of aluminum-pigmented dope for the flight, bearing Department of Commerce number 11717 on its tail and wings.[7]

Slowly, Roy nestled his frame into the cockpit, checked the controls and engine instruments and taxied away. Aiming the nose upwind, he applied full throttle and 110 horsepower thrust the ship across the field like a slingshot. In what seemed only a few moments it was airborne, clawing its way into the Kansas blue.

Roy pulled the steel downlock pins from their sockets and briskly moved the gear handle, retracting the wheels neatly into the fuselage. The CR-2 continued to accelerate as her pilot carefully checked

the Warner's vital signs and then proceeded to find out just what she could do.

Controls were checked in all three axes, especially the roll axis as Liggett simulated pylon turns. Throttle was intentionally conserved on this flight, since all-out speed tests were scheduled to begin in a few days.

Satisfied with the ship's handling, Roy brought the sleek monoplane in for a landing, rolling to a stop near the admiring crowd. Naturally, one of the first questions asked by the spectators was, "How fast did she go?" Liggett's only reply was, "Well, I'd say I was going fast, pretty fast." Pilots like Anderson and J. Earl Schaefer (who also saw the flight) estimated the CR-2's speed at about 125-150 mph.

Cessna, pleased with the initial flight of his racer, was anxious to get on with final testing so he could unleash the ship in two weeks at the Omaha Air Races. Speed tests were not made public, but the airplane was hitting around 190 mph at full power. Liggett made repeated high speed dives that probably hit or exceeded the double century mark as the ship blistered across the sky like a silver bullet. [It should be mentioned here that the Scarab radial was turning up almost 2,500-2,700 rpm in the CR-2, pulling almost 150 hp from an engine designed to operate at 2,050 revolutions per minute and 110 hp. The propeller pitch was lowered to allow the increased rpm without sacrificing maximum speed of the aircraft. This practice was very common for a pylon racer, where the only thing that really counted was speed.]

On May 25th, the CR-2 was honored at a special meeting of the Women's Aeronautical Association in Wichita, held near the Stearman factory. The ship was towed to the reception area wearing a fresh, brilliant red paint job, except for the cowling which remained aluminum in color.

Standing in front of the airplane with a bottle of water in her hand (prohibition was still in effect), Clyde's daughter baptized the CR-2 saying, "With best wishes for the success of the plane and for Wichita, I hereby christen the ship, "Miss Wanda". She struck the bottle against the propeller hub with success, shrinking back as water flew everywhere amidst great applause.

Just aft and slightly below the cockpit, lettered in graceful script style were the words, "Miss Wanda". Following the ceremony, Clyde Cessna and other local dignitaries made short speeches and then Liggett took off for a few crowd-pleasing flybys, all at reduced throttle.

On May 26th, Roy flew "Miss Wanda" to Omaha, accompanied by Clyde and Eldon in the grandaddy of Cessna racers, NR7107, along with George Harte in his modified DC-6A (c/n 226, NR6441) who had Walter Beech along for the ride.[8]

The Omaha races were somewhat controversial in that it was the first time in air racing history that women were permitted to compete on an equal basis with their male counterparts. However, very few female pilots attended and none placed in the money.

But the men were there in force. Great names in racing like Benny Howard, Harold Neumann, Art Chester and Johnny Livingston, who was flying his modified Monocoupe with a new set of very short wings. The "Hollywood Hawks", an aerobatic team consisting of Frank Clarke and Roy Wilson in two

speedwing Travel Air biplanes were there, too, ready to give their sensational aerial routine complete with smoke.

When Liggett and the CR-2 flashed across the field at Omaha, they turned lots of heads and the little red racer attracted much attention on the ground. It was recognized as a radical departure in aircraft design for Clyde Cessna, and elicited many questions and comments from its admirers.

The Cessna camp struck first blood when George Harte won the ATC event at 121.33 mph on Friday, May 27th, while Eldon managed fifth spot in the ATC 800 cubic inch displacement-class (cid) competition the next day. Saturday also saw the baptism of fire for "Miss Wanda", as Liggett placed fourth in the 500 cid race at 166.08 mph, behind Livingston's Monocoupe which flew the course at 170.44 mph.

The CR-2 was a new airplane with a new pilot, and it would take some time before the two got to know each other. Some break-in period was expected, and the racer had not done badly in its first outing against some very tough competition.

Sunday's unlimited Free-For-All was won by Russell Boardman in the new Gee Bee Model Y racer, with Liggett having to settle for fifth place, again behind Livingston. The CR-2's final effort at Omaha came on Monday, when another Free-For-All speed dash found Liggett back in fifth place once again, but this time behind Earl Ortman in the speedy Keith-Rider R-2 "San Francisco". Liggett's speed was 172.21 mph; up slightly from the first day's events but still out of first-place contention. He had nothing to be ashamed of, since the airplanes he finished behind had more horsepower, all the way up to 450 in the Gee Bee.

Despite this power disadvantage, less than 10 mph separated "Miss Wanda" from the winner's circle, and after returning to Wichita, Clyde Cessna sought a way to close the gap.

After discussions with Eldon and Liggett, Cessna consulted the Warner engine company in Detroit about installing a 145 hp "Super Scarab" in the CR-2. According to Warner's engineers, the 35 extra

The Cessnas were constantly improving the CR-2 in an effort to obtain that slight edge over their competitors. In August and September of 1933, a new Warner was installed that Cessna claimed produced more than 145 hp and a special, blister-cowl installed that hugged the Super Scarab very tightly. Landing gear doors identical to those on the CR-3 were added before the ship left for the Chicago races. This is one of the last photographs taken of "Miss Wanda" before it crashed. (Truman C. Weaver)

horsepower would translate into a 15 mph increase in speed for the racer.[9]

That's all Clyde needed to hear. Somehow, he was going to get the 499 cid powerplant for his racing machine. But for now, there were other races to be won against more balanced competition, so the 110 hp engine was retained with hopes that the Super Scarab could be installed by fall for the National Air Races.

On June 18th, the Cessnas suffered a setback when a full-blown Kansas tornado ripped through southeast Wichita that night, venting its worst wrath on the Mooney factory building and the Stearman facility nearby.

The roof of the Mooney building was swept away, parts of the walls collapsed and steel girders fell on five airplanes Cessna had stored in the hangar, including the CR-2 and Eldon's Model AW. Fortunately, the racer escaped with no damage, but the other four monoplanes were not so lucky. Old '99' reportedly took a girder across the cockpit, crushing the landing gear, but could be repaired. Equipment and machinery in the building was almost untouched by the twister. As for Stearman's facility, it suffered damage to some sections of the factory but was not incapacitated by the storm.

After the Cessnas had removed all aircraft, tools and equipment from the building, it was razed and a new home for the company was found in Unit "D" of the empty Travel Air factory on East Central Avenue. By June 28th, the C.V. Cessna Aircraft Company was back in business, and one interesting thought must have passed through Clyde's mind, perhaps even causing him to chuckle, as he set up shop in his new quarters...by a strange twist of fate, Cessna was building monoplanes in a plant originally constructed by Walter Beech to produce biplanes, while at the same time Beech was building biplanes in a factory built by Cessna to produce

Johnny Livingston's Cessna CR-3 racer soon after rollout from the Travel Air factory in June, 1933. Powered with the Super Scarab radial from Livingston's Monocoupe, the little ship differed from the CR-2 in having a shoulder-mounted wing to reduce airspeed loss during tight pylon turns as suggested by Dwane Wallace. Original canopy with fold-down side pieces was later removed by Livingston. Note tube ahead of windshield to route fresh air into cockpit. (Truman C. Weaver via Bob Pickett)

monoplanes.[10]

Meanwhile, Liggett was back east competing at the Niagara, New York air races, where he placed third in one race. He was doing better on the pylons than ever before, but still had to take a back seat to Johnny Livingston and his Monocoupe.

Eldon had his racer back in the air very soon after the tornado incident, and by July 4th he was at Emporia, Kansas, competing in the Independence Day celebration races there. He and George Harte collected some cash at the event, with Eldon winning the ATC race for planes with engines up to 500 cid, while George Harte won the Pony Express Free-For-All event. The Pony Express race was unique in that it required the entrants to fly the specified number of laps, landing at certain intervals to eat a sandwich before taking off again. Whoever could fly, land, eat and takeoff in the least amount of time was the winner.

The Cessnas had been busy with NC7107 since October, 1931, when they began a modification program to make the ship into a winning racer. The original Warner (serial number 26) was removed and another 110 hp Scarab (serial number 566) and a NACA cowl was installed along with a set of wheel pants and a highly streamlined windshield that weighed three pounds less than the original unit.

On December 7th, the ship was flight tested by Eldon and Department of Commerce Inspector Joseph E. Boudwin who found that the changes did not affect the flight characteristics in any way. Empty weight increased to 1,295 pounds, while the gross weight was limited to 2,260 pounds. 45 gallons of fuel could still be carried if only the pilot was aboard, but this amount was reduced to 33 gallons with four people and a maximum of 51 pounds of baggage.

On June 23rd, Eldon had landed at Richards Field in Kansas City when he was hit by C.E. Norton, who was also taxiing his airplane. NC7107 incurred serious wing damage, and Clyde elected to build a new wing instead of repairing the old one. By late summer, the airplane had joined the CR-2 on the race circuit.

In August, "Miss Wanda" had yet to win a major race against her primary competitors like Johnny Livingston, Benny Howard and S.J. "Steve" Wittman, but she would get another chance at the

National Air Races in Cleveland, Ohio, August 27-September 5th, 1932. Unfortunately, the 145 hp Super Scarab engine installation was still not a reality and the CR-2 would have to face her foes with the same 110 hp Warner.

Roy Liggett would be handling the stick once again, bending the CR-2 around pylons while Eldon competed in the major cross-country event associated with the races that year, the Cord Cup challenge. There were two divisions, each one starting from opposite coasts and meeting in Cleveland to finish the race.

The victor in each division would be a rich man or woman by Depression standards. The Cord Corporation, builders of high-quality and high-priced automobiles, was putting up $2,000 cash, a 12-cylinder Auburn speedster and permanent possession of the Cord Cup to the overall national winner, while the leader of the other division would receive $1,000 cash, an eight-cylinder Auburn speedster and a plaque of the Cord Cup.

Eldon Cessna, flying his newly-modified Model AW, entered the Western Division race and led it all the way to Lubbock, Texas, but relinquished the lead to Roy Hunt in a Cirrus-powered Great Lakes biplane at St. Louis. The Warner developed a problem with one of its valve rocker mechanisms, and Eldon was forced to improvise a fix that was sufficient to get him into Cleveland for a second-place win worth $500. Hunt was given the keys to that fabulous 12-cylinder Auburn and drove away with the Cord Cup resting in the seat beside him.[11]

Clyde Cessna planned to enter the CR-2 in any event open to airplanes with engines up to 800 cid. To prepare the scarlet monoplane for the big national competition, every inch of its airframe and engine were meticulously inspected, some minor changes made to better streamline the ship and then Liggett was off for Cleveland on August 27th.

The CR-2 went up against its old foe, Johnny Livingston's highly-modified Monocoupe, in the Cincinnati Trophy Race. This event was flown between Cleveland and Cincinnati, with a landing at the latter city before the return flight.

Liggett was doing very well in this event until he

Front quarter view of CR-3 racer shows the shoulder-mounted wing to good advantage, including the root fairings that were installed after first flight. Original propeller shown here was specially built by Hamilton Standard. Livingston paid Clyde Cessna $2,700 for the racer, less engine and propeller. (Truman C. Weaver via Bob Pickett)

landed at Cincinnati. He didn't insert the downlocks properly and the landing gear twisted upon touchdown, making it inadviseable to attempt to retract it for the trip back to Cleveland.[12]

Roy had to fly that leg with the gear down, causing him to fall from first place to third in the final standings. He flew the round trip in 2 hours, 32 minutes, 39 seconds and won $300 while S.J. Wittman placed second earning $500. Johnny Livingston's victorious Monocoupe took 2 hours, 17 minutes, 29 seconds and pocketed $900.

Roy Liggett and the CR-2 probably could have won the race if the extended gear had not exacted the speed penalty on the second leg. Clyde Cessna was visibly unhappy about the whole incident, but thankful that the gear didn't collapse putting "Miss Wanda" out of contention entirely for the remainder of the races.

Liggett next entered the 510 cid Free-For-All and placed second behind Ben O. Howard in his Menasco-powered monoplane "Ike", winning $225 and showing "Miss Wanda's" tail to Livingston for the first time at the finish line.

Next up was the Frank Phillips' race for the Woolaroc Trophy, which was hotly contested by Liggett in the CR-2, Benny Howard in "Ike" and Ray Moore flying the Keith-Ryder racer. Moore won and received $1,125 with a speed of 182 mph while Liggett managed third at 176.5 mph winning $375.

Eldon wrapped up Cessna winnings at Cleveland by taking first place and $270 in a speed race at 114.8 mph, clearly demonstrating the speed and efficiency of the AW and Warner engine over its Monocoupe, Great Lakes and Stinson competitors.

In all, Roy and "Miss Wanda" had won $900 and Eldon nailed down $770 for the week of racing in Ohio. After the conclusion of the Cleveland Nationals, both airplanes hopped over to Sky Harbor,

The CR-3 after minor modifications at Aurora, Illinois in late June, 1933. Metal panels were installed over the wheels and faired flush with the fuselage when the gear was retracted, an all-new cockpit enclosure was installed including a low-profile windshield and the fresh air tube was removed since the cockpit was open to the airstream. (Harold G. Martin via Bob Pickett)

Another view of the racer showing the metal wheel panels. The CR-3 used 20 x 4 inch wheels instead of the 20 x 3 inch units on the CR-2. Race #27 was used by Livingston since it reflected part of his pilot license number; T1427. (Truman C. Weaver)

Michigan, to compete in the American Legion Charity Air Meet on September 8th.

Both the CR-2 and the speedy AW did well, with Liggett placing second in a Free-For-All race and Eldon winning the Sportsman Pilot event. Then it was homeward-bound for the two airmen and Clyde Cessna. Eldon capped off his winning season by clinching first-place in the handicap race at Coffeyville, Kansas, on October 3rd in his Model AW racer.

Reflecting on the fall's successes and failures, Clyde and Eldon believed they had done well with their first thoroughbred racer. They had shown the big boys that Kansas airplanes could go fast, too, and actually put the fear of Cessna into Messrs. Livingston, Howard, Wittman and other patriarchs of the sport.

But one fact remained: "Miss Wanda" was too slow. In order to become a winning racer she would have to hit 200-plus mph consistently, even on the racecourse. With that in mind and enough cash in the bank, a Super Scarab was finally installed by December.[13]

The new engine necessitated some changes, foremost among these being an increase in the fuselage length to satisfy weight and balance requirements since the powerplant weighed 30 pounds more (dry weight) than the standard Scarab. The outside diameter was also larger and required a slightly bigger cowling. More streamlining and drag reduction was done in an effort to make the racer break 200 mph.

On December 28th, the airplane was flight tested and reportedly was clocked at 255 mph according to Clyde Cessna. Like the previous engine, the big Scarab was turning almost 2,700 rpm and was probably developing close to 175 hp to achieve this speed.

Cessna was charged with enthusiasm by the monoplane's performance, and wasted no time getting the airplane down to Miami for the 1933 All-American Air Races, accompanied by Eldon in the AW.

"Miss Wanda" kicked off the new year with the biggest win of her short career, capturing the Colonel E.H.R. Green Trophy at an average speed of 194.056 mph. The combination of Super Scarab engine, reworked streamlining and superior airmanship by Roy Liggett did the trick.[14]

Johnny Livingston placed second, realizing then and there that the days of his beloved Monocoupe were numbered. The CR-2 dusted Johnny off with little trouble, and that wasn't something that he could accept easily. If winning races meant flying a Cessna racer of his own, then so be it, and John began thinking seriously about a talk with Clyde Cessna.

Liggett's winnings didn't stop with the Green race, however. He placed second in the Unlimited Free-For-All behind Jimmy Wedell's hot #44, making 195.25 mph and picking up another $200. While Eldon and his wife did some vacationing in Florida after the races, Liggett flew to Love Field, Dallas, Texas, where he had a fuel tank leak repaired enroute to Wichita. "Miss Wanda" was resting in the Cessna hangar by January 19th, having proved herself to be the best of the breed in Miami.

With Clyde back in town, the Cessna Aircraft Company called its board of directors meeting to order on January 18th, and had very little to discuss in the way of airplane sales but did need to elect a new president, as Thad C. Carver had died of bronchial pneumonia the previous month.

Charles G. Yankey became the new president, with Horace Carver, vice president; A.B. Sanders, treasurer and A.S. Swenson was elected secretary. Clyde Cessna nominated Walter H. Beech to become a director of the company and the nomination was unanimously approved.

In March, Johnny Livingston flew his Monocoupe (c/n 533, NR501W, Mono Aircraft Corporation) to Wichita, landing at Travel Air Field to pay Clyde Cessna a special visit. The Cessnas knew he was coming and they knew what he wanted: a racer. Johnny had decided the only way to survive in the world of air racing was to fly a Cessna speedster of his own, so on March 9th he placed his order for the third racing ship built by Clyde and Eldon, known as the CR-3.

Livingston wanted Cessna to incorporate a few changes into the aircraft, such as higher gross weight, 20 x 4 inch wheels (slightly larger than those on the CR-2, to handle the increased weight) and a shoulder-mounted wing.

The wing's location was decided upon after Johnny consulted with Dwane Wallace, who recommended the configuration because it was known to minimize airspeed loss during tight, high-G pylon turns.

Work on the ship began quickly, and by April 21st the fuselage was welded up and sitting on the landing gear, the wings were almost completed and Livingston was back in town with the Monocoupe for an engine exchange.

The Super Scarab from Johnny's airplane was removed and installed in the CR-3, with the CR-2's original 110 hp Scarab reportedly being installed in NR501W, which was then sold to Jack Wright of Utica, New York.

John H. Livingston learned to fly in Waterloo, Iowa, in the 1920s, and picked up his mechanics license to boot, having a penchant for taking things apart, improving them, then putting everything back together again. He sold airplanes, too, and became the owner of Midwest Airways at Waterloo with branches at Aurora and Monmouth, Illinois.

Johnny had been associated with Waco airplanes for quite some time by 1930, piloting the company's biplanes in the 1926, 1929 and 1930 Ford Reliability Tour, winning the '29 event. He had a talent for air racing, and became one of the nation's all-time top money winners by 1933.

During the race seasons spanning 1928 to 1931, Livingston took the checkered flag 79 times, placed second on 43 occasions and third only 15 times. He finished out of the money only twice. In 1932 he continued his winning ways, using the Monocoupe that he had transformed from a 130 mph stock ship into a 190 mph racing champion.

With the CR-3, Livingston intended to push speeds far above what the old, faithful 'coupe could do, and had plans for even bigger engines and more horsepower in his never-ending quest for racing supremacy.

The warmth of a Kansas May ushered in the genesis of another season of speed, and the CR-3 was ready for final assembly by the 17th of the month, and Clyde Cessna expected the craft to be ready for its maiden flight within 10 days. Livingston, who had been touring the mid-west area with the American Air Aces in recent weeks, returned to Wichita at the end of May to oversee and assist the Cessnas in completing the ship.

The racer was painted in the same colors his Monocoupe had worn; bright yellow with red trim. Department of Commerce number NR57Y was painted red on the wings and yellow on the rudder. A very tight-fitting NACA-type cowl, featuring valve rocker blisters, encircled the Warner.

The CR-3 was virtually finished by June 1st, except for the oil tank that was left out intentionally until Livingston sat in the cockpit and the monoplane's center of gravity determined. Then, the tank was placed aft of the seat for final balance and the horizontal stabilizer was adjusted to have no up or down force acting on it during straight and level flight.[15]

The airplane was rolled out of the shop on June 2nd for the local press, who took their share of photographs and asked lots of questions. Johnny told them very little, except to describe the racer's length of 17 feet, wingspan of 18 feet, 11 inches and empty weight of 750 pounds. He paid the C.V. Cessna Aircraft Company $2,700 for the airframe, with the engine and propeller supplied by Livingston bumping up the final cost to $5,000.

On June 11th, the airplane was ready for its first flight. Johnny checked everything in the cockpit and the Warner was started, belching puffs of black exhaust as all seven cylinders joined together in ear-splitting harmony.

Tex LaGrone (right) and Livingston (center) pose with a friend and the CR-3 before cockpit and landing gear changes were made. Livingston is wearing his parachute in this view, but he often just sat on it when flying from one race town to another. (Truman C. Weaver via Bob Pickett)

He taxied out, checked the magnetos and then eased in the throttle. As expected, the ship shot forward in an immediate burst of speed and jumped into the air effortlessly. Within seconds, however, the horizontal stabilizer began to vibrate so badly that Livingston moved the stick around, searching for a position that would stop the flapping act behind him.

No matter where he placed the controls, the vibration continued unabated, so the pilot brought the craft around and landed, keeping the airspeed close to 100 mph all the way to touchdown to ensure adequate pitch control.

Taxiing back to the hangar, Johnny climbed out of his seat and joined Clyde Cessna in searching for the cause. They quickly concluded that the wing root fairings, left off for the test flight, had to be installed since without their streamlining effect on the wing's airflow, severe turbulence and burbling was created that pummelled the empennage.

With the fairings in place, a second flight was made and the vibration had disappeared, but now longitudinal stability was so sensitive that even the slightest fore and aft stick movement caused Johnny to hang on the safety belts or get slammed down in his seat. He also tried a rapid aileron roll, but the CR-3 refused to go beyond an 80 degree bank in either direction. Livingston realized that some sort of aerodynamic force was preventing the ailerons from doing their job, and he suspected a disruption of airflow over the wing as the culprit.

After another landing and conference with the Cessnas, it was decided that perhaps the cooling baffles between each cylinder were inhibiting airflow over the wing, so the cowling and baffles were removed and another flight made.

This time, aileron rolls were swift and exact, the racer responding to its master's every wish. Back on the ground, the cowling was installed along with another set of baffle plates that permitted more airflow through the cowl. No further trouble was encountered, and Livingston was anxious to hit the air race circuit, convinced that his new mount could conquer any opponent he expected to meet.

In addition to the CR-3 project, Clyde and Eldon had also been overhauling the CR-2 in another effort to squeeze more performance out of the scarlet racer. During June, the wings were recovered and slight changes made to the fuselage, cowling and turtledeck/cockpit structure to enhance streamlining.

The vertical stabilizer size was reduced and given a smooth, graceful curve to its leading edge, blending in very nicely with the fuselage spine. Lastly, a factory-fresh Super Scarab radial was purchased and installed in place of the previous powerplant, covered by a silver cowling.

The necessity for this revamping of an already-winning airplane was actually precipitated by the Cessnas. When they built the CR-3, they also created their fiercest competition. There was no time or money available to design and construct a second-generation racer, so the changes made to "Miss Wanda" would hopefully do the job and keep her in the money.[16]

Just how much trouble the CR-3 was going to be for everyone else in 1933 was clearly illustrated at the Omaha races in mid June, when Livingston easily held his own against Harold Neumann in Benny Howard's "Mike", although the Cessna was still so sensitive longitudinally that its full potential couldn't be utilized.

At various air races held during June, Johnny was able to defeat his opponents but was not fully satisfied that the airplane was achieving its design maximum speed of around 230 mph. He flew the ship to Kansas City to confer with his friend and well-known aviation personality, Tex Lagrone.

The propeller used on the CR-3 since its first flight was a specially-built steel unit made by Hamilton-Standard, designed to give good thrust while being short enough to permit tail-up takeoffs and wheel landings, if desired.

Johnny felt that the combination of the Monocoupe's Super Scarab and propeller were right for each other, and decided to install the original propeller on the CR-3 for a speed test. He found that maximum speed did increase slightly, but the longer blades made three-point takeoffs and landings a necessity. He decided to stay with the shorter propeller since ground clearance was an important consideration at the many unfamiliar airports the ship would be visiting that season.

With the Chicago races coming up on the Fourth of July holiday, Johnny was anxious to make some important improvements to his little monoplane,

On August 1, 1933, Johnny had to bail out of the CR-3 after the landing gear refused to lock in place. The red and yellow Cessna smashed into the ground near Columbus, Ohio and was totally destroyed as shown here after all the airplane's remnants were collected. In less than 60 days of existence, the CR-3 had won every race it competed in and had earned a place in history as one of the great racers of the Golden Age. (Truman C. Weaver)

which had not lost a race since the beginning of its short career. Returning to his Aurora, Illinois, home base, Livingston set about modifying the CR-3.

The longitudinal instability problem was quickly remedied by using a piece of copper tubing, slit along its length so that it would fit over the leading edge of the horizontal stabilizer.

The tubing set up a small down load on the stabilizer by disturbing the airflow, and worked perfectly in flight tests. The large, Pyrolin cockpit canopy that was originally installed was removed and a high, but short, headrest and fairing was built in its place. To streamline the cockpit, two metal panels, designed to hinge upward and close around the pilot, were installed. The landing gear also received a change, getting a small, metal skirt fixed over each wheel to smooth airflow across the gear wells during flight.

Back in Wichita, the CR-2 was prepared for the trip to Chicago, being more fit for any race competition than ever before. Clyde Cessna flew to the windy city along with Eldon and his wife in NC7107, which now had a 125 hp Warner radial up front. Arthur J. Davis was now in command of "Miss Wanda", as Roy Liggett was unable to pilot the ship due to other flying commitments.

At the Chicago races, Livingston won the Baby Ruth Trophy Race at a speed of 201.42 mph, while Art Davis, who was a highly competent race pilot himself, nailed down second at 200.76 mph. Just as Livingston and Cessna knew would happen, the two Wichita racers were going to butt heads in wingtip to wingtip fights for the money.

On July Fourth, in the Aero Digest Trophy Race, it was another battle of the Cessnas, with the CR-3 and the CR-2 looking like one airplane as they rounded the course, but Livingston was able to pick up precious seconds on the turns thanks to that shoulder-mounted wing. He won the $2,250 first prize while Davis locked up second spot again, earning $1,250, with less than 3 seconds and 3 miles per hour separating the two sister ships.

Johnny Livingston was flushed with victory as he and the CR-3 dominated the Chicago scene. To top off their already sterling display of airmanship, the duo went out on July 5th in an attempt to set a record for airplanes using engines of less than 500 cid. The record was held by Benny Howard and his "Ike" at 213.8 mph, but the yellow and red Cessna made it obsolete by attaining an average speed of 237.40 mph over a 1.932-mile course.

Only 30 days after it first flew, the CR-3 had enjoyed a meteoric rise to fame and fortune at the hands of Johnny Livingston. After the Chicago triumph, the racer went on an air show tour while also bringing in some cash by winning races.

On August 1st, Livingston pre-flighted the monoplane and prepared to leave for Columbus, Ohio. He tossed his parachute into the cockpit where it served as a seat cushion for the flight. After takeoff, the tailskid, which was designed to retract on the CR-3, refused to come up.

Thinking there was little to worry about, Johnny proceeded to his destination, announcing his arrival in the classic Livingston style by buzzing the field flat out and zooming toward the heavens. He cranked the gear down without difficulty but couldn't insert one of the downlocks.

After several unsuccessful attempts to snap the stubborn gear into position by bouncing the good gear on the ground, Johnny tried high-G pull-ups from dives to snap the struts into place, but this failed, too.

As a last resort, he took a screwdriver and punched holes into the fuselage sheet metal, hoping to get a visual determination of the gear's position. If he could see how close it was to being down, then perhaps he could manually force it the rest of the way and insert the downlock pin.

Unfortunately, he couldn't see the gear system clearly enough, and circled Columbus for 30 minutes, pondering his next move. Livingston made the painful decision to abandon his little racer, since it couldn't be landed gear-up due to the high risk of a crash and serious injury or death to himself.

Johnny dropped a note over the airport explaining that he would fly north and bail out. His message was acknowledged, so he climbed the ship high enough for a safe exit. Cinching up the parachute straps, it was time to abandon ship, but the CR-3 had a surprise in store for her pilot.

Just as Livingston stood up to jump, his body so disturbed the airflow that the ship snapped into a spin, pinning Johnny against the fuselage. He struggled back into the cockpit and recovered from the spin, climbed back up to altitude and again tried to leave the stricken craft, but the Cessna spun again as it tried to keep its master from saying goodbye.[17]

Recovering from the second spin, Johnny figured a way out of his dilemma. He threw the ship into knife-edge flight, holding full throttle and top rudder, then jammed the stick forward, popping himself out of the cockpit.

Free at last, he pulled the ripcord and watched the white canopy blossom into fullness above him. Searching for the CR-3, he saw it diving straight for the ground, with observers estimating its speed at over 300 mph. Not one piece separated from the racer as it sped to its death. It hit the earth with tremendous force, penetrating the ground several feet.

Johnny made a safe descent and looked sadly at the mass of wreckage above and below the ground. Investigation revealed the cause of the gear failure to be a cold weld in a tubing cluster that prevented the downlock from engaging.

Had the CR-3 survived, Livingston intended to make further modifications that would allow the airplane to hit the 300 mph mark. Some of the anticipated changes were: reducing empennage size by almost 50%, trimming down the fuselage and squeezing it at midpoint and installing one of the new 165 hp Warner radials without increasing the frontal area.

New wings were already on the drawing board, featuring a slightly more narrow chord, a new airfoil section and spanning only 16 feet. Just how well the reborn CR-3 would have performed with these changes will never be known, but nobody doubted Livingston's intentions.

Having earned the distinction of winning every race it was entered in during its short, but dynamic, career, the CR-3 went down in history as one of the great air racers of all time, along with its skilled pilot who made it all happen.

Clyde Cessna, however, had his own set of plans for the CR-2, and hauled the airplane back into the

Marcellus Murdock, noted publisher of the Wichita Eagle newspaper, bought the C-3 from Walter Anderson in April, 1936. Murdock had high praise for the ship, stating that it was the best flying airplane he had ever owned. Murdock sold the C-3 to Andrew "Andy" Bland in March, 1945. It was destroyed by fire in December of that year. Note the different design of the cockpit area compared to the earlier Cessna monoplanes. (Bob Pickett Collection/Cessna Aircraft Company)

shop after the Chicago races to work more miracles through yet another remodeling.

After 30 days of hard work, "Miss Wanda" emerged from behind closed doors sporting a new, dark red paint job, a completely revised cockpit enclosure including a canopy and small, metal panels over the wheels almost exactly like those used by Livingston on the CR-3. Another set of doors were attached to the inboard, lower fuselage and mated with the wheel panels when the gear was retracted, completely enclosing the wheel wells during flight.

The 145 hp Super Scarab radial engine was retained, but Cessna stated that the power had been increased enough to yield another 10 mph to the maximum speed. Hugging the Warner was a totally new cowling with large, tapered valve rocker blisters that were very prominent. The leading edge of the cowl wrapped around the cylinders and formed a smaller intake area than the previous assemblies. Known as the CR-2A in its modified form, the racer was now registered to R.A. Herman but still owned by Cessna.[18]

Roy Liggett performed speed trials with the airplane on August 30th. He was clocked flying upwind at 250 mph, with 270 mph being indicated on some runs, according to Cessna. He departed Travel Air Field at 4:30 P.M. that afternoon for Chicago, where the International Air Races were being held from September 1st through the 4th.

Liggett arrived without mishap and met Clyde and Eldon Cessna. They prepared the racer for the qualifying heats, and "Miss Wanda" easily earned her place in the starting lineup. Roy flew the heats with reduced power, wishing to save the engine until it was really needed.

Even then, the racer clipped around the course at 183 mph, and when the events began, Liggett warmed up by taking second place in the 550 cid race at 191.14 mph. At least four races remained that were ideally suited for the CR-2A when tragedy struck.

On Saturday, September 2nd, high winds blew across the Curtiss-Reynolds Airport as "Miss Wanda" took off for a speed dash across the field. Flying at about 300 feet altitude with the airspeed hitting nearly 175 mph, a section of the cowling reportedly flew off and hit the wing, breaking it off near the root.[19]

The CR-2A whipped into a vicious, rapid roll, diving into a nearby cornfield. Roy Liggett was killed instantly. The airplane suffered total destruction, its steel structure gripping Liggett's mangled body so tightly that special saws were employed to extricate the corpse.

Clyde Cessna had witnessed the accident. He was distraught over having lost a friend, but the loss was made more painful because it was one of his creations that had taken a life. Something within his being also perished that day. Never again did Cessna possess that dynamic drive and interest toward airplanes and flying he had displayed for the past 22 years.[20]

The Cessna CR-series racers were a special breed of airplane, flown by a special breed of pilot who was not afraid to take himself and his machine to their limits. History will remember the CR-2 and CR-3 as classic examples of the Golden Age of air racing when sheer speed and courage won the day.

---

[1] Of the 44 aircraft and engine builders located in Wichita between 1927 and 1931, only Stearman was still actively engaged in the airplane business by 1933.

[2] Jack Northrop's all-metal monoplanes, with catchy names like "Alpha" and "Beta" were among the very first aircraft of their type constructed. Northrop was another member of the huge United Aircraft and Transport Corporation along with Stearman, and the Burbank, California-based firm was moved to Wichita and merged with Stearman in September, 1931. In 1933, the factory was producing component parts for the revolutionary Boeing 247 transport.

[3] Clyde Cessna claimed the landing gear design was his own and that it was patented. In the CR-1, there was no room in the thin wings for the gear and the fuselage was the only place it could be stowed. It is also interesting to note that Cessna's firm was known as the "Clyde Cessna Aircraft Company" at this time as well as the "C.V. Cessna Aircraft Company." No state charter was ever filed, and the business was set up as a partnership between Clyde, Eldon and a few other unknown individuals.

[4] Eldon was well educated in mechanical systems design and knew a great deal about aerodynamics, but to tackle a complex job like designing a high-speed racer was apparently more than his father thought he could do. In any case, Eldon made contributions to the CR-1's concept and design. Also, government files on the racer call it the "C-1", and this may have been the official designation by Cessna, but CR-1 has been the popular name for over 50 years. Garland Powell Peed, Jr. was a highly respected test pilot and project engineer for Alexander Eaglerock in 1930, when the advanced Eaglerock "Bullet" low-wing monoplane was introduced, having retractable landing gear. Peed may have picked up some experience with such mechanisms there which were later put to use on the CR-1 project.

[5] Two eyewitnesses to this flight claim that Clyde Cessna was very concerned about turning Eldon loose with a ship like the CR-1. Eldon was a good pilot, but he was accustomed to the docile Model AW and not the capricious ways of the little racer.

[6] Eldon did well to handle the little airplane and get it back on the ground. Clyde Cessna was greatly relieved, too, and decided that the ship was probably just too dangerous for anyone to fly in its original configuration.

[7] The number 11717 was first issued to Travel Air's fifth Model "R", sent to Italy in the summer of 1931. This was strictly used for export purposes only, and once the airplane left America the number was again available. According to Department of Commerce records, the CR-1 racer had two hours of flight time and the engine had accumulated 185 hours prior to Liggett's test flight.

[8] Walter H. Beech and his wife Olive Ann teamed up with K.K. Shaul and Ted Wells to start the Beech Aircraft Company in April, 1932. Beech had tired of the executive life with Curtiss-Wright, and Wells had designed a negative-stagger biplane that could hit 200 mph and land at 60 mph. Returning to Wichita that spring, Beech rented Building "A" and "B" of the closed-down Cessna factory to begin construction of the Model 17R. Harte's DC-6A featured a full cowling, streamlining around the cockpit area and large wheel fairings to increase speed.

[9] Warner's engineers may have been optimistic in their estimate of a performance gain from another 35 hp, but the CR-2 reportedly flew faster after the engine change.

[10] In late 1933, Beech entered into a lease agreement with the Cessna Board of Directors for the two buildings he had been renting since April, 1932. He paid $75 per month to use the facilities. In April, 1934, Beech purchased the old Travel Air factory complex and moved operations there.

[11] Modifications to Cessna 7107 were slowly accomplished over a period of two years. In 1931, the airplane was still basically a stock ship, but later that year a program to streamline the airplane began, and by 1933 it was the fastest AW in the world at more than 140 mph maximum speed.

[12] Liggett wisely elected to leave the gear down instead of risking a jam or damage during retraction. Apparently, the first indication Clyde Cessna had of the trouble was after "Miss Wanda" finished the race. There is some hint that Liggett may have received a lecture from Cessna about his mistake with the downlocks.

[13] The Warner Scarab received a tougher crankshaft in 1929 along with a boost to 128 hp. The Super Scarab appeared in 1932 and featured a larger bore of 4 5/8 inches and a stroke just over 4 1/4 inches. It weighed 305 pounds compared to the Scarab's 275. Both engines were among the best American-designed radials.

[14] Some sources say Liggett won $6,500 for the race, while others indicate only $300 was paid for first place.

[15] The oil tank location was a critical step in the determination of the CR-3's center of gravity (CG), since the racer was designed to have neutral static stability in flight so that it could be maneuvered with very little input from the pilot. This was desireable for a racer since it had to be capable of changing attitudes instantly, such as rolling into a pylon turn in a dive or climb.

[16] Clyde and Eldon Cessna knew that the CR-3 would be a direct competitor to their own racer, but a sale was a sale and the two men countered the CR-3's threat by working a few more wonders with "Miss Wanda". They were very successful since the CR-2A was almost a duplicate in performance of Livingston's ship.

[17] The trouble Johnny Livingston experienced trying to bail out of the CR-3 clearly illustrates just how high-strung and sensitive the Cessna racers were to any airflow disturbance. The CR-2A and CR-3 were not forgiving airplanes and their pilots knew that all too well. If Livingston or Liggett had ever been forced to hit the silk, their chances of an easy exit from the cockpit were not very good.

[18] R.A. Herman was married to Clyde's sister, Hazel, and may have been a financial supporter and member of the partnership known as the C.V. Cessna Aircraft Company. This may explain, at least in part, why Herman was registered as the owner but did not actually have possession of the racer.

[19] According to the accepted story, the wing was severed by the cowling, but the Associated Press stated that it was the strong, gusty winds that seemed to cause the aircraft to crash. Eldon Cessna said he was not present when the crash occurred, but that his father mentioned the cowling separation as the probable cause. Liggett left a wife and two children behind, and they were reportedly cared for (to some extent) by Clyde Cessna's financial support over the next few years.

[20] People who knew Clyde Cessna before and after the CR-2A crashed believe that the accident simply drained much of his remaining interest in aeronautics.

CHAPTER TEN
Revival

After the Chicago races concluded, Clyde and Eldon Cessna returned home, still stunned from the loss of Roy Liggett and the CR-2A. For Clyde, the respected air pioneer, there was little left in aviation to hold his interest.

However, the same was not true of his nephew, Dwane Wallace. He was high on enthusiasm and long on ideas, had a fresh sheepskin in his hand from Wichita University and a sincere desire to get into the airplane business.

Dwane L. Wallace was born at Belmont, Kansas, on October 29, 1911. His father, Dr. Eugene Wallace, was a pioneer physician, and his mother, Grace Opal Cessna Wallace, was Clyde Cessna's younger sister. Dwane grew up around his air-minded uncle, and probably caught the flying bug from him.

He took instruction from George Harte while studying at college in Wichita, soloing a Travel Air biplane on March 18, 1932, at the Travel Air Field on East Central Avenue.

Graduating in May, 1933, with a degree in aeronautical engineering, Dwane sought a position with one of Wichita's aircraft manufacturer's to gain some important experience. Knocking first at Stearman's door, he was reluctantly turned away by Mac Short. He then tried Ted Wells at the Beech firm, but got the same treatment.

However, Wallace was persistent with Mr. Wells and finally got the nod in May, hiring on as the third engineer on the payroll, along with Wells and Jack Wassal. He worked on layout, drafting and stress analysis at first, then progressed into engineering projects for the Model B17L and A17F.[1]

Dwane was glad to have a job, especially one in aviation where he was using his hard-earned knowledge, but he wanted to do more than just work in the old Cessna airplane factory; he wanted to revive it, to bring it back to life again.

To do that, Dwane knew he would have to plan out a strategy that would accomplish three critical things: wrest power from the incumbent board of directors, invite Clyde Cessna to be an active participant in the new venture and design an airplane that would sell in the Depression marketplace.

Before any plans were firmly made, Dwane sought his uncle Clyde's thoughts on the proposal, and the two men had many discussions over the months between May and December, 1933, on what would have to be done to resurrect the company and reopen the plant. Meanwhile, Clyde and Eldon were still busy completing a custom-built monoplane known as the C-3.

Walter L. Anderson (of White Castle Hamburgers) ordered the ship built to his requirements, and the fuselage of a Model AA, c/n 124, NC5335, produced in the summer of 1928, was utilized as the basis for the ship. The C-3 was powered by a 125 hp Warner (serial number 916) and, according to Civil Aeronautics Authority records, was completed on October 14, 1933.[2]

The C-3 was one of Clyde Cessna's last aeronautical projects. He and Eldon worked together on the design and construction of the ship, but the C-3 and the CR-3 were the final effort by the father-son team. Walter Beech was planning to move into the vacant Travel Air factory in just a few months, and Clyde was no longer interested in constructing airplanes. Instead, he channeled his efforts into helping his nephews reopen the Cessna factory.[3]

Dwane's brother Dwight was also very interested in getting the company back on its feet, and he had been an integral part of the overall effort from the start. He was a lawyer and knew the legal re-

The Beechcraft Model 17R had speed, range and good looks when it first flew in November, 1932, with Pete Hill at the wheel. Designed by Ted Wells, the classic biplane was built in a rented portion of the closed-down Cessna factory. (Beech Aircraft Corporation)

The first Model C-34, c/n 254, X12599, stands ready to fly at Cessna Field in August, 1934. Note absence of landing gear strut fairings and trim paint on the all-blue monoplane. Ship was the first Cessna factory product since the EC-2 of 1931. (Bob Pickett Collection/Cessna Aircraft Company)

quirements that would have to be satisfied if the takeover was to be successfully carried out. Dwight was two years older than Dwane, being the first-born of Dr. and Mrs. Eugene Wallace on June 19, 1909. He and his brother worked together very closely as they made their bid for the Cessna Aircraft Company.

Both Dwight and Dwane exchanged ideas and thoughts while formulating their plans, part of which entailed writing letters to stockholders of record explaining reasons for reopening the plant. Clyde Cessna agreed to sign the documents as author, but made it clear to his nephews that he wanted no serious involvement in the venture.

By late 1933, despite the bleak and discouraging economic climate that worked against opening the factory, special letters were mailed along with a proxy to hopefully gather sufficient votes to oust the presiding board of directors. Here's what one of the letters said, quoted in full:[4]

"Dear Sir:

A short time ago, I mailed you a letter enclosing a proxy, which no doubt gave you a good idea of what has been going on at the Cessna plant for the past three years under its present management."

"I feel that I should write you more in detail of what I intend to do after I'm back in control of our company. There is no doubt but that the airplane industry could be a paying one today if handled properly. Good examples of which are represented by the Waco, Monocoupe, Douglas and Northrop airplane companies, as well as various others."

"Through the fact that I have been engaged in the

By July, 1935, c/n 254 had been thoroughly flight tested, granted its Approved Type Certificate and given a coat of trim paint. While the C-34 shared many design and construction features found in earlier Cessna monoplanes, it set a new standard for speed and comfort in the four-place, single-engine market. (Bob Pickett Collection/Cessna Aircraft Company)

airplane business for the past two decades and having always been recognized as one of the pilgrims in the airplane industry, I have made many valuable contacts in the field of aviation in the last three years with various companies and large distributing agents for airplanes, and with these connections I am sure that I can sell a large number of planes."

"I intend to re-design and develop the 4-place Warner ship to such an extent that it will develop a speed of approximately 185 mph and yet keep its present stability, airworthiness and other grand features that made it so popular. This ship will have many wonderful selling points, such as the low cost of maintenance and operation, upkeep and high cruising speed."

"I am sure you realize that our stock is practically worthless today. A complete liquidation would pay only a very small per cent back on our original investments, while if you cooperate with me, the Cessna Aircraft Company will again be doing a good business and our stock on the market rise accordingly."

"I am enclosing another proxy in case you did not receive or have misplaced the other one, and I will appreciate your executing the same and returning it to me in the self-addressed envelope which is enclosed."

Very Truly Yours,
Clyde V. Cessna

In addition to the letters, Dwane Wallace visited every person in Wichita who held more than 100 shares of stock, stating that the times were right for Cessna airplanes and that their support now would lead to profits later.

Dwane and his brother knew it would take more than proxy votes to gain control of the company, and they got a big boost for their side when they bought 6,000 shares of outstanding Cessna stock from the C.M. Keys brokerage firm in New York City. However, the Thad Carver family held over 20,000

shares and Clyde Cessna had 12,000, with 67,000 total shares outstanding.

By the end of 1933, the time had come to see if Dwane and Dwight Wallace had succeeded in their bid to take over the company. At the annual stockholders meeting held on January 17, 1934, they won by only a narrow margin.

Election of the new board of directors took place that day, with Clyde V. Cessna, Roscoe Vaughan, Dwight Wallace, A.S. Swenson and A.B. Sanders accepting positions. Officers were elected from the board that evening, with Clyde Cessna, president, Vaughan, vice president, and Dwight Wallace, secretary and treasurer.

Dwane Wallace, who had resigned his job with Beech on December 31, 1933, was general manager. The hardest battle had been fought and won. The Wallace brothers had an airplane company, but what they needed was a new aircraft to build in the Franklin Road facility. Fortunately, Dwane had just what they needed.[5]

Since his senior year in college, he had been thinking about a new cabin monoplane, formulating what virtues it should possess as compared to the Model AW. Although Dwane recognized that the AW was a well-designed airplane, he was also cognizant of some shortcomings inherent in it, such as the cramped cabin with its difficult entry and exit through small doors, restricted visibility and high noise level in the cabin.

On March 5, 1934, Clyde Cessna officially announced that the company's new airplane would be known as the C-34, indicating the rebirth of the Cessna company in 1934. Engineering on the monoplane was progressing well as of that date, and he expected the prototype aircraft to be under construction within two weeks.

A very small group of workers, led by Dwane Wallace, took up residence in the factory and began the slow, painstaking task of transforming a paper airplane into wood, metal and fabric. Almost every piece of the ship had to be made by hand, as there were almost no jigs, fixtures or tooling extant to ease the job. By late spring, the fuselage and cabin design were nearly completed and the wing layout was approaching its final configuration.

Two separate front seats and one bench-type back seat provided ample comfort for the four occupants. Soundproofing materials were used in the cabin, along with fresh air vents and a heating system. A small baggage compartment was to be situated behind the rear seat that could hold up to 64 pounds.

The new airplane featured a spruce horizontal and vertical stabilizer with a plywood leading edge, while the rudder and elevator were made of welded steel tubing and sheet.

Dwane also planned to replace the M-12 airfoil, which had low drag but also possessed less lift than desired, with a new 2412 section that improved the overall lift of the wing.

The spruce spar was made of built-up laminations that formed one continuous unit when finished, with truss-type ribs built of spruce and plywood. Double brace wires were employed to give the required torsional stiffness to the assembly, and the leading edge was covered with plywood. Like the earlier "A"-series wings, the C-34 wing was a very solid, rigid assembly when completed, and did not require plywood cover-

Left: Dwane L. Wallace put his aeronautical engineering talent to work and designed the C-34 along with help from Tom Salter and Jerry Gerteis. Under Wallace's guidance, the Cessna Aircraft Company weathered the Great Depression and went on to become the world's largest manufacturer of light aircraft. (Dwane and Velma Wallace)

Right: Dwight Wallace worked side by side with brother Dwane to reopen the Cessna Aircraft Company factory. He later resigned from his law practice and became a full-time company employee during World War Two. (Dwane L. Wallace)

ing over its entire length like many cantilever-winged airplanes of the era did. There was more than ample torsional strength in the wing, allowing it to be covered with fabric, saving time, money and weight.

Choice of a powerplant for the airplane was the easiest decision Dwane faced. He intended to use the dependable Warner "Super Scarab" radial engine of 145 hp turning a fixed-pitch propeller.

The landing gear would consist of a cantilever assembly on each side, eliminating the cross-tubing and elastic shock cords of the earlier "A" series monoplanes. Each gear assembly used an oil-spring shock strut with 21-inch wheels. Cable-operated brakes were standard, and an 8-inch, full-swiveling, non-steerable tailwheel was employed.[6]

By April 10th, the wings and fuselage were approaching completion, but production of essential sub-assemblies and components was hampered because the tooling and jigs were being hand-made one at a time as construction progressed. Some of the original Cessna factory employees were fashioning the new-generation monoplane, including Karl Boyd and John Pickering, who used their talents with wood to construct the wing.

Although Dwane Wallace was hard at work on the monoplane's basic design and did a large part of the engineering work, he hired Jerry Gerteis to assist him with the stress analysis and later, in the spring of 1934, signed up Tom Salter as the third member of Cessna's engineering department.

Eldon Cessna had been retained by Dwight and Dwane Wallace at the request of his father, but his involvement with the project was centered around the design and layout of some sub-assembly components along with some drafting work.[7]

The prototype C-34 was completed on August 9th, licensed NX12599, (c/n 254 - a continuation of the numerical sequence from 1931) and made ready for its maiden flight. Rolled from the factory at 7 A.M. on August 10th, a small group of people gathered in the still, cool, air to witness the event. Clyde Cessna was not among the spectators, but Dwane Wallace was, combing every detail of the all-blue ship before

Closeup of c/n 301 shows good detail of the full- cantilever landing gear...a feature that Dwane Wallace believed was one of the airplane's most innovative features. Note the fairings around the cable-operated brake mechanisms. (Bob Pickett Collection/Cessna Aircraft Company)

it took to the air.

George Harte had been asked to take the C-34 on its first trip into the sky, and he was soon airborne over Cessna Field for a short test hop. After landing, he told Wallace that the ship was a real performer, and showed promise of hitting the maximum speed of 165 mph Dwane had calculated for the airplane.

No speed tests were run that day, but tests conducted in the next few days showed a high speed of 162 mph, with a cruising speed of 145 mph. That was terrific performance on 145 hp, and it looked as though the new Cessna Aircraft Company had a winner.

In the next few weeks, Harte began flying the engineering flight tests on the ship, accompanied on many occasions by Dwane Wallace, who observed the airplane's behavior while recording data on performance.

Jim Peyton was the Civil Aeronautics Authority

Miss Betty Browning poses with the C-34 she flew at the 1936 National Air Races, winning the Amelia Earhart Trophy. The airplane is c/n 320. (Bob Pickett Collection/Cessna Aircraft Company)

Early production C-34 instrument panel layout showing engine and flight instrumentation. Throttle is large knob at lower center, with magneto switches and starter button at left. Although electric flaps were not available on the C-34, this airplane apparently had the electrically-controlled system since it has the flap select switch visible on the left side of the panel. (Bob Pickett Collection/Cessna Aircraft Company)

representative assigned to fly the C-34, and he worked closely with Dwane Wallace and George Harte as the airplane's flight tests progressed, including the spin demostration.

To be certified, six turn spins to the left and the right had to be successfully completed, with recovery from the spin occurring in no more than one and a half turns after the controls were neutralized. No control reversal, such as opposite rudder to stop rotation, could be employed during recovery. The C-34 passed its spin tests with flying colors.

With the factory open and operating on a small scale, a promising airplane design ready for production and hope for the future, Dwane Wallace still had to surmount one last obstacle: the Civil Aeronautics Authority stress analysis and engineering drawings that had to be approved before commercial sales began.

In the fall of 1934, all of the necessary paperwork was completed and Dwane set off for Washington, D.C., with a round- trip bus ticket and a very small amount of cash in his pockets plus a file full of engineering data under his arm.

Arriving in the nation's capital, the young Kansan got a room for $2 a day at the Ambassador Hotel. The next day, he went to the Civil Aeronautics Authority and was introduced to engineer Al Vollmecke. For the next five weeks the two men poured over the stress analysis, ensuring every detail met the demands for certification.

Occasionally, changes had to be made to the stress analysis for clarification and amplification of details. To cope with this requirement, Dwane made many trips to the local blueprint shop where the necessary revisions were made.

Finally, the Department of Commerce seal of approval was stamped on the C-34 and Dwane returned to Wichita armed with government approval for his airplane and renewed enthusiasm for the future.

Wallace realized that the company was not going to have customers standing in line to buy the C-34, so a repair station certificate was obtained soon after the factory opened which kept the small workforce busy making repairs to many types of aircraft.

Dwane Wallace and Eldon Cessna were both earning $100 per month from January, 1934, until that summer. The harsh realities of the airplane business in the Depression demanded that both men take a substantial pay cut.

Wallace accepted the reduction and asked Eldon

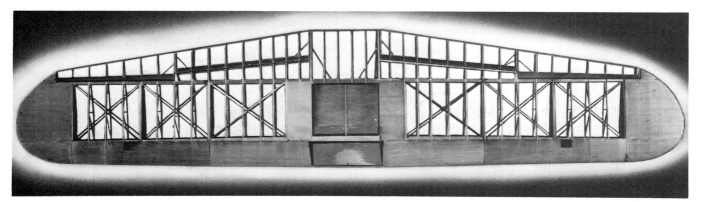

to do the same, but he declined, electing to leave the company instead. Dwane related the situation to Clyde Cessna, telling him that he had done all he could to explain the financial situation to his cousin, but to no avail. Clyde understood the position of both his nephew and his son, and accepted the fact that Eldon would have to leave the firm. Eldon soon found work with an aircraft company in California, leaving Cessna in the fall of 1934.[8]

For Dwane Wallace, living with no salary wasn't a comforting experience, but he managed to get along by eating lots of hamburgers, which cost only five cents in 1934. Dwight Wallace was able to support himself with his law practice, and uncle Clyde had enough money in the bank to live comfortably.

In the summer of 1935, the All-Kansas Air Tour was scheduled for a 1,000 mile trek through the Sunflower State, and George Harte was there with the C-34, giving the public its first real view of the new Cessna. One feature of the tour was a 25-mile free-for-all event that Harte won easily.

Approved Type Certificate number 535 was issued for the C-34 on June 8, 1935, and the prototype C-34 was sold to the Sundorph Aeronautical Corporation of Cleveland, Ohio, later that year. In 1937, Eiler C. Sundorph had designed a four-place cabin monoplane aimed at the businessman-pilot market, and entered it in the Bendix Trophy Race that year.

Powered by a 285 horsepower Jacobs radial powerplant, the craft flew using the wing and empennage surfaces from the first C-34. The registration number on the ship was R2599; very close to the NC12599 of c/n 254.

Wearing race #17 for the contest, the "Special" was flown by Eiler Sundorph to sixth place at the unimpressive speed of 166.21 mph (winning speed was 258.24 mph). As Sundorph dove the ship across the finish line, the wing began to flutter but remained intact and the airplane landed safely. Dwane Wallace, who witnessed the wing's flapping act, went to Sundorph's hangar after race. After talking with Sundorph, Wallace discovered that the aileron balance weights had been removed to save weight, but caused the entire wing to flutter at high speeds such as those encountered in the dive to the finish line. Further modifications were made to the hybrid aircraft after the races; however, no significant performance improvements were made and the ship was not entered in competition again. Eventually, the wing and tail found their way back on NC12599, and more than half a century later the airplane is still airworthy and flying regularly with its original wing.

Wallace knew very well that the C-34 was an efficient airplane for its power, and he sought to

The wing for the C-34 was little changed from the full-cantilever design developed by Clyde Cessna in 1927. Note steel straps between spars necessary for torsional rigidity of the structure. (Bob Pickett Collection/Cessna Aircraft Company)

publicize the ship's capabilities on a national scale by entering the fourth production airplane (c/n 301, NC15462) in the Detroit News Trophy Race at the 1935 National Air Races in Cleveland, Ohio.

The race was run strictly on the basis of an airplane's overall efficiency, with four main categories of competition: 1. A cross-country flight of 200 miles to determine fuel efficiency and economy of operation; 2. A speed race around a five-mile, triangular course; 3. Obstacle hurdling that consisted of takeoff and landing over a 50-foot high barrier, with the shortest distances for takeoff and landing determining the winner; 4. Accomodations and comfort of each airplane for the pilot and passengers.

George Harte flew the blue and orange Cessna C-34 to victory, amassing a majority of points for the four areas evaluated. He then capped off that feat by winning the sweepstakes race for airplanes powered by engines of not more than 550 cubic inch displacement (cid).

The first production C-34 (c/n 255, NX14425) was sold through H.O. Claywell to Ross E. Colley in Tuxpan, Mexico, in November, 1935. It was reregistered XB-AJO when George Harte and Dwane Wallace delivered the ship, paying only $15.24 for fuel while

Tests were conducted on the unique Di Cesare propeller using a C-37 as the testbed. The propeller's over-and-under blade and hub design reduced overall diameter. S.J. "Steve" Wittman (right) and Mr. Di Cesare pose in this wintertime photograph. (Bob Pickett Collection/Cessna Aircraft Company)

104

C-37 instrument panel showed very little change from C-34 layout. Electric fuel guage at right was activated by pushing left or right button below it to read each tank's quantity. Spark, mixture and carburetor heat controls are at left. (Bob Pickett Collection/Cessna Aircraft Company)

averaging 16.9 miles per gallon.

By late in the year, three C-34s per month were rolling out the door, and it looked like that figure would go even higher based on the ever-growing customer interest being shown the attractive monoplane. The company finished 1935 with 11 airplanes built, including two uncompleted DC-6B models that were still in storage at the factory.

The Cessna company had already been victorious in the Detroit News Trophy Race in 1931 when Eldon Cessna flew a Model AW (NC7107) to victory. The event was not held in 1932, 1933 or 1934 because of tough economic times, but the 1935 competition saw a Cessna win for the second time, with George Harte and his C-34 defeating all comers.

Since the company had already won twice, it seemed only natural to try for a third triumph and permanent possession of the trophy. Dwane Wallace flew c/n 320, NC15852, down to Florida for the 1936 Miami All-American Air Races which featured the Detroit News events.

The sleek, speedy monoplane and its lanky pilot outflew everyone else, clinching permanent possession of the trophy and earning the title "World's Most Efficient Airplane" for the C-34.

The Model C-37 prototype was X17070, c/n 330. Principal change was a four-inch increase in cabin width at the front spar that improved interior space and comfort, especially for the pilot and front seat passenger. First flight was made by Dwane Wallace on December 22, 1936. Note Hodge wind-driven generator in right wing leading edge; it was standard equipment on all C-37s. (Bob Pickett Collection/Cessna Aircraft Company)

Wallace also decided to have a go at the Argentine Trophy Race, consisting of a 5-mile triangular course marked by pylons. Dwane had virtually no experience in that type of flying, but had prepared himself well before leaving home by practicing on a piece of the world's biggest race course: Kansas.

He picked out a simulated triangular course, five miles in length with a windmill for a pylon and a county road intersection for a marker. There he became accustomed to the ground-hugging, high speed style of flying required to win such events. He must have taught himself well, for the Pee-Wee green Cessna took home $350 for its victory in the race.

Wallace knew that there were few stock airplanes in the 550 cid class that could best the C-34 in a battle around the pylons. The 145 hp Monocoupes were the most serious threat, often beating the Cessna off the ground because of its lighter weight and faster acceleration.

But once the prairie-bred speedster built up a head of steam, it left the little Monocoupe and the rest of the field behind and usually took the checkered flag with a comfortable lead. Wallace also went up against cabin Waco biplanes and Fairchild 24 monoplanes on many occasions, beating the Fairchild with sheer speed and usually besting the Waco ships as well.

After two years in business, the company had delivered 42 C-34s and also found a successful export market for its product. Nine airplanes were shipped abroad, including two each to England and South Africa and a total of five going to Mexico, Argentina, Australia, Canada and Portugal.

Cessna's upper management experienced a change in the fall of 1936, when Clyde V. Cessna stepped down as president of the company after a quarter century of dedicated involvement with designing, building and flying airplanes. He officially resigned his position on October 28, 1936, choosing to retire at his farm near Adams, Kansas.

Wallace replaced his uncle at the helm of the firm, and Albin K. Longren, also an airplane pioneer that hailed from the Topeka, Kansas, area, continued in the vice president spot that he had occupied since being elected April 13, 1935. Dwight Wallace was reelected as secretary and treasurer.[9]

Additional personnel arriving on the scene by the end of 1936 were Cecil Lucas, who took the reins as sales manager and sometimes doubled as a production test pilot. President Dwane Wallace himself

It wasn't long until pilots like Hollywood actor Robert Cummings bought a C-37 of their own. "Spinach II" was Cummings first Cessna, c/n 369. Aircraft in background is original "Spinach" ship, a Porterfield monoplane. (Bob Pickett Collection/Cessna Aircraft Company)

The C-37 featured electric flaps that are shown extended to the full down position. (Bob Pickett Collection/Cessna Aircraft Company)

still did most of the experimental and production flight testing.

Late in 1936, company engineers began rethinking the C-34 into an improved model, christened the C-37. The thirty-second production airplane (c/n 330) was used as a prototype and registered X17070. Dwane Wallace and Tom Salter aimed their redesign efforts at enlarging the C-34's cabin, smoothing out the ride of the landing gear and reengineering the flap system.

Completed on December 8, 1936, the airplane looked much the same externally, but the internal modifications it embodied set it apart from its progenitor.

The fuselage was widened four inches at the front wing fittings, the engine mount was lowered two inches while the firewall bay was narrowed one inch. Two inches were added to the fuselage width at the rear corner of the entry door and the flaps were electrically operated (the manual system became an option).

Improved baffles were fitted in the NACA cowl along with minor changes to the carburetor heater assembly and the landing gear featured a seven-foot tread with 6.50x10 Warner wheels, still using mechanical brakes. All of these changes required a new type certificate, and the Civil Aeronautics Authority issued ATC Number 622 for the C-37 on February 8, 1937.

The first production C-37 (c/n 342, NC17059) rolled off the assembly line on January 22, 1937, and was one of 46 airplanes built through December, 1937, at the peak rate of seven per month by June of that year.

When properly loaded and trimmed for cruise flight, the C-37 exhibited rock-solid stability in smooth air, and this characteristic sooned earned it a job in the aerial photography business.

Factory modifications consisted of large windows in the forward fuselage section and cabin floor, providing ample room for camera mounting and operation. Seven of the type were constructed specifically for this purpose:

1. c/n 363, NC18037
2. c/n 366, NC18047
3. c/n 368, NC18049
4. c/n 379, NC18594
5. c/n 381, NR18596
6. c/n 383, NC18598
7. c/n 386, NC18589

In addition to the photographic mission, the C-37

was also approved for water operation when equipped with Edo 44-2425 floats. Dwane Wallace flew a C-37 back to Edo's factory near North Beach in Flushing Bay, New York, where the pontoons were installed and flight tests commenced.

Just like the land-based airplanes, the seaplane model had to demonstrate a six-turn spin left and right, with recovery within a turn and a half after controls had been neutralized. Wallace flew the spin tests without any problems arising, and the Civil Aeronautics Authority gave their blessing to the modification. Although the C-34 was later approved for floats, the C-37 led the way as the first model to receive seaplane approval. The Curtiss-Reed metal propeller was standard equipment for the float version since it had more diameter and a lower pitch setting to provide more thrust for takeoff. With pontoons installed, the gross weight was 2,500 pounds, with an empty weight of 1,560 pounds.

Despite the popularity of the C-37, Cessna engineers were not satisfied with the airplane, donning their thinking caps and coming up with still more improvements that resulted in the C-38 model introduced in 1938.

The C-37 was flight tested on Edo floats in 1937 by Dwane Wallace and was the first of the series to be approved for water operations. NC18590, c/n 375, was later sold to Thor Solberg, Cessna distributor for Norway. (Rudy Arnold via Bob Pickett)

Its drag flap fully extended, this C-38 (N19459, c/n 412) comes in for a landing at Spokane, Washington, in September, 1964. (Peter M. Bowers via Bob Pickett)

Model C-38 instrument panel was very clean and functional, with all controls positioned for easy identification. Parking brake handle is under panel at far left, with drag flap pump handle under center of panel. (Bob Pickett Collection/Cessna Aircraft Company)

Constructor number 400 (X18048) served as the prototype, manufactured on October 11, 1937. The C-38 was the first of the new generation Cessnas to be called "Airmaster", the name now associated with all airplanes back to the first C-34. It was an appropriate word for an airplane that did, indeed, master the air in every way.

Basically very similar to the C-37, the C-38 incorporated a major refinement to the landing gear by use of a heat-treated, curved sponson tube that increased the gear's width 10.5 inches. The tube was a one-piece unit of 4130 chrome molybdenum steel, measuring 3 inches outside diameter with a 5/32 inch wall thickness.

The oil-spring shock struts were also improved. A piston with four metering ports allowed more oil flow for better shock absorption on landing and a steel spring handled taxi loads while permitting a full six inches of strut travel.

Other changes included rubber Lord mounts between the engine and the redesigned, detachable mount which reduced vibration to the cabin area. A new tailwheel lock was developed that used a spring-mounted pin to secure the 8-inch tire in the trailing position until the pilot released it for full-swiveling action.

The C-38 also introduced use of a single, large flap mounted on the lower fuselage under the cabin, replacing the wing trailing edge flaps used on the C-37. The new device was actually more of a speed brake than a flap, since it gave the desired drag for landing but contributed virtually nothing to lift. It was hydraulically operated by a pump handle located under the instrument panel, positioned so that it could be easily reached by the pilot from either front seat.

The flap was hinged on ball bearings and featured a cable-operated indicator on the cockpit floor that informed the pilot of the flap's position. When extended or retracted in flight, the flap caused very little pitch change and required only a small amount of retrimming.

Back on the tail, the metal fairing extending from the fuselage under the rudder was now fixed to the fuselage, and did not move with the rudder as the C-34 and C-37 fairings did. The vertical stabilizer and rudder were also slightly larger than previous models.

To reduce system friction in the Cessna's controls, ball bearings were employed on the aileron hinges and the elevator push-pull tube.

In the cockpit itself, the control sticks were moved forward six inches along with a tubular steel cross member that permitted easier entry/egress from the front seats, which now featured moulded, whipped-rubber cushions for better comfort.

Instrumentation included a Kollsman tachometer, altimeter, airspeed indicator, magnetic compass, oil temperature and pressure gauges. Plexiglass replaced the Pyrolin cabin windows and windshield, improving visual clarity for the pilot and passengers.

Standard equipment remained much the same as on the C-37, with the Hodge wind-driven generator being retained in the right wing but the standard propeller was the metal Curtiss-Reed unit. Warner 6.50 x 10 semi-balloon wheels, complete corrosion proofing of the fuselage tubing, float fittings, radio bonding straps and engine ignition shielding for a radio were also standard.

Performance was almost identical to the C-37, with a maximum speed of 162 mph (at sea level), cruising at 75% power yielded 143 mph and the large, belly-mounted drag flap panel reduced the landing speed to 49 mph. Price at the factory was $6,490 for the standard airplane, and the float-equipped version sold for almost $10,000.

Approved Type Certificate #668 was issued for the C-38 on June 25, 1938, but was retroactive back to October 30, 1937, to cover the prototype and initial production examples. Only 16 of the first "Airmaster" model had been built when production ceased in August, 1938. According to Cessna company records, none were exported.

The C-38 was also popular as a camera plane, with six ships being converted for aerial photography. They were:

1. c/n 402, NC18795
2. c/n 406, NC18798
3. c/n 408, NC19455
4. c/n 409, NC19456
5. c/n 412, NC19459
6. c/n 415, NC19463

As 1939 approached, the Cessna engineers huddled together in yet another effort to brainstorm improvements to the highly successful "Airmaster". It wasn't an easy task, for the basic design was so sound that only minor refinements could be implemented to make it any better.

For the first time since 1935, a choice of engines was offered with the reliable 145 hp Warner 'Super Scarab' as the basic powerplant and the new 165 hp version as an alternate. A change in the airplane's

Instrument panel of the C-145/C-165-series was unchanged from the C-38. Elevator trim control is on left sidewall, parking brake handle at lower left, cabin entry assist handle on right side of panel. (Bob Pickett Collection/Cessna Aircraft Company)

designation was made to reflect which engine was installed, known as either the Cessna C-145 or C-165. Actually, Cessna had intended to use "C-39" as the official name, but dropped the year-designator system in favor of the powerplant title.

Fuselage length on the C-165 increased slightly to 25 feet as opposed to the 24 feet, 8 inch length of the C-145. Empty weight for the 165 hp ship was 1,400 pounds and 1,380 pounds for the 145 hp version. Gross weight was 2,350 pounds for both models.

Cable-operated, mechanical brakes found on all airplanes since the first C-34 were adequate, but needed frequent adjustment for effective operation. The new monoplanes used hydraulic brakes operated by heel pedals in the cockpit, and were a distinct and very welcome improvement. A lever permitted the brakes to be set for parking.

Minor changes were made to the wing panels to accomodate flaps mounted immediately aft of the mid-chord position on the lower surface. They were electrically actuated and fully synchronized to extend and retract together. The aft cabin windows were curved to improve both appearance and viewing area. Baggage capacity remained at 64 pounds for both models.

The C-145 and C-165 airplanes were finished in a combination of two colors unless the customer ordered a custom paint scheme, which cost extra. Cessna offered at least 27 different colors, some of the most popular being "Pee Wee Green", "Drake Blue", "Diana Cream" and "Yellow Oxide".

Normal factory finish consisted of three brush coats of clear dope on the virgin fabric, followed by two spray coats of clear dope for final taughtening. Then, two coats of aluminum-pigmented dope were cross-sprayed, followed by water sanding and then three cross-sprayed coats of final color, yielding a lustrous, shiny finish that reflected the high standard of workmanship found throughout the Airmaster series. Only two coats were normally applied to the fuselage, horizontal stabilizer and elevator bottom surfaces to save weight.

There was very little difference in performance between the C-145 and C-165 models. Maximum speed for the C-145 was 162 mph while the C-165 added only seven mph to that figure. Rate of climb was slightly higher with the 165 hp engine as was service ceiling, giving around 925 feet per minute at sea level and topping out at 19,300 feet.

All of the optional equipment offered on the C-38 was also available on the latest models. 1939 prices

at the factory were $7,875 for the standard C-145, and $8,275 for the C-165, jumping to $10,635 and $11,035 respectively for the float-equipped versions.

On September 10, 1938, c/n 450, NC19464, was completed as the prototype C-145 with the prototype C-165 emerging from the assembly lines on April 22, 1939. Both models were built concurrently and shared constructor numbers until 1941, when production ceased after 42 C-145s and 38 C-165s were built.

Three C-145s were exported, going to Brazil (c/n 452, PP-TEH), Finland (c/n 464, OH-YNB) and Puerto Rico (c/n 576, NC25481). Only two were built as camera ships, c/n 457, NC19487, and c/n 465, NC19496, costing $8,315 for the basic conversion.[10]

The C-165-series experienced some interesting variations, including three with 175 hp Super Scarab radial engines and Hamilton-Standard constant-speed propellers known as C-165D. All were manufactured in 1941 and possessed performance improvements over the standard airplanes although the Curtiss-Reed, fixed-pitch propeller-equipped C-165 was faster than the Model C-165D because of differences in effective thrust between the two propeller designs. Here's a list of the three C-165D ships built:

1. c/n 579, NC25484
2. c/n 584, NC32451
3. c/n 586, NC32453

Perhaps the most fascinating C-165 ever built was not a Cessna Aircraft Company project, but that of a car manufacturer that mated an Airmaster to an unusual engine just prior to World War Two.

Detroit's automobile giant, General Motors, developed an experimental aircraft powerplant called the X-250 in 1940. This novel engine featured a

In late 1938, the Model C-145 was introduced for the 1939 sales year. Fresh from the factory, NC19464 served as the prototype and shows off its interior with Laidlaw fabric seats. (Bob Pickett Collection/Cessna Aircraft Company)

Cessna also offered a special panel arrangement for training instrument pilots in blind flying techniques. The false front was deleted with a gyro-operated attitude and heading indicator installed in its place. Note the radial lines painted on airspeed indicator at left; redline is 215 mph with yellow line (caution) at 150. (Bob Pickett Collection/Cessna Aircraft Company)

Cessna also custom-built instrument panels such as this example found in a late-model Airmaster. Note the radio gear mounted below the panel. (Bob Pickett Collection/Cessna Aircraft Company)

new twist on the old two-stroke concept of reciprocating powerplants by having a common combustion section for each pair of eight pistons. It produced 175 hp and looked like a promising design, so General Motors went shopping for a modern, aerodynamically-clean airframe to hang it on for testing.

They found just what they needed in the Cessna Airmaster, and purchased c/n 568, licensed NX25463, in August, 1940. Cessna installed the third X-250 engine on the ship, and it was first flown on September 27th.

Known as the "GM Special", the airplane was flown by famed racing and test pilot Anthony "Tony" LeVier. Flight tests were conducted by the General Motors Research Laboratories in Detroit, Michigan. The original cowling installed by Cessna was removed by GM and replaced by one with more intake area. Flight tests continued on the X-250 during 1940, but the impending global conflict forced cancellation of the project.

Ignacio Nogueira bought this attractive Model C-145, later registered PP-TEH, c/n 452, for personal use in Rio de Janiero, Brazil. Ship was nicknamed "Queimado II". (Bob Pickett Collection/Cessna Aircraft Company)

Only one export C-165 can be found in Cessna company records, c/n 576, NC25481, sold into Puerto Rico in October, 1940, but eight of the type were sold as camera ships:

1. c/n 482, NC20758
2. c/n 488, NC21910
3. c/n 556, NC21916
4. c/n 558, NC21942
5. c/n 559, NC21943
6. c/n 579, NC25484 (C-165D)
7. c/n 580. NC25485
8. c/n 584, NC32451 (C-165D)

During the seven-year production life of the Cessna Airmaster monoplanes, a total of 186 aircraft were constructed, and 23 of that amount (roughly 12%) were camera-equipped versions. There is no doubt that the airplane earned a solid reputation as an excellent photographic platform, capitalizing on its inherent stability and altitude capability.

The Airmaster was a pilot's airplane, and everyone who flew the Cessna soon learned that it was designed to perform at its best all the time, at low altitude or high, on rough, grass strips as well as smooth, paved runways.

For the state-of-the-art in 1940, the C-165 represented one of the best examples of a four-place airplane found anywhere in the world. No other single-engine monoplane could equal its overall

capabilities, efficiency and customer appeal.

Its large cabin door made entry for the pilot and passengers easy. Visibility from the pilot's seat was good to the left, but a blind spot existed to the right and straight ahead because of the Warner's cowling and required caution when taxiing. On takeoff, the locking tailwheel helped the airplane track straight down the runway until airborne.

Once in its element among the clouds, the Cessna had no peer. It climbed eagerly and required little of the pilot once it was trimmed up. In cruise, the airplane flew through the sky straight as an arrow, using its excellent longitudinal stability to good advantage for a smooth ride. Once the ship was trimmed, hands-off flight in smooth air was commonplace.

For roll control, the Airmaster was blessed with ailerons that were quite light and pleasant. When the stick was moved to bank the craft, response was immediate and predictable. Rudder and aileron were well harmonized, and a small amount of adverse aileron yaw present did not spoil that balance.

The Airmaster had good stall characteristics with the wings level, although some tendency to drop a wing during the stall was common. If the pilot allowed the wing to drop far enough, the ship would usually fall into a spin, but would recover quickly when opposite rudder and forward stick were applied.

Pre-stall tail buffet was almost totally absent, with little or no oscillation of the nose as the stall occurred. The tapered wing did not feature much washout, and the tips would stall right along with the root. Flaps did not cause much change in stall behavior. Retracting the flaps after stall recovery did not produce any surprises, as the ship picked up airspeed quickly and climbed eagerly for altitude.

If there was one area that pilots had to get accustomed to with the Airmaster it was the heavy elevator pressures at slow airspeeds and on landing. Holding about 75 mph on final, the Airmaster pilot had to crank in lots of elevator trim, with 70 mph over the fence. As airspeed decreased, pitch forces increased and became progressively heavier.

The elevator condition was aggravated when only the front seats were occupied and fuel load was low, and this characteristic, coupled with the clean aerodynamics of the ship, made some novice Airmaster pilots overshoot the runway. The airplane was fast and it was hard to slow down. Speed management was a critical part of becoming a good Cessna

NC19496, c/n 465, was built as a photoplane featuring both side and belly-mounted vision windows. Stable flight characteristics and good high altitude performance made the camera-equipped Airmasters very popular for such demanding work. (Bob Pickett Collection/Cessna Aircraft Company)

pilot, and it didn't take long for newcomers to learn that the airplane meant business when it came to airspeed control.

At slower speeds, the airplane gave no sensation of losing its sterling stability, and could be easily trimmed up for a final approach to landing. The rudder was effective for slips even at landing speeds and the flaps, whether of the trailing edge type on the C-34 and C-37 or the fuselage flap of the C-38, gave lots of drag to slow the approach speed when deployed.

Mort Brown demonstrates room and comfort of the C-145/C-165 Airmaster's back seat. Note single lap belt for both passengers. (Bob Pickett Collection/Cessna Aircraft Company)

Paint shop in the Cessna factory during production era of the Model C-37. Note straight-leg landing gear on the airplane at left. (Bob Pickett Collection/Cessna Aircraft Company)

With full flaps extended, the Airmaster had little tendency to float down the runway, but if flaps were retracted it would dally just above the surface for quite some distance before deciding to land.

One man who probably knows the Airmaster as well as anyone else is Morton W. Brown, chief production test pilot for the Cessna Aircraft Company from 1939 until his retirement on July 29, 1972. Brown has vivid memories of how well the airplane flew, especially the C-145 and C-165 ships.

Mort flew many of the Airmasters coming off the production line, giving them a thorough flight test to detect any problems before delivery to the customer. A typical check consisted of a series of speed runs at various throttle settings, a complete stall series and perhaps a spin to ensure that the aircraft would recover with proper control inputs.

A checklist was strictly adhered to for these flights, and all 'sqawks' observed for each airplane were recorded for correction. Mort kept very busy at his job, accumulating almost 1,000 hours per year at the stick.

Dwane Wallace's creation earned a distinctive niche in history as not only the "World's Most Efficient Airplane", but also a truly classic flying

General Motors bought NX25463, c/n 568, as a testbed for the experimental X-250 aircraft engine under development in 1940. The original cowling design is shown here. Tony LeVier was the test pilot. (Bob Pickett Collection/Cessna Aircraft Company)

machine. The Airmaster kept the Cessna Aircraft Company in business when the times were tough, winning praise and admiration from all who flew it.[11]

Although the Airmaster had been a great success, it was a seven-year old design that had reached its limit of development. What the company needed was a follow-on airplane that could carry five people at speeds approaching 200 mph with a price tag of about $30,000, aimed at the airline feeder and charter market.

Wallace had been thinking seriously about just such an aircraft back in 1937, and put Tom Salter and his engineers to work on the basic design in the fall of that year, supervising the entire project himself.

Eighteen months later, the first twin-engined Cessna was ready to fly. It had no name; just the designation "T-50". The low-wing, conventional gear ship was constructed of very similar materials and processes as the Airmaster, with a welded, chrome-molybdenum steel tube fuselage, faired with spruce formers and fabric covered.

A full-cantilever empennage group was utilized, using spruce framework for the horizontal and vertical stabilizers and mahogany plywood for covering. The elevator and rudder were made of welded steel tubing with fabric covering. It is interesting to note that the original T-50 mockup had twin tails ala the Beech Model 18 and Lockheed 10, but the design was dropped in favor of a conventional empennage configuration.[12]

The full-cantilever wing was also wood, with laminated spruce spars, spruce and plywood truss-type ribs. Fabric was used for covering the entire wing except for the leading edges which were plywood. A NACA 23014 airfoil section was selected for the root of the wing, which tapered in planform and thickness with a NACA 23012 section at the plywood wingtips. The elevator, rudder and aileron were provided with adjustable trim tabs.

For the first time since the CR-series racers, a retractable landing gear was used, being operated electrically with a manual crank for alternate extension capability. Toe-operated hydraulic brakes were fitted to the 8.50 x 10 wheels that rode on air-oil shock struts of eight-inch travel. A full-swiveling tailwheel was included that could be locked in the trailing position from the cockpit.

For power, the T-50 sported two seven-cylinder Jacobs L-4MB radial engines of 225 hp each on welded steel tube mounts, swinging Curtiss-Reed fixed-pitch propellers.

Cabin appointments were an important factor in

the airplane's design, with the front seats being adjustable and dual controls standard. The big cabin was almost 10 feet in length and featured nearly five feet of width and height to accomodate its occupants. Fresh air vents and a cabin heater were provided to keep the pilot and passengers comfortable year round.

A baggage compartment that could hold up to 300 pounds was located behind the rear seat and was accessible in flight and through a door on the left side for loading and unloading on the ground.

Three large plexiglass windows on each side gave lots of visibility, as did the two-section windshield. A 28 inch x 49 inch entry door on the port side featured a recessed section at the top that permitted graceful entry and exit from the airplane.

Licensed NX20784 and given c/n 1000 in the Cessna production sequence, the first flight of the T-50 was conducted on Sunday, March 26, 1939, with president Dwane Wallace at the controls accompanied by factory manager Bill Snook for the 20-minute jaunt. The next day, Wallace flew the twin for one hour, 40 minutes, probing its speed and handling characteristics.

A six-month flight test program and pre-production evaluation dictated some changes, including a rounded, two-piece windshield, revised empennage shape and the aft side window trailing edge was curved for increased viewing area.

One year after the T-50's maiden flight, Approved Type Certificate #722 was issued on March 24, 1940. The Cessna Aircraft Company had an airplane that would sell, but the aviation business was still a constant struggle as the decade of the 30s ended.

In the previous seven years, profits were thin at best and it was a never-ending battle to keep the firm solvent and the payroll met. Fortunately, good

A dynamic duo...Dwane L. Wallace (left) and Walter H. Beech pose with a Cessna C-165 and Beech C-45 not long before World War Two put both men and their companies to work for victory. (Bob Pickett Collection/Cessna Aircraft Company)

management kept losses to a minimum. For example, for the four months ending March 31, 1939, the company showed a net loss of only $1,123.

Cessna's twin was born into a world at war. Hitler was advocating a "Thousand-Year Reich" and Japan her "Hakko Ichiu" that would bring all the world under Nippon control. Yet, America rested in her isolationism, unaffected by events across the seas until a fateful day in December that awoke a sleeping giant. ✈

---

[1] Walter Beech was still building Model 17 biplanes in the Cessna factory until the end of 1933. Only four ships are thought to have been built there: the two production Model 17R aircraft, the first A17F, powered with a nine-cylinder Wright R-1820 of 690 hp and the prototype Model B17L with retractable landing gear and 225 hp Jacobs engine. It is interesting to note that the A17F was known around the factory as the "thumbtack" because of its large radial engine tacked onto a slender fuselage.

[2] The Cessna C-3 was sold by Walt Anderson to Marcellus Murdock, publisher of the Wichita Eagle newspaper, on April 29, 1936. Murdock had high praise for the ship, with its cruise speed of 120 mph and gentle handling qualities. Although built as a four place airplane, Murdock said it was very tight for four people, but very comfortable for three. He sold it to Andrew V. Bland, who had worked for Dwane Wallace since 1934, on March 19, 1945. By that time the ship was restricted to three occupants and Bland intended to completely refurbish the aircraft and had replaced the 125 hp Warner with a 145 hp Super Scarab by September. The airplane was destroyed in a hangar fire at Wilson Field, Wichita, Kansas, on December 22, 1945.

[3] Clyde Cessna was willing to help his nephews, but wanted no more than a ceremonial participation in the company. Dwane Wallace clearly remembers that his uncle was reluctant to help him at first, then changed his mind and agreed to sign the proxy letters and act as interim president.

[4] The brothers met in the evenings at Dwight's law office to write letters and discuss the amount of stock they could afford to buy. The office served as a base of operations for the two men in their quest for control of the Cessna Aircraft Company.

[5] Although untrue, a story has persisted for decades that the Wallace brothers took advantage of Clyde Cessna's financial and emotional condition when they obtained the company. On the contrary, Cessna was glad to see someone in his own family lay claim to the factory and firm that he worked so hard to establish.

[6] Despite the fact that retractable landing gear technology was available to the C-34 designers, Dwane Wallace flatly states that no consideration was ever given to retracting the gear since he believed the cantilever fixed gear used on the C-34 was in itself a breakthrough in lightplane design.

[7] Dwane Wallace conceived the C-34 and took it from paper to reality with help from Jerry Gerteis and Tom Salter. Eldon Cessna did accomplish some engineering on the airplane but was not involved with its basic design.

[8] When Eldon Cessna declined to take the cut in salary, he decided to leave the Cessna company but claims that he was never compensated for engineering work he performed on the C-34. Dwane Wallace states that Eldon was given the equivalent of his back pay in tools and equipment when he departed.

[9] Albin K. Longren was building airplanes in Topeka, Kansas, at the same time Clyde Vernon Cessna was flying them in Enid, Oklahoma. Longren came on board at Cessna in 1935 as vice president, after exchanging his metal forming and stretching process for about $22,000 in Cessna stock. He was given a small area of the factory for experimenting, and did build an all-metal fuselage biplane powered with a Martin engine. Dwane Wallace flew the ship on several occasions. Longren's sheet metal technology included methods for making butt-joined, flush-riveted structures that Cessna considered applying to future airplane designs, but the process was not used. Longren took no active part in the company's management.

[10] Cessna's export agency was Aviation Equipment and Export, Incorporated, 25 Beaver Street, New York, New York.

[11] As of 1985, there were about 20 airworthy examples of the Cessna Airmaster-series in the world, with most of them in the United States. Of the 186 built, approximately 35-40 are still extant, many undergoing slow restoration or languishing in hangars and barns. On August 10, 1984, 50 years to the day after George Harte flew the C-34 prototype, a small flock of Airmasters and their owners celebrated the event at Cessna Field in Wichita, Kansas.

[12] According to Cessna correspondence dated March 31, 1939, the T-50 specifications originally submitted to the Civil Aeronautics Authority on September 20, 1938, called out Warner engines and a design gross weight of 4,500 pounds.

CHAPTER ELEVEN
Cessna At War

In the winter of 1940, Europe was quiet. Poland had long since fallen, part of Finland was under Soviet rule and a brief but tranquil three month period known as the 'phony war' settled over the continent.

At Cessna Aircraft Company, Dwane Wallace and the board of directors realized, as did many other Americans, that the fighting across the Atlantic Ocean threatened to plunge America into a war that she was unprepared to fight.

When Germany attacked Denmark, Norway and the Low Countries in April and May, the ugly reality of Uncle Sam's involvement in the conflict seemed even more likely. Only France and Great Britain stood between the Fuhrer and the Statue of Liberty.

If America was forced to fight, then she would need airplanes flown by trained pilots, and many of those pilots would be flying medium and heavy, multi-engine bombers like the North American B-25, Consolidated B-24 and Boeing's B-17. Cessna management saw the T-50 as a strong candidate for possible advanced trainer contracts, and started preparations for large scale production in case the war came to Wichita's front step.

In June, the company announced an expansion program that would allow mass production of the

The first T-50, X20784, c/n 1000, flew on March 26, 1939, with Dwane Wallace in the left seat. Design work began in 1938 with Warner Super Scarab engines proposed, soon superseded by Jacobs L4MB radials of 225 hp. Note V-shaped windshield found only on the prototype. (Bob Pickett Collection/Cessna Aircraft Company)

light twin and the Airmaster, although little need for the popular single-engine ship was anticipated in the military marketplace. An assembly building with 28,000 square feet of work space was under construction that month, costing $50,000.

Simultaneously, the first of 13 T-50s for the Civil Aeronautics Authority were completed, with seven delivered by December, 1940, while commercial operators and private individuals flew away with seven of the fast, comfortable twins.

Although civil sales of the Jacobs-powered monoplane were good and promised to get better, Wallace realized that the aircraft's real potential was in the military market.

He concentrated on making the T-50 a prime contender for trainer contracts, talking with government and military officials about the plane's qualifications for the job. Previously, the army had used obsolete airplanes for multi-engine training, but recognized the need for a specialized aircraft, tailor-made for the task.

The army liked Cessna's twin, but couldn't get appropriations from a cost-conscious Congress to buy any. However, the fall of France and the Battle of Britain soon changed that. President Roosevelt vowed to help the British, realizing that such a move could jeopardize America's neutrality. In May, he called for the manufacture of an unprecedented 50,000 airplanes, and it wasn't long before Congress began to loosen its pursestrings.

Slowly, but with increasing speed, Uncle Sam began to modernize its armed services. The U.S. Army sought to build up its air fleet as quickly as

NC20784 as it appeared in December, 1939, after being modified to production standards. Windshield has been changed to a rounded, smooth contour and rear cabin window sports curved trailing edge. (Bob Pickett Collection/Cessna Aircraft Company)

This view of c/n 1000 shows the clean mating of wing to fuselage, landing gear and engine details. Propellers are Hamilton Standard 2B-20-213 hydraulic, constant-speed, non-feathering units. Flaps are fully extended. (Bob Pickett Collection/Cessna Aircraft Company)

possible, and, just as Cessna management expected, twin-engine trainers were high on the priority list.

On July 19th, Louis Johnson, Assistant Secretary of War, announced that Cessna would build 33 airplanes for advanced training, to be known as the AT-8. The contract was valued at over $800,000, and represented the largest order the company had ever received up to that time.

The AT-8 was also one of the first airplanes built for the army that was designed expressly for multi-engine training. It was a virtual copy of the commercial Model T-50, but added windows to the cockpit roof and exchanged the Jacobs radial engines for 290 hp Lycoming R-680, 9-cylinder powerplants swinging metal Hamilton-Standard, constant-speed propellers.

Other changes included hydraulically-operated Sperry autopilots, the usual government furnished equipment (GFE), special radio gear and overall aluminum color paint scheme.

As Britain reeled under the might of Goering's Luftwaffe that summer and fall, gallant pilots from England were joined by their comrades from Canada, Poland and the United States. To keep the United Kingdom supplied with pilots, England, Canada and Australia conceived the British Commonwealth Air Training plan that was designed to pool the pilot resources of the three nations.

For flight training, Canada was foremost among the group, being far from the front lines. It represented a continent-sized airbase that stood little chance of being attacked. Would-be aces and bomber pilots flocked to the country, where many of them would learn their deadly trade in twin-engine Cessna airplanes.

The Royal Canadian Air Force sent a contingent to Wichita in the summer of 1940 to evaluate the T-50 as a possible advanced trainer. To the men who flew the ship, it represented not only a modern airplane, well suited to the job, but it also possessed economy of operation, was built from non-strategic materials, could be easily repaired in the field and would be ready for mass production in only a few months.

The RCAF wanted the T-50, and awarded Cessna its biggest single order in company history in September, signing on the dotted line for 180 aircraft, designated Crane I. It was also the largest order for airplanes that the Air Capital had ever received.

As the chill air of fall settled in, the Cessna Aircraft Company had a $5,000,000 production backlog but a small factory campus to meet the exploding demand for its products. Under terms of the contract, Cessna was to deliver the first AT-8 before the end of December, and the RCAF expected to fly its first Crane by Christmas.

Even though the new building greatly enlarged the factory's manufacturing capacity, more room was desparately needed along with the manpower to keep production rolling.

Early in September, Dwane Wallace announced the second expansion program in the last three months. A new final assembly structure, 400 feet long and 200 feet wide plus a two-story administration facility were to be built as soon as possible. Walter A. "Pop" Strobel, Cessna's head of plant engineering, was charged with overall responsibility for the layout of the facility and completion of the project targeted for late fall.[1]

As Cessna grew, so did its number of employees. By September, the workforce of men and women increased from 200 in July to over 500, and hit 710 by Thanksgiving. Many of these workers came from Kansas areas, but there was a growing population of out-of-state people who came to the prairie city to build the wings of war.

Cessna wasn't the only Wichita company with big contracts and a shortage of workers. Beech Aircraft Corporation and Boeing's Stearman Division were also experiencing the boom in business caused by the government's rearmament program. Beech was producing the AT-11 bombardier trainer and C-45 pesonnel transports while Stearman's successful primary trainer design, the Model 75, was in production for the army as the A75N1 (PT-17, 17A, B and C) and the navy took the same model as the N2S-1 and N2S-4. The three Wichita-based manufacturer's combined had a total backlog of more than $30,000,000 at the end of 1940.[2]

Cessna's new plant buildings were completed in November, after a two-month long, round-the-clock 'blitz' by contractors to get the job done. As fast as the floorspace was released to Cessna, workers moved in equipment to build airplanes.

The hectic pace that had become commonplace at the Pawnee Road factory paid off in December, when the first AT-8 was delivered to the army and flown

Cessna's first retractable gear airplane since the CR-3 racer, the T-50 used an electric motor driving chains and a jackscrew actuator to raise and lower the gear, which is not completely retracted in this view. (Bob Pickett Collection/Cessna Aircraft Company)

away to Wright Field in Dayton, Ohio, for operational evaluation less than six months after the contract was signed.

Hot on the heels of the AT-8 came the first Crane I, being delivered to the RCAF in less than 90 days from the order date. As the number one ship winged its way north that December, the Canadians announced that a further 360 Cessnas would be ordered, bringing the total Crane I backlog to almost 540 airplanes.

The Crane I differed from its American counterpart in several areas: it utilized the 225 hp Jacobs engine with wooden, fixed- pitch propellers, military radio sets and special equipment for dealing with the extreme low temperatures found in the cold country, such as removeable baffles for the engine that allowed cylinder head and oil temperatures to remain at near normal levels, and oil radiators that helped keep the oil warm.

As the fateful year of 1941 began, 1,500 Cessna

An early T-50 wing under construction at the Cessna factory. Spars were laminated spruce with spruce and plywood truss-type ribs. The leading edge and outboard wing tips were covered with plywood sheet. (Bob Pickett Collection/Cessna Aircraft Company)

Commercial T-50 instrument panel shows the layout of engine and flight controls, instrumentation and systems switches. Parking brake is against left sidewall. (Bob Pickett Collection/Cessna Aircraft Company)

workers labored in three shifts to build AT-8 and Crane I trainers. Knowing about the war's worsening situation for England as she fought alone against the Nazi juggernaut, everyone worked just a little harder for the cause of freedom.

The newspapers carried stories of General Erwin Rommel's famed 'Afrika Corps' and its march toward the Nile River in Egypt, pushing the British forces eastward until their backs were against the Mediterranean Sea.

Of even more concern, however, to most Americans was the worsening relations between the United States and Japan, the latter's leadership being bent on vast expansion and by 1941 was threatening peace in the Pacific Ocean.

Few people contemplated a war with Japan or Germany, and the mood at the Cessna plant was one of optimism for the future. Leading the company into its second year of growth were Dwane L. Wallace, president, Thomas B. Salter, vice president and chief engineer and Dwight S. Wallace, secretary and treasurer. Joining these men on the board of directors were John C. Kelley and Will G. Price, Sr.

It took more than just top management to make the Cessna Aircraft Company a success. There was a second echelon of men who got the sales, kept the books and managed the plant. Among these were Donald C. Flower, in charge of sales. He came to Cessna with 14 years experience in commercial aviation and learned the business as a mechanic, foreman, service manager and salesman, as well as being known as an ace glider pilot.

All of those pennies the company was earning by 1941 had to be accounted for, and it was Arthur L. Vermillion's job to keep track of all finances and run the accounting department. He gained experience working for the U.S. Treasury Department and the Farm Credit Administration before joining the Cessna team.

The double expansion programs of 1940 required a rapid buildup of qualified workers, and it was Myron E. Russ who tackled the job of hiring labor to build the advanced trainers as head of the personnel section.

Harold E. Reed and David E. Brehm were in charge of production at Cessna, while Arthur H. Sheldon was the factory superintendent with Andrew "Andy" Bland as his assistant. O.C. Helvy was night shift superintendent.

Purchasing agent William H. Whipple had to be sure that thousands of parts were on the production lines for the Airmaster, T-50 and military ships. The critical job of aircraft inspection was headed up by

Sherman Graves and his 16 assistants, who supervised 53 other inspectors in the plant's 14 departments. These men worked side by side with Flight Lieutenant W.J. McGrandle, chief inspector for the Royal Canadian Air Force and Gale Savage, who commanded a force of nine government inspectors who made sure the army got what it paid for.[3]

Morton W. Brown and Mel A. Couer were the chief test pilots for the company, but most of the every-day production flight testing was handled by assistant test pilots Victor D. Gibson, Gail Storck, Harald Thomas, Ivan Spong, Ralph Fehring, Haskell Shaw, Norman Blake, Ralph Primo, Don Richardson, R.P. Tucker and Lawrence Enzminger. Most of these pilots were hired by Don Flower to ferry Crane Is from Wichita to Trenton and Winnipeg, Ontario, for delivery to the RCAF, but they also filled in around the plant as required for production flights.[4]

In May, the 100th Crane I was delivered to the RCAF, and employment had increased to 1,900 people, followed in June by Dwane Wallace's announcement of a third plant expansion program. More room was needed for woodworking and assembly of the twin engine airplanes, and construction of a 3,750 square foot building for that purpose was soon underway and was completed by late summer.

A very important facet of the new program was to construct a cafeteria capable of preparing enough food to feed the ever-growing family of Cessna workers. When finished in August, the unit was among the most modern in all of the mid-west, with the latest in refrigerators, ranges, baking ovens, steam cookers, electric food processors and even automatic dishwashing equipment.

Dwight Wallace realized that it would be very difficult for employees to leave their job stations and come to the chow line without seriously disrupting production schedules, so he decided the food would have to go to them.

Wallaces' brainstorm was known as the 'rolling cafeteria', and consisted of 14 specially designed carts that were electrically heated to keep food piping hot. When mealtime came, the carts were dispatched from the cafeteria and served each department in only five minutes, leaving 20 minutes for everyone to enjoy their food before returning to their jobs. Cessna's 'meals on wheels' was the only known one of its kind in any American aircraft factory up to that time.

In 1941, company engineers initiated a program to improve performance of the T-50 and AT-8/Crane I, and in the spring a new airplane design tagged the "P-7" was taking shape (the letter "P" was used by Cessna for experimental projects. The P-7 was also known as the T-50A).

Two 300 hp L-6MB Jacobs engines were installed, along with plywood skin over the entire wing surfaces. Since higher wing loadings and speeds would be encountered by the P-7, the extra torsional strength of the plywood was necessary. Gross weight of the airplane was higher than production machines, requiring a new landing gear to support the craft. Cessna reportedly purchased North American AT-6 landing gear components and modified them to fit the T-50 gear wells to handle the extra weight.

Flown by Mort Brown on June 2, 1941, the one and only P-7 exhibited a marked improvement in takeoff,

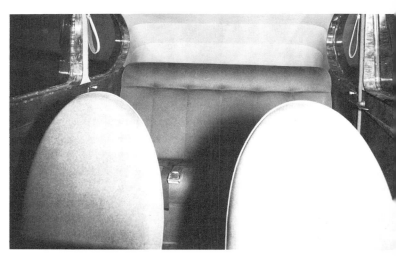

Spacious cabin of the Cessna twin featured lots of legroom and thickly-padded seat for rear passengers. Large windows gave a good view outside. (Bob Pickett Collection/Cessna Aircraft Company)

climb and maximum speed, the ship hitting just over 200 mph in flight tests. The aircraft was used for further testing through the summer months and was often the mount Dwane Wallace preferred due to its higher performance. The airplane was not put into production because the army and the Canadians were happy with their Cessnas in their original form and weren't interested in an improved model.

On October 6th, another experimental airplane known as the P-10 took to the air, again with Mort Brown at the controls. Designed as a high-performance twin-engine trainer, the P-10 made extensive use of T-50 components and featured a bubble-type canopy and side by side seating. It also shared the P-7's plywood wing covering but the span was reduced slightly. The fuselage was also plywood-covered.

Powered with two 300 hp Jacobs engines and standing on North American AT-6 landing gear, the P-10 had excellent visibility and performance, but the government already had all the training aircraft on order it needed for the forseeable future and no production contracts were forthcoming. Mort Brown

The Cessna Board of Directors in 1942 are shown here, left to right: Tom Salter, vice president and chief engineer; John C. Kelley; Dwane L. Wallace, president; Dwight S. Wallace, secretary-treasurer; Will G. Price, Sr. (Mrs. Dwight S. Wallace)

The army trained thousands of multi-engine pilots in AT-17s during World War Two. It proved to be a rugged airplane that did the job with little fuss. Shown aloft for a test flight is army serial number 238715, Cessna c/n 2924. (Bob Pickett Collection/Cessna Aircraft Company)

continued flying the ship during further tests until Carl Winstead took over late in the year so Brown could devote most of his time to production flying. Both the P-7 (c/n P-7, NX34750) and the P-10 (c/n P-10, NX34751) were dismantled on October 14, 1941, at the factory and never flew again.

Later that fall, the army completed its evaluation of the first 33 AT-8s and gave Cessna an order for another 450 aircraft with the designation AT-17. The only changes incorporated into the new trainer were additional windows in the cockpit roof and the exchange of Lycoming engines back to the 225 hp Jacobs R-755-9 radials. The Jacobs engine was more readily available and became the standard powerplant on the American and Canadian trainers.

In keeping with the practice of nicknames for military airplanes, Cessna held a factory-wide contest to find a name for the AT-17. After combing

Cessna won a contract for 33 AT-8 advanced trainers in July, 1940. Equipped with 225 hp Lycoming R-680 radials, the airplanes featured ceiling windows and were equipped with Sperry autopilots. The first AT-8, c/n 1030, army serial number 41-5, stands ready for flight. (Bob Pickett Collection/Cessna Aircraft Company)

through hundreds of suggestions, "Bobcat" was selected and met with approval from just about everyone, including the army.[5]

Social life for Cessna's employees was an integral part of the company's in-house program for morale and labor-relations. The Cessna Employees Club sponsored many special events like picnics and dances and encouraged comraderie and friendship among the more than 2,000 workers at the plant by November, 1941. Bowling, softball, baseball, basketball, trapshooting and use of a completely equipped gymnasium were just a few of the off-hours activities available to all.

Yes, there was a lot of joy around the plant, but there also a lot of worry, fear and uncertainty about the immediate future. Tokyo and Washington were further apart diplomatically than ever before, and scuttlebutt about America's entry into World War II was openly discussed not just at Cessna, but across the nation.

In October, the company purchased 320 acres east of the main plant that permitted much more room for takeoffs and landings and removed the problem of taxiing across a county road to get to the old runway area, a practice Cessna pilots had to endure since 1940.

November saw yet another expansion of the plant, this time to the south of the final assembly building. An extension was added that totaled 20,000 square feet inside and brought Cessna's total factory floorspace to more than 360,000 square feet.

To prepare for what was called the "impossible days" of war, Cessna formed the Home Guard, a small band of less than 100 employees who volunteered their free time to learn combat tactics, maneuvers and how to repel attacks from parachute troops or fifth column insurgents.[6]

All the gossip about war with Japan became fact on December 7, 1941, when the Imperial Japanese Navy attacked the U.S. Pacific Fleet at Pearl Harbor, Territory of Hawaii.

President Franklin D. Roosevelt spoke to the

117

nation that Sunday, galvanizing Americans into a determined people with but one resolve: to defeat Japan. Thousands of Wichitans listened to that radio broadcast, including men like Walter Beech, J. Earl Schaefer and Dwane Wallace. They knew that the war would demand far more of their companies than any of them ever dreamed about in peacetime. And they were right.[7]

Even as the wreckage of Pearl Harbor still smoldered, Cessna received huge orders for AT-17 advanced trainers and Crane Ia ships for the RCAF. Commercial T-50 production was halted entirely by June, 1942, to devote the entire factory effort toward military contracts.

Cessna had delivered 25 commercial T-50s in 1941 and early 1942, including six to the Civil Aeronautics Authority and 14 to Pan American Airways. The Pan Am ships were actually Canadian Crane trainers that were sold to the airline, and were built to standard Crane Ia configuration (same as army AT-17A).

Another victim of the war was Cessna's highly publicized "Family Car of the Air" project, announced in late 1941. The company planned to design, build, certify and produce a four-place airplane that would be easy to fly, possess safety features more advanced than any plane then in existence and sell for about the same price as a 1941 Chevrolet.

When the war interrupted all design work, the project was shelved but not abandoned. However, it was much more important to defeat the Axis powers than fly a family flivver and the fanfare quickly died away, not to be heard again until after the war.

To produce thousands of airplanes for the army and the RCAF, Cessna had to enlarge the factory once again. In 1941, the plant had grown by 358%, employment by 679% and equipment by 522%, yet 1942 demanded more than that to meet the task ahead.

Stock issues were offered to the public in March, with 21,445 shares at $11.50 per share available through Cessna's broker at the New York Stock Ex-

change. The offer was part of 71,446 shares owned jointly by Dwane and Dwight Wallace. Their sale provided Americans with an opportunity to invest in the defense of America.

Production of the AT-17 was in full swing by May, 1942, with the new buildings all completed and operating at maximum capacity on a 24-hour basis.

From January, 1941 until December, 1942, Cessna built 1,839 airplanes for the military. The breakdown is as follows:

Crane I - 640
Crane Ia - 190
AT-17 - 450
AT-17A - 33
AT-17B - 466
AT-17C - 60

The Crane Ia airplanes were virtually identical to the army's AT-17s except that the Canadian ships had slightly different electrical systems. The first 63 AT-17s were limited to a gross weight of 5,100 pounds because of wing spar structural restrictions until c/n 1763, after which the gross weight was increased to 5,700 pounds. However, some airplanes built after c/n 1763 also suffered from gross weight restrictions of 5,300 pounds and carried the designation AT-17E. The only difference between AT-17, A, B and C models was special equipment such as radios and flight instrumentation. The gross weight restrictions centered around the safety factor of the T-50's wing. As originally certified by the Civil Aeronautics Authority, the wing design limited the gross weight to 5,100 pounds, and the AT-17 was introduced with this wing.

The army operated the airplanes at 5,200 pounds gross weight for a few months after initial deliveries, found no problems and then cleared the AT-17 for

In 1942 the army ordered 450 AT-17 "Bobcats" for multi-engine training. Note cockpit ceiling windows, Hartzell fixed-pitch, wooden propellers and anti-glare paint on these ships inside the final assembly building. (Bob Pickett Collection/Cessna Aircraft Company)

An early production C-78, army 258125, Cessna c/n 3616, shown in olive drab and gray camouflage scheme. Note early national insignia without bars. No AT-17/UC-78 ships had feathering propellers; if an engine failed, the checklist called for high pitch on the dead engine propeller while maintaining an airspeed of 90 mph. Single-engine ceiling was about 5,000 feet. (Bob Pickett Collection/Cessna Aircraft Company)

a 5,300 pound gross weight. Most of the AT-17 and UC/C-78 series were built with a wing designed for a commercial gross weight of 5,400 pounds, but were operated by the military at 5,700 pounds.

Only the original production AT-17 aircraft were delivered with Hamilton-Standard constant-speed propellers, with Hartzell wooden propellers being standard equipment on the vast majority of the other models because critical metals such as aluminum and steel were being reserved for combat aircraft.

Of the 550-airplane Crane Ia order of 1942, only 182 were delivered to the RCAF before the Army Air Force took over the balance of the order after Pearl Harbor. Of the remaining 368 aircraft, 41 were delivered as AT-17A, 60 as AT-17C, 131 as AT-17D and 136 as UC-78C models.

The first of the C/UC-78 series was built in 1942, carrying the original designation C-78 for light cargo and personnel transport work, which included flying the 'brass' when necessary. 330 ships were delivered to the army as C-78s before the designation was upgraded to UC-78 in 1942, the "U" indicating utility service. Gross weight of both models was 5,700 pounds, and the C/UC series were the first Bobcats to receive the olive drab and gray paint scheme.

Uncle Sam later ordered more UC/C-78 ships, with 937 going to army service and 67 were transferred to the U.S. Navy with the designation JRC-1. According to Cessna records, all of the navy ships had Hamilton-Standard constant-speed propellers. Some of these airplanes wore overall aluminum paint, while others were painted with two-tone light blue and white or a dark blue and white scheme.

By far the largest batch of airplanes built during the war by Cessna, the UC-78B numbered 2,156 strong by the time production ended in 1944. Sporting an overall aluminum color, some were constructed with metal, constant-speed propellers, but the majority featured wooden units. The UC-78B was also plagued by wing spar weight limitations, with the designation UC-78E given to those ships restricted to 5,300 pounds gross weight.

AT-17 instrument panel was well equipped for 1942 with full blind flying instrumentation. Note landing gear position indicator left of throttles, propeller controls at right, mixture controls and carburetor heat levers on quadrant. (Bob Pickett Collection/Cessna Aircraft Company)

The AT-17B model was produced in 1942 with an order for 655 ships, but the last 189 airplanes in the production run were changed to UC-78B models before delivery. Some AT-17Bs were limited to a gross weight of 5,300 pounds, being redesignated as the AT-17G.

Being built at the same time as the AT-17B, the AT-17C production run was originally intended for lend-lease to the RCAF, but the army absorbed the entire order for 60 aircraft. When held to 5,300 pounds gross weight, the type was known as the AT-17H. All AT-17Cs received Hartzell, fixed-pitch wood propellers.

In addition to the total of 1,052 AT-8 and AT-17-series airplanes, plus the 3,160 UC/C-78/JRC-1 aircraft, all 40 of the commercial T-50s were impressed by the government for the duration and were assigned United States Army Air Force serial numbers.

Many of the civil Airmasters and even the veteran and aging Model DC-6-series monoplanes were also impressed into government service during the war. The following listing provides all of the known Cessna airplanes that served in a military capacity: *

Cessna C/N	License	Model	Military Number	Designation
c/n 238	NC302M	DC-6A	42-38290	UC-77
c/n 232	NC654K	DC-6A	42-46637	UC-77
c/n 231	NC6449	DC-6A	42-46638	UC-77
c/n 226	NR6441	DC-6A	42-46639	UC-77
c/n 211	NC631K	DC-6B	42-38292	UC-77A
c/n 219	NC633K	DC-6B	42-38293	UC-77A
c/n 290	NC14452	DC-6B	42-38294	UC-77A
c/n 200	NC9865	DC-6B	42-38295	UC-77A
c/n 321	NC16402	C-34	42-78021	UC-77B
c/n 309	NC15470	C-34	42-78025	UC-77B
c/n 381	NC18596	C-37	42-78023	UC-77D
c/n 366	NC18047	C-37	42-78024	UC-77D
c/n 347	NC17087	C-37	42-97412	UC-77D
c/n 591	NC32458	C-165	42-107400	C-94
c/n 558	NC21942	C-165	42-78018	UC-94
c/n 562	NC21946	C-165	42-78022	UC-94

* (Information courtesy Ray Ruhe and Bob Pickett)

In 1942, the allies began to plan 'Operation Overlord', the invasion of Europe. A key factor in that assault was the use of gliders to airlift troops behind enemy lines.

The aircraft picked for the job was the CG-4A

Some JRC-1s featured a two-tone blue and white paint scheme like this ship. Gross weight was 5,700 pounds with performance the same as UC-78 series. (Harold G. Martin via Bob Pickett)

Cessna produced a grand total of 5,399 twin-engine advanced trainers from 1941 through 1944, when production was terminated. Among that number were these six AT-17s, running up their Jacobs engines prior to a test flight at the factory. (Bob Pickett Collection/Cessna Aircraft Company)

designed by the Waco Aircraft Company of Troy, Ohio. Waco was a very familiar name in American aviation, going back to the early 1920s. But now it was hard pressed to build enough of the powerless aircraft for the big show, so the government turned to subcontractors for assistance.[8]

In June, 1942, Cessna, Beech and Boeing were tapped for their talents with mass production and ordered to give the glider program top priority, with 1,500 of the craft to be built and delivered by October, but half of the order was later cancelled.

Responsibility for the program was divided, with Beech assigned to build the inner wing panels, tail surfaces, all forgings and castings. The company subcontracted most of the work to outside firms, who delivered the parts on time and to specifications.[9]

Cessna's part in the program involved construction of the outer wing panels, but there was simply no room to build them within the factory. Acting swiftly to remedy the problem, Dwane Wallace announced the purchase of 110 acres of land east of Hutchinson, Kansas, 50 miles northwest of Wichita, as the site for a special facility dedicated to the glider project.

In just over 30 days, a 108,000 square foot factory was erected and almost immediately began producing the wing panels. Three shifts labored hard hours to meet the deadline. Karl Boyd was supervisor at the Hutchinson division, overseeing 315 workers initially and then more than twice that number as the job got rolling.

As Beech and Cessna completed their parts and assemblies, they shipped them to J. Earl Schaefer's Plant II at the Boeing, Wichita Division factory. There, the gliders were assembled and delivered to the army, on time.

The fact that the three aircraft manufacturers cooperated so well toward accomplishing a common goal was not surprising, since Wallace, Beech and Schaefer were friends and knew how to make their companies pull together for victory. But the glider program was, perhaps, most difficult for Schaefer.

His outfit was not only building Waco CG-4As but also rushing to tool up for mass production of the highly-advanced Boeing B-29 'Superfortress', constructing a million square-foot factory to house the big bomber's assembly lines and reengineering the airplane all at the same time.[10]

As 1943 arrived, Cessna management was looking ahead to the day when demand for the AT-17 and UC-78 would decline, leaving the company without a product to build. The engineering department had been working on another airplane that could take over where the Cessna twin left off. They came up with a proposed transport ship that could be built of non-critical materials, possess good overall performance and would operate out of short, unimproved airfields that were common in battle zones.

Cessna used North American AT-6 landing gear on the P-10 and installed a full-vision sliding canopy for the two-man crew. Although the airplane had good performance, the army wasn't interested and the ship was dismantled in 1941. (Bob Pickett Collection/Cessna Aircraft Company)

Waco CG-4A troop/cargo gliders were an integral part of the Allied plan for invasion of Europe in June, 1944. Cessna, Beech and the Wichita Division of Boeing were instructed to build 750 of the powerless aircraft in June, 1942. The three companies worked together and delivered their quota on time to the army. (Bob Pickett Collection/Cessna Aircraft Company)

The army liked the C-106 and intended to order at least 500 airplanes, hence the national insignia on wings and fuselage during flight tests. (Bob Pickett Collection/Cessna Aircraft Company)

Designated the P-260 project and nicknamed the "Loadmaster", the design featured the characteristic Cessna all-wood, full- cantilever wing mounted on top of a welded, chrome-molybdenum steel tube fuselage.

The landing gear was fully retractable into each nacelle, which mounted two 600 hp (takeoff rating) Pratt & Whitney R-1340S3H1 radial engines with two-bladed, constant-speed propellers.

The forward fuselage around the cockpit and the nacelles were the only areas utilizing aluminum, with the rest of the fuselage covered by fabric. The wings were covered with plywood, as were the fixed, wooden horizontal and vertical stabilizers. Ailerons, rudder and elevator were made of welded steel tubing and covered with fabric.

Given the designation C-106 by the U.S.A.A.F., the prototype flew for the first time in January, 1943. It was the largest Cessna ever built up to that time, and Deed Levy was brought in to help evaluate the airplane's handling characteristics.[11]

Levy's suggestions were coupled with those of the Army Air Force and a second airplane was constructed. Tagged the C-106A, it featured three-bladed, constant-speed propellers, geared engines and a refined fuselage

End of the line. Rows of war-weary Bobcats await their fate at a storage depot after the war. Fuselage numbers are probably some kind of storage code. There are at least three olive drab airplanes in this group. (Bob Pickett Collection)

As a result of flight tests on the C-106, the C-106A was built embodying improvements such as full-feathering Hamilton Standard propellers, geared Pratt & Whitney engines of 550 hp and a slightly redesigned fuselage. Note gearbox on right engine, carburetor air intake on top of nacelle. (Bob Pickett Collection/Cessna Aircraft Company)

design that included a larger cargo door.

Spanning 64.7 feet with a length of 51.1 feet, the new Loadmaster weighed in empty at 9,000 pounds, and could be loaded up to a gross takeoff weight of 14,000 pounds. Flown on April 9, 1943, the C-106A transport earned Cessna a contract for 500 of the 195 mph (maximum speed) airplanes.

Unfortunately, the government could not justify enough priority for materials to build the monoplane and quickly lost interest in the C-106A. The contract was cancelled and both airplanes were cut up for scrap at the factory.

Cessna was also heavily involved in rebuilding, repairing and maintaining the military's AT-8, AT-17 and UC-78 aircraft. As the war progressed into its third year, the company leased the main hangar on Hutchinson airport, previously used by U.S. Navy personnel for aircraft work.

In April, the hangar was refurbished and turned into a smooth- running overhaul depot. The government snapped up the opportunity to let the Wichita-based manufacturer maintain, rebuild and repair its own products, releasing military personnel for other duties while saving the taxpayer some cash. The Hutchinson facility operated from April, 1943 until the end of the war.[12]

1944 saw the allies on the offensive around the globe, with Germany and Japan on the defensive, fighting to retain every foot of ground they had taken from their enemies. At Cessna, the production line was no longer crowded with chrome-yellow Crane Ia, silver AT-17 and olive drab and gray UC-78s. The day of the trainer was over.

Now, it was the day of the bomber. Heavy and medium bombers that dealt the Fuhrer and the Emperor death and destruction from high and low altitude, severely damaging their ability to wage war.

In the Peerless Princess of the Prairie, Boeing's Wichita Division had been building control surfaces for the mighty Flying Fortress during 1941 and 1942, but in 1943 it was struggling against gigantic odds to build the B-29 on time and deliver them to General Hap Arnold's bomber boys.

To do the job, Boeing needed help. Cessna answered the call of its brother across the airport and built 1,400 vertical stabilizers, 1,894 rudders, 1,658 heat exchangers, 1,619 pilot and co-pilot instrument panels, 1,536 dorsal fairings, 1,567 elevators, 1,343 wing leading edges and 1,583 sets of rudder pedals for the 60-ton behemoth of the sky.

Both Cessna and Beech also built parts for the Douglas A-26 "Invader" medium bomber. While Beech built 1,635 wing assemblies for the attack airplane, Cessna contributed by constructing 6,500 engine cowlings and 2,046 landing gear sets for the speedy and maneuverable Douglas machine.

Then, in what seemed like only a short time to some people, but an eternity to others, the war was over. Japan lay in ruins having twice suffered the horror of atomic weapons. Germany was so thoroughly ravaged that it was split in two between its conquerors.

For Cessna employees, they could look back with pride and the satisfaction of a job well done, as could every other aircraft worker in Wichita who had helped Uncle Sam win the war. The time that Dwane Wallace and the board of directors had known would come finally arrived: it was time to revert to peacetime production.

That meant massive layoffs of personnel, and the ax fell quickly on the thousands of workers who made Cessna a name known the world over. Peak employment during the war reached 6,074, dropping to 1,800 after V-E Day, falling to only 450 following the surrender of Japan.

During the previous four years, Cessna and the Beech Aircraft Corporation had cooperated many times in getting the job done for democracy, setting aside their peacetime rivalry. In July, 1945, the aviation world was surprised to learn that the two companies were discussing a merger.

Beech director and financial advisor Thomas D. Neelands got the two firms together and started the ball rolling. Reasons for a linkup seemed rational: both companies were located in Wichita, both had the same auditors and fiscal years, both wanted very much to survive in the postwar marketplace and neither organization had any debts and owned their factories outright.

As proposed by Neelands, Beech would trade 233,000 shares of its stock, worth $3,500,000 for $5,000,000 in Cessna facilities and working capital.

Airborne allies. Canadian Crane Ia (c/n 2399) leads an army AT-17 on a production test flight. Crane Ia and AT-17 were identical in construction. Tail stripes on the army ship quickly disappeared after Pearl Harbor. (Bob Pickett Collection/Cessna Aircraft Company)

Some ex-war Bobcats were put on floats and made their living on water, like this Canadian ship, registered CF-GGQ, Cessna c/n 2377, previously a Crane Ia (FJ-176, RCAF 8827), captured out of its element at Vancouver in 1955. (Peter M. Bowers via Bob Pickett)

Beech also would be entitled to Cessna's tradename and sales potential that amounted to about $1,000,000 annually.

Meetings were held, but directors disagreed on just about every point and the whole proposal fell flat on its face by August. Both companies announced that discussions had ceased, and then went back to work as before with no hard feelings.

Probably the greatest challenge facing Beech and Cessna in 1945 was what kind of airplane to build for the post-war market. Thousands of surplus aircraft like the Aeronca "Chief", Piper "Cub" and the Taylorcraft light, single-engine ships, some of which had been used in the war for liason and reconnaissance work, would be available for sale, driving prices down and making it very difficult for any new, more expensive models to survive.

Walter Beech introduced the famous Model 35 "Bonanza" in 1946, while Cessna engineers labored to design and develop two new aircraft simultaneously; the Model 190/195 and Model 120/140, which formed the nucleus of the company's product line and were highly successful in the post-war marketplace. In 1947, the Model 170 emerged from the drawing board and took its place on the production lines along with the other models.

To better explain how each airplane fits into the Cessna story, they will be treated separately by model type, along with a look at their development, production span, price and service use.

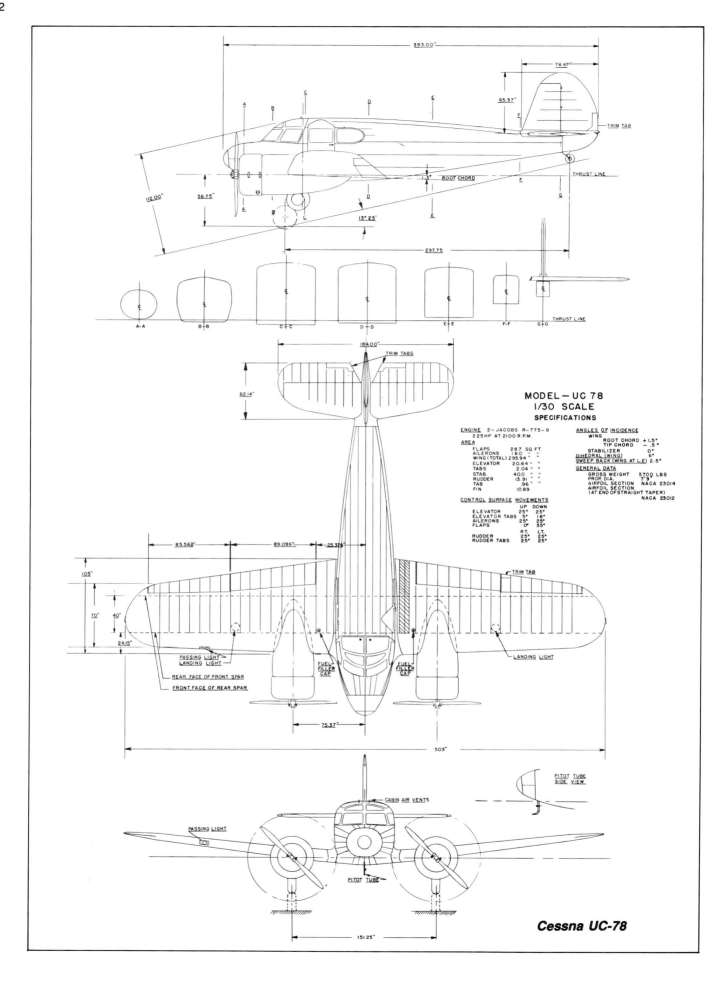

MODEL — UC 78
1/30 SCALE
SPECIFICATIONS

ENGINE 2-JACOBS R-775-9
225HP AT 2100 R.P.M.

AREA

FLAPS	28.7	SQ.FT.
AILERONS	18.0	"
WING (TOTAL)	295.94	"
ELEVATOR	20.64	"
TABS	2.04	"
STAB.	40.0	"
RUDDER	13.91	"
TAB	.96	"
FIN	10.89	

CONTROL SURFACE MOVEMENTS

	UP	DOWN
ELEVATOR	25°	25°
ELEVATOR TABS	5°	18°
AILERONS	25°	25°
FLAPS	0°	35°
	RT.	LT.
RUDDER	25°	25°
RUDDER TABS	25°	25°

ANGLES OF INCIDENCE

WING
ROOT CHORD +1.5°
TIP CHORD −.5°
STABILIZER 0°
DIHEDRAL (WING) 6°
SWEEP BACK (WING AT L.E) 2.5°

GENERAL DATA
GROSS WEIGHT 5700 LBS
PROP. DIA. 7'9"
AIRFOIL SECTION NACA 23014
AIRFOIL SECTION
(AT END OF STRAIGHT TAPER)
NACA 23012

Cessna UC-78

THE BOBCAT AT WAR

Cessna's venerable "Bobcat" distinguished itself during the war in every major theatre of action. It was used for transport of people and parts in Europe and the Pacific, flying from land bases that ranged from modern, well-equipped military fields to rough, dirt strips hacked out of the jungle by natives. The vast majority, however, spent their war-time years at American bases in the advanced trainer role.

5,399 AT-8, Crane I/Ia, AT-17 and C/UC-78 airplanes emerged from the Cessna factory from 1940 to 1944, each batch having some differences in gross weight, equipment and color scheme. The accompanying table lists all military models and specific production information:

that were included in the NC license kit:

1. Rewiring of the generator switch circuit to make it a part of the master switch circuit (parts and wiring diagram included in NC license kit).
2. Removal of navigation light resistors, replacing them with switches (parts and wiring diagram included with NC license kit).
3. Removing military instrument markings and replacing them with Civil Aeronautics Authority-approved markings (parts and instructions included with NC license kit) on the following instruments only:
A. Cylinder head temperature gauge - 275 to 575 degrees F.
B. Oil temperature gauge - no marking

MODEL	CESSNA C/N	BUILT	A.A.F.#	GROSS WEIGHT	VOLTS	COLOR
AT-17/AT-17E	1701-2150	1-1-42 to 6-29-42	42-2 to 42-451	5,100	24	Silver
AT-17A/AT-17F	2301-2490	12-16-41 to 7-27-42	42-13617 to 42-13806	5,100	12	Yellow
	2551-2583	12-19-42 to 12-23-42	42-13867 to 42-13899	5,700	12	Yellow
AT-17B/AT-17G	2901 to 3011	6-29-42 to 12-19-42	42-38692 to 42-38802	5,100	24	Silver
	3012 to 3366		42-38803 to 42-39157	5,700	24	Silver
AT-17C/AT-17H	2491 to 2550	7-25-42 to 8-14-42	42-13807 to 42-13866	5,100	12	Yellow
UC-78	3601 to 4031	7-13-42 to 3-26-43	42-58110 to 42-58540	5,700	24	Olive Drab
	4801 to 5373	3-26-43 to 12-11-43	43-7281 to 43-7853	5,700	24	Olive Drab
	5701 to 6050	12-11-43 to 3-17-44	43-31763 to 43-32112	5,700	24	Silver
UC-78B/UC-78E	3367 to 3555	1-13-43 to 3-1-43	42-39158 to 42-39346	5,700	24	Silver
	4161 to 4800	3-2-43 to 7-22-43	42-71465 to 42-72104	5,700	24	Silver
	5374 to 5700	9-1-43 to 10-25-43	43-7854 to 43-8180	5,700	24	Silver
	6051 to 6700	7-22-43 to 1-15-44	43-32113 to 43-32762	5,700	24	Silver
UC-78C/UC-78F	2584 to 2850	1-26-43 to 5-28-43	42-13900 to 42-14166	5,700	12	Silver
	4101 to 4160	5-28-43 to 6-7-43	42-72105 to 42-72164	5,700	12	Silver

NOTE: All of the UC-78 series airplanes were equipped with Hamilton-Standard constant-speed propellers and a 30-gallon auxiliary fuel tank mounted under the rear seat.

After the war, thousands of ex-military airplanes were declared surplus and offered for sale, including AT-17s and UC-78s. Cessna sent information packets to interested buyers and to aircraft operators who had already bought one of the twin engine monoplanes. Many of the Crane I and Ia airplanes were also sold off by the Canadian government. The AT-8 trainers, although identical to the commercial T-50, were not eligible for commercial license.

Cessna's correspondence explained what steps had to be taken to transition the airplanes from military to commercial status. All of the modifications were of a non-structural nature and could be easily accomplished by most repair stations as the Cessna factory was too busy completing government contracts to handle the conversion workload.

Here's a listing of the required changes, including a notation about parts and instructions

required.
C. Airspeed indicator - Maximum dive speed - 200 mph, cruise - 168 mph and flaps extended - 112 mph.
4. Replacement of the tail navigation light with an approved type (parts and wiring diagram included in NC license kit).
5. Modification of the landing gear warning horn circuit and/or installation of a warning horn in accordance with Cessna Service Bulletin #94 (parts and instructions included in NC license kit).
6. Installation of fuel selector valve sealing plates (parts and instructions included in NC license kit).
7. Installation of a datum locator plate on the base of the front spar for weight and balance computations (parts and instructions included in NC license kit).
8. Installation of a bungee spring in the elevator control system (parts and instructions included in NC license kit).
9. Removal of all military markings from instrument panel and the installation of a Civil

Aeronautics Authority decal showing limitations (parts and instructions included in NC license kit).

10. Inspection and replacement (if required) of the engine throttle and mixture control cables where they passed through the nacelle structure to ensure the cables did not foul on the landing gear during retraction, in accordance with Cessna Service Bulletin #95 (bulletin furnished in NC license kit).

11. Inspection and replacement (if required) of the carburetor heater muff gasket, in accordance with Cessna Service Bulletin #88 (parts and bulletin furnished with NC license kit).

12. Installation of additional drain holes in the wing fuel tank compartment, in accordance with Cessna Service Bulletin #96 (bulletin furnished with NC license kit).

13. Installation of additional fasteners on the fuel selector valve housing cover, in accordance with Cessna Service Bulletin #92 (bulletin furnished with NC license kit).

14. Stamping the date of manufacture and date of conversion to commercial status on the data plate mounted on the co-pilot window sill frame.

15. Inspection of the wing to determine the airplane's gross weight status. There were two gross weight/wing spar limit classes for the military: 5,100 pounds and 5,700 pounds. Cessna did not recommend the purchase of an airplane with a wing limited to a weight of 5,100 pounds because it would carry a lower payload compared to the heavier wing.

To confirm the wing's classification, a small access door (located on the lower surface of the wing, forward of the inboard end of the flap) was opened to allow the rear spar face to be viewed. If the spar was spruce planking, it was a 5,100-pound wing; if the spar face was plywood, it was a 5,700-pound wing. This was a very important inspection for the prospective buyer to make, since it determined the ultimate usefulness of the airplane in commercial service.

Cessna also built a liason/transport version of the AT-17 known as the C/UC-78. Over 2,100 were delivered to the U.S. military forces. This UC-78B, army 332169, Cessna c/n 6107, has the red border around the national insignia that was deleted after September, 1943. (Bob Pickett Collection/Cessna Aircraft Company)

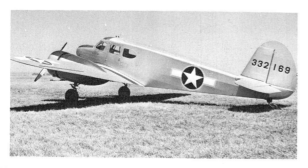

16. The second most important inspection centered around inspection of the wing leading edge rib spacing, as called out by Cessna Service Bulletin #48. The steps were:

1. Removal of nacelle cover and a small plate adjacent to the first rib outboard of the nacelle leading edge.

2. If the ribs were spaced four inches apart, the wing had been modified at the factory; if the spacing was eight inches, the wing had not been modified and Cessna again recommended against purchase of the airplane with this condition. Service Bulletin #48 could not be accomplished in the field, effectively eliminating these ships from potential commercial service.

17. A complete weight and balance check of the aircraft to provide a record for the operations manual (instructions and operations manual included in NC license kit).

18. A 100-hour inspection was to be performed on the airplane and a Form ACA 319 completed by the inspecting mechanic. Cessna provided a "Service Hints Manual" detailing all special areas deserving careful inspection as part of the NC license kit.

Cessna also provided guidance on the airplane's equipment status as delivered to the armed forces, and made recommendations to make the ship commercially suitable.

The front seats of the AT-17 and UC-78 series were designed to accept a standard military parachute. Since this would be unacceptable for civilian operations, Cessna offered a complete interior upholstery and trim kit for installation.

If the ship was to be used for charter work at night, the Civil Aeronautics Authority required three Class II flares and one Class I flare (added by the operator at his discretion).

All AT-17 and UC-78 models featured battery/magneto ignition as specified by the military. Many of the post-war "Bobcats" retained this type of ignition, which had the battery firing one set of spark plugs and the single magneto firing the other set on each engine.

Cessna also recommended that the oil radiators installed in some of the early AT-17 and UC-78 ships be removed to save 38.5 pounds. The radiators were originally installed on all Canadian Crane I and Ia ships to warm the oil during cold weather operations, but were included as standard equipment in the early production runs for the U.S. Army until finally deleted later in the war. Removal instructions were outlined in Cessna Service Bulletin #49.

Regarding paint finishes, Cessna was frank about the poor protection against ultraviolet rays by the camouflage schemes applied to approximately one third of all army airplanes. When the navy bought the JRC-1s, they painted their camouflage directly over the army's. Camouflage was not a good base paint and finishes applied over it did not last very long. A careful inspection and fabric test of each airplane purchased was highly recommended along with a complete repainting.

MODEL 190 AND 195

Cessna had originally counted on the "Family Car of the Air" project to be its premier airplane after peace returned, but the proposal was dropped in 1945 in favor of a more promising design known as the P-780.

This aircraft was strictly a proof-of-concept ship, employing as many T-50 parts and assemblies as possible while adhering closely to the venerable Airmaster's layout. With these guidelines to go by, the experimental department was soon humming with activity as the prototype went from the drawing board to sheet metal in only six months.

It greatly resembled an enlarged Airmaster, blessed with a larger cabin and resting on Cessna's brand-new spring steel landing gear.[13]

Because of the rush to build the airplane, the fuselage was made of welded steel tubing and fabric covered, but the full cantilever wing was all metal, using Alclad aluminum sheet. Powered by a 245 hp Jacobs radial engine surrounded by a T-50 cowling, the monoplane made its first flight in December, 1944.

Dubbed the Model 190 in 1945, development continued, with the biggest change being an all-metal fuselage of semi-monocoque construction and a complete overall streamlining from spinner to rudder. A second ship was built that featured these refinements and was flown on October 15, 1945, with a 300 hp Jacobs radial engine thrusting the sleek machine to a maximum speed of nearly 180 mph at sea level.

Further development yielded a third aircraft, powered by a 240 hp Continental radial powerplant, that flew in June, 1946. Both the Jacobs and Continental-powered ships had good performance, so the company decided to produce two versions, the Model 190 with its 240 hp Continental and the Model 195 with its 300 hp Jacobs.

The Model 195 received Approved Type Certificate #790 on June 12, 1947, with the Model 190 following on July 1, 1947. That year, combined sales of 84 airplanes got production off to a good start, with 1948 sales jumping up to 205 airplanes and to 186 in 1949.

Although the Model 195 was selling well, Cessna improved the breed by doubling the flap chord, restyling the interior, adding a spinner to the propeller, slightly reshaping the elevators and changing to a 245 hp Jacobs engine. The 195A was approved under the parent 195 type certificate on January 6, 1950.

Sales for the new version hit 190 in 1950 but fell to 96 in 1951. Horsepower was increased to 275 in 1952 when the Model 195B made its sales debut powered with the new R-755 radial and was approved under the original Model 195 ATC on March 31, 1952.

The Model 190 was built alongside the 195B until 1953, when it was dropped due to lackluster sales. It was soon joined by the 195B, which disappeared from the production lines in 1954 after two years of steadily declining customer interest and orders.

During the Model 190/195-series eight-year production life, it served not only its civilian owners well but its military masters, too. In 1949, the United States Air Force needed a rugged airplane to perform flight duty in the Arctic, and shopped around for an off-the-shelf design that met its requirements.

Instrument panel of a 1952 Model 190 shows neat, logical arrangement of engine and flight instruments. Notice the throwover control wheel. (Bob Pickett Collection/Cessna Aircraft Company)

In the fall of that year, Uncle Sam selected the Model 195 and gave Cessna an order for 15 aircraft under the designation LC-126A. Floats and skis were delivered with the airplanes in January, 1950, with the only salient differences from the commercial version being radio gear, emergency escape hatch for the pilot, paint and spartan interior appointments.

The government was back for more Model 195s in 1951, buying five for duty with the National Guard. Designated LC-126B, these airplanes were identical to the Air Force LC-126A except for radio equipment.

Another order came to Cessna in 1952, when the U.S. Army bought 63 Model 195s designated as LC-126C. A different interior, designed to accomodate two stretcher patients requiring a much larger baggage door for entry/exit of the patients was the primary change along with different radio gear. All 63 ships were delivered to the army between May and October, 1952.[14]

Including these 83 airplanes, a total of 1,183 (including the prototype and military aircraft) Model

The P-780 served as a developmental test bed for the Model 190 series airplanes. It was powered by a 245 hp Jacobs radial engine and featured a welded steel tube fuselage and all metal wing. Note spring steel landing gear and T-50 cowling. (Bob Pickett Collection/Cessna Aircraft Company)

126

Big brother to the 190 was the Model 195, also introduced in 1947. With its 300 hp Jacobs radial pulling it along at 180 mph maximum speed at sea level, the 195 was bullish on performance and had good looks as well. (Bob Pickett Collection/Cessna Aircraft Company)

190, 195, 195A and 195B were built from 1947 to 1954. Of this total, the Model 190 accounted for 233 examples, while 866 Model 195, 195A and 195B ships were flown away from the factory by their proud owners.

MODEL 120 AND 140

In 1945, the United States government realized that thousands of returning GIs would be seeking a new life after the war, and approved educational funds to help them get reestablished in the mainstream of American society.

One of the areas authorized to receive financial assistance was flight training. Cessna management was quick to recognize that the market for training aircraft would be great, even though the small, two-seat light airplanes built by competitiors like Aeronca, Taylorcraft and Piper would also be vying for their share of this potentially lucrative market.

What the Cessna Aircraft Company had to do was make their trainer design more attractive, modern and appealing than the older, pre-war ships they would compete against while keeping the price as low

Cessna developed the very popular Model 140 in 1945 as a two-place trainer and sport aircraft. The prototype, NX41682, c/n 8000, is shown here in its original configuration. Chrome-vanadium spring steel landing gear was initially developed by S.J. "Steve" Wittman who sold the manufacturing rights to Cessna. (Bob Pickett Collection/Cessna Aircraft Company)

Powered by a Continental C-85-12, four-cylinder opposed engine of 85 hp, the Model 140 could hit 110 mph and cruise at the century mark. Note the original cowling design found on the first prototype only and absence of aft window incorporated on production ships. (Bob Pickett Collection/Cessna Aircraft Company)

as possible.

It didn't take the engineering department long to come up with an airplane that fit those requirements perfectly, - the Model 140. Designed around the small, reliable and economical four- cylinder, opposed, Continental engine of 85 hp, the 140 prototype featured an all metal fuselage but retained a fabric covered wing of semi-cantilever construction to save weight and production costs.

Side-by-side seating was cozy yet comfortable for the two occupants, and visibility was good all around through large, plexiglas windows in the doors as well as the windshield.

The chrome-vanadium spring steel landing gear was employed on the Model 140, with the prototype (c/n 8000, NX41682) making its first flight on June 28, 1945. A complete flight test program followed, and two additional aircraft were built in the fall that incorporated changes dictated by operational experience with the first ship.

A slight redesign of the fuselage was accomplished that included a new tail cone, addition of a rear cabin window and an entirely new engine cowling.

In 1950, the U.S. Air Force bought 15 Model 195s under the designation LC-126A for work in the Arctic region. The military ships were very similar to their civilian counterparts except for radio equipment and utilitarian interior. (Bob Pickett Collection/Cessna Aircraft Company)

Instrument panel of c/n 8000, the prototype Model 140. Magneto switches are at left behind control wheel. (Bob Pickett Collection/Cessna Aircraft Company)

Cessna's use of aluminum alloy for spars and ribs shows up well in this view of a Model 140 wing without its fabric covering. (Bob Pickett Collection/Cessna Aircraft Company)

Announced in the spring of 1946, the 140 represented a real value at only $3,385, equipped with a complete electrical system, manually-operated wing flaps, deluxe upholstery and rear quarter windows. The wing incorporated aluminum spars and stamped aluminum ribs, greatly reducing both time and labor for these components.

The Model 140 received Approved Type Certificate #768 on March 21, 1946, and began rolling off the assembly lines that month, hitting a production rate of 22 ships per day by August. Sales of the 140 were excellent and the airplane was an instant success, making the competition's tube and rag, 65 hp ships look quite antiquated by comparison.

Cessna dealers couldn't get enough of the 1,450 pound gross weight aircraft, and flew them away day after day from Cessna Field throughout the summer and early fall of 1946. Peak production reached 30 airplanes per day in September, and Cessna had increased their employment to over 1,800 employees, going full blast to build the handsome little

monoplanes.

In 1949, the Model 140 became the Model 140A with the change to aluminum wing skin and a single lift strut replacing the dual struts of the original version. The 140A was awarded Approved Type Certificate 5A2 as an amendment to the Model 140 ATC and sold for $3,495 with the 85 hp engine and $3,695 for the 90 hp Continental C-90-12 model. By 1951, when production of the Model 140 was phased out, 4,905 airplanes had been built, compared to 124 Model 140A with the 85 hp engine and 401 sales of the 90 hp version.

Cessna also offered a spartan version of the Model 140 called the Model 120. It had no wing flaps or rear quarter windows, the upholstery was plain and the electrical system was optional. Otherwise, the two

A sea of aluminum and doped fabric typifies the production pace Cessna experienced as dealers and customers waited in line to get their Model 120 or 140. The factory was turning out up to 22 per day by August, 1946. (Bob Pickett Collection/Cessna Aircraft Company)

128

In March, 1947, both the Model 120 and 140 were approved for Edo floats, opening up yet another world of flying fun for Cessna pilots. Note paddle secured to the left float. (Harold G. Martin via Bob Pickett)

Beautiful inflight shot of a 1950 Model 140A, showing off its optional overall paint scheme and wheel fairings. Note landing light in left wing leading edge. Production of the 140A ceased in March, 1951. (Bob Pickett Collection/Cessna Aircraft Company)

airplanes were virtually identical in construction and overall appearance.

The 120 was approved under the Model 140's type certificate and sold for only $2,845. It was popular with flight training schools and fixed base operators, and many were scooped up for that purpose, destined to suffer the ups and downs of teaching fledglings to fly. Production of the Model 120 ceased in 1949, after 2,171 airplanes had been delivered.

MODEL 170

To capture a share of the emerging businessman-pilot market that was becoming increasingly attractive by 1947, Cessna designed the Model 170, using its experience and technological know-how with sheet aluminum gained from the Model 120/140 program.

Powered with a 145 hp Continental C-145, six-cylinder, opposed engine, the prototype took to the air in September, 1947, and received Approved Type Certificate #799 on June 1, 1948.

The Model 170 featured an all-metal fuselage and empennage with aileron, rudder and elevator also

Fine profile view of a Model 140 illustrates the airplane's clean lines, full-cantilever landing gear and semi-cantilever wing. Over 4,900 140s were built. In 1948, the horsepower was increased to 90 with introduction of the C-90-12. Maximum speed was 125 mph, cruise speed 105 mph. (Bob Pickett Collection/Cessna Aircraft Company)

of aluminum construction. The fabric covered wing was built around aluminum spars and ribs, utilizing dual lift struts. Flaps were manually operated with four positions and featured a maximum extension of 40 degrees.

Entering production in March, 1948, 729 were sold that year before Cessna decided to revamp the design for the 1949 model year, giving the 170 an all-metal wing, large, sweeping dorsal fairing on the tail section, increased fuel capacity from 37.5 gallons to 42 gallons and a new designation of Model 170A.

The new ship sold for only $5,995 in its basic form and remained in production until 1952, when the Model 170B was introduced, incorporating new, single-slotted, high-lift flaps and minor interior styling changes. Continental's engine designation was changed to 0-300, and still retained 145 hp and a fixed-pitch metal propeller.

In 1952, 1,108 170Bs were built, followed in 1953 by 666 ships that had a revised cowling design. Only 467 170Bs were produced (including the prototype) in 1954, and production was terminated in 1956 when Cessna swapped the tailwheel for a nosewheel and the ubiquitous Model 172 was born. Including the prototype ships, a total of 5,173 Model 170-series airplanes were built.

Instrument panel of N2142V shows little change from earlier 140 models. Note airspeed redline at 140 mph, yellow arc from 115 mph to redline and white arc for flap extension from 45 to 80 mph. (Bob Pickett Collection/Cessna Aircraft Company)

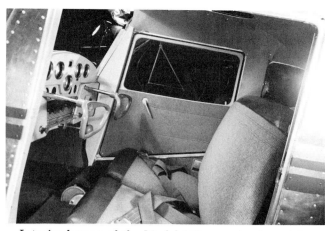

Interior layout of the Model 140 was simple and functional. Seats were padded for comfort and upholstery covered much of the metal structure in the cabin. (Bob Pickett Collection/Cessna Aircraft Company)

A TRIBUTE TO CLYDE CESSNA

The Cessna Aircraft Company had come a long way since the days of the First Street and Glenn Avenue factory. It had survived the Great Depression, helped to win a global war and by 1954 had emerged as one of the largest airplane manufacturers in the world.

Founder and past president Clyde Cessna had watched the company grow from a tiny one-room workshop on Wichita's west side to a sprawling factory campus on the east side of town. Since his retirement in 1936, Clyde had been enjoying the farmer's life he had known so well as a young man in southcentral Kansas.

Yet, Dwane Wallace and others in the Cessna organization clearly remembered the air pioneer and his tireless efforts to make the company successful from 1927 until 1936. Clyde and Europa Cessna were honored at a banquet on February 28, 1953, held at the Broadview Hotel in downtown Wichita.

Many famous aviation personalities sent their best wishes to the couple, and even President Dwight D. Eisenhower dispatched his personal congratulations, praising Cessna for his long and illustrious career in aeronautics. Throughout the evening, Clyde said little, choosing only to listen and smile as others told stories of days long past.

In 1954, Mr. Cessna was a guest of honor at the dedication ceremonies for Wichita's new municipal airport, located on the southwest side of the city, not far from the first Cessna factory. It was his last public appearance. He continued his quiet, reserved lifestyle until his death on November 11, 1954, at his home near Norwich, Kansas.

His passing was mourned by not only his family, but many friends and public dignitaries who knew him well, not to mention untold thousands of airmen to whom the name "Cessna" had come to symbolize flying itself.[15]

The 1949 Model 170A featured an all-metal wing, dorsal fairing forward of the vertical stabilizer and a single lift strut for each wing. Base price was only $5,995. (Bob Pickett Collection/Cessna Aircraft Company)

Above: In 1948, Cessna began deliveries of the new Model 170; a four-place airplane aimed at the private and businessman pilot. The fuselage and wing structure were aluminum alloy, but the latter remained covered with fabric. (Bob Pickett Collection/Cessna Aircraft Company)

Below: Instrument panel of a Model 170 shows general arrangement and enlargement from 140 series. (Bob Picket Collection/Cessna Aircraft Company)

Below: Dwane L. Wallace and his famous flying uncle pose for the camera in 1953 in front of a Model 180. Cessna helped his nephew regain control of the Cessna company and Wallace built it into one of the largest manufacturers of airplanes in the world. (Bob Pickett Collection/Cessna Aircraft Company)

Left: Clyde and Europa Cessna relax and reminisce in their rural Kansas farm home in December, 1941. Cessna rarely visited the Wichita factory after his retirement from aviation in 1936, preferring to spend his time enjoying the simple life. (Bob Pickett Collection/Cessna Aircraft Company)

FLIGHTS OF FANCY

During the years 1938-1945, the engineering department at Cessna was busy creating fresh, innovative aircraft designs. Unfortunately, some of the proposed models never got off the drawing board. Let's take a look at some interesting Cessnas whose only flights were in the minds of their creators.

Cessna wanted to be ready for the expected post-war airplane boom and designed the "Family Car of the Air" in the early 1940s. Known as the P-370, the airplane never progressed beyond the mockup stage shown here. (Bob Pickett Collection/Cessna Aircraft Company)

PROJECT 370

P-370 was the number assigned to the "Family Car of the Air" that never progressed beyond the mockup stage in 1944 and was finally cancelled in 1945. General specifications and predicted performance were:

Gross weight - 2,100 pounds
Wingspan - 35.5 feet
Wing Area - 182.5 square feet
Engine - Six-cylinder, opposed Franklin 6-ACG-298, 160 hp at 3,250 rpm geared down to produce 2,050 propeller rpm
Fuel capacity - 40 gallons
Maximum speed - 165 mph
Cruising speed - 140 mph
Range - 500 statute miles
Service ceiling - 18,000 feet
Landing speed - 50 mph
Price - Intended to be competitive with a typical family automobile in 1945

MODEL CTP-1

Envisioned as a pilotless torpedo plane, the CTP-1 was designed for catapult launch from a land base with its own internal guidance system leading it to the target some 200 miles away.

Flying at 200 mph, when the one-way aircraft reached its destination the wings would be blown off by an explosive charge and the fuselage would plummet downward to hit the target with its 500-pound warhead.

Since the aircraft had an intended useful life of only one hour, construction materials were not only non-critical to the war effort but very inexpensive, too. The steel tube fuselage framework was arc-welded and covered with pre-doped fabric, which was pulled over the structure while the dope was still wet and then

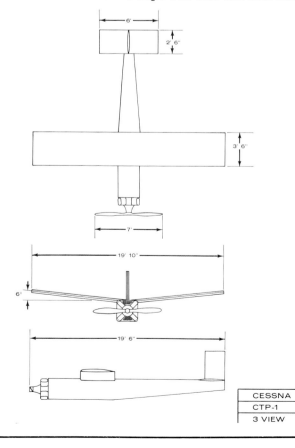

CESSNA
CTP-1
3 VIEW

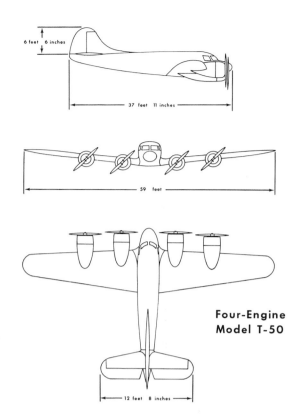

6 feet 6 inches

37 feet 11 inches

59 feet

Four-Engine Model T-50

12 feet 8 inches

drawn down tight using a simple drawstring at each end.

The wings featured a steel tube spar with stamped steel ribs designed to be welded quickly and easily in a special jig. Pre-doped fabric also covered the wings, using drawstrings at the root and tip to pull the fabric into place.

Empennage surfaces were wood, with a plywood covering and the elevator and rudder were deflected using small electric servo motors to control the flight path.

Gross weight was 1,500 pounds, with a 200 hp engine driving a wood, fixed-pitch propeller at 2,500 rpm. Service ceiling was 21,000 feet and rate of climb 1,500 feet per minute. No CTP-1s were built as the concept apparently never gained much favor with the military.

Exactly how effective the weapon would have been in combat is impossible to determine, but it probably stood little chance of hitting its target with the crude and unsophisticated guidance system originally planned for it.

MODEL T-55

Designed in May, 1941, as a two-place version of the T-50, the T-55 was scheduled to use two Jacobs L-6 radial engines of 300 hp each. Wingspan was 42 feet, length 31 feet, two inches and gross weight was 5,750 pounds. Calculated maximum speed was 225 mph. No mockups or prototypes are known to have been built.

FOUR-ENGINE T-50

In 1942, Cessna engineers took a standard Model T-50, gave it two more engines, room for

six occupants, eliminated the aft cabin side windows and exchanged the trusty Jacobs radials for more powerful Pratt & Whitney 'Wasp' Jr. T1B3 powerplants to create the first four-engine Cessna.

The airplane was proposed as a heavy bomber trainer, intended to teach future B-17, B-24 and B-29 pilots how to handle all those throttles. Gross weight was expected to be 12,000 pounds, empty weight 8,000 pounds with 466 gallons of fuel carried in wings that spanned 59 feet with 470 square feet of area.

Construction was essentially like the T-50 using welded steel tube fuselage and wood wings with plywood covering replacing the T-50's fabric. The empennage surfaces were plywood.

While the basic design looked promising, no development was forthcoming probably because of the company's commitment to building twin-engine trainers for the war effort. Predicted performance at sea level boasted a maximum speed of 240 mph, cruising speed of 200 mph at 75% power, 2,700 feet per minute rate of climb with a service ceiling of 31,000 feet. Range at 70% power was expected to be 800 statute miles at 212 mph.

MODEL T-70

In 1941, Cessna proposed a low-wing, cabin monoplane powered by two Pratt & Whitney R-1340 radial engines of 600 hp each as a possible navigator trainer. Seating 10 in its spacious interior, the airplane had a design gross weight of 12,000 pounds, wingspan of 60 feet with 600 square feet of area.

The T-70 was expected to hit 220 mph and

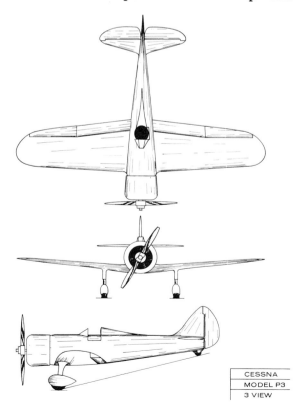

CESSNA
MODEL P3
3 VIEW

carry 200 gallons of fuel while teaching fledgling navigators their trade. Cessna did not pursue the T-70 with the military forces since other aircraft like the Beech AT-11 were already in service.

PROJECT P-3

As early as 1938, Cessna was working on a single-engine fighter design aimed at the domestic or export market. Dubbed the P-3, there were four versions originally planned, each one differing in powerplant, wood or metal construction and fixed or retractable landing gear.

The only known drawing of the P-3 depicts the full-cantilever, low-wing monoplane with a Pratt & Whitney 'Wasp' SB4-G radial engine of 450-500 hp swinging a metal, constant-speed propeller. No prototype is known to have been built. Specifications and performance information are unknown.

[1] Walter A. "Pop" Strobel was no newcomer to aviation when he joined Cessna after the company's rebirth. He had been one of the original employees at Matty Laird's company and took part in construction of the early Swallow biplanes designed by Laird. He and Bob Phelps developed a jig for building wing ribs that worked so well they could produce a full set of ribs every day. Strobel was a key man in Clyde Cessna's organization in 1927, and helped run the First Street and Glenn Avenue factory. Along with Phelps, he deserves recognition as one of Wichita's earliest and most experienced aviation mechanics.

[2] When the government broke up the gigantic United Aircraft and Transport Corporation in 1934, The Boeing Aircraft Company, then a subsidiary of the conglomerate, pulled out and absorbed the Stearman company as a subsidiary of its own. In 1938, the company became The Stearman Aircraft Division of Boeing and J. Earl Schaefer became vice president and general manager. In 1941, the name was changed to the Wichita Division of the Boeing company. Schaefer's outfit had some very impressive numbers at the close of World War II: 8,584 PT-series trainers plus enough spare parts to build another 1,762 ships; the armed forces accepted 44% of all training airplanes during the war from the Wichita plant, and credited the 'Kaydet' biplane with teaching more pilots to fly than any other airplane; 1,644 B-29 bombers with enough spare parts to construct another 125; an employment of 29,402 at the peak point in January, 1944, of which 11,620 were females, and hit a production rate of 4.2 B-29s per day by July, 1945, and nine PT aircraft per day in April, 1943.

[3] By 1942, Major G.T. Chadwell and Captain B.S. Ray were added to the roster of military inspectors, representing the Army Air Force. Gale Savage was still chief inspector. The Civil Aeronautics Authority stationed J.D. Davis on site to handle all liason between Washington and Cessna. The company earned the Army-Navy E Award five times during the war and was the first to be given the accolade. The award was based on quality of the airplanes, avoiding work stoppages, labor relations and other considerations. Beech Aircraft Corporation and Schaefer's Wichita Division of Boeing also collected five E awards.

[4] These pilots were kept very busy ferrying the Canadian monoplanes to their home in the north country. Most of the Crane I ships were used for multi-engine and navigator training and operated in severe cold as well as high heat conditions with little difficulty.

[5] The company baseball team was named the "Bobcats" and even had a caged, live example for a mascot at the games.

[6] The Home Guard was not just for fun; they meant business. Any employee between the ages of 21 and 45, who was physically fit and ready to devote 200 hours per year of his free time toward learning military tactics was eligible to join. The goal was to have two battalions totaling 450 men. However, their equipment was not the most modern. Their standard weapon was the 1873 model Springfield 45-70 rifle, one of the last blackpowder firearms in the U.S. arsenal.

[7] In 1941, Dwight Wallace left his successful law practice to work at the Cessna plant full time. Meanwhile, brother Dwane tied the knot with his long-time secretary, Velma Lunt. He was elected Chairman of the Board on August 19, 1964 and retired from the company in 1982.

[8] The big Waco glider was built by 16 manufacturers during the war, totaling 13,909 units by war's end. It could carry 15 fully equipped troops in its capacious interior, suspended in flight by an wing of 83 feet, 8 inches. Gross weight was 9,000 pounds with a maximum towing speed of 150 mph. The usual tugs were Douglas C-47 or Curtiss C-46 transports. The British also used the type and called it the "Hadrian."

[9] Beech was busy building AT-10 multi-engine pilot trainers, AT-11 bombardier trainers and UC-45 transports when the glider contract hit. They allowed their subcontractors to do the work so the production lines would not be disrupted. Almost 6,000 people were working for Walter and Olive Ann Beech during the war years.

[10] The story of what Boeing called "The Battle of Kansas" is both a unique and gallant example of American know-how and ingenuity. Briefly stated, Boeing expected J. Earl Schaefer and his people to build the super bomber almost overnight when the Seattle engineers had yet to lock-in much of the engineering details. Tooling started in November, 1941, and finally involved 130,000 individual fixtures and jigs by 1944, when the task of building all the required pieces was completed. The first 100 airplanes took over 157,000 man-hours to build, while the last 100 ships only took 17,000 man-hours. Wichita's first B-29 flew on June 29, 1943. The first B-29 raid of the war was made by Wichita-built B-29s on June 5, 1944, when they plastered Bangkok from five miles up. Ten days later, on June 15th, the first raid on the Japanese homeland was made, when Wichita-built bombers hit the steel mills at Yawata. General H.H. Arnold visited the plant and congratulated Schaefer and his employees on a job well done. The last B-29 rolled from the factory in October, 1945.

[11] Deed Levy was called in by Cessna to evaluate the C-106's flight characteristics since he was experienced with larger airplanes from his past flying experience. He did not do any actual engineering on the C-106A variant, but did contribute to the improvements made in the ship.

[12] After the war, the Hutchinson plant was closed until the summer of 1946, when it was reopened to build wings and tail surfaces for the booming Model 120/140 airplanes. This was followed a year later by a contract with the Air Force to build furniture for use at overseas bases. The Wichita plant also built the wood and aluminum desks and chairs. The Hutchinson factory was later turned into Cessna's Industrial Products Division including hydraulic controls and equipment, known as the "Fluid Power Division".

[13] Sylvester "Steve" Wittman pioneered the use of chrome-vanadium spring steel landing gear on his many experimental aircraft designs of the 1940s. He sold the manufacturing rights for the gear design to Cessna, and the company also bought all rights to the four-place Wittman WD "Big-X", which was under negotiation for production with Fairchild, thereby eliminating any potential competition the airplane could have offered.

[14] In 1949, Cessna flew its Model 305 that later became famous as the L-19 "Bird Dog" two-place liason airplane. 2,466 were built from 1950 to 1955, with the army getting most of them but the navy managed to purchase 60 for the Marines by 1953. A little-known Cessna product, the Model 325, was an agricultural variant of the L-19. Only four were built.

[15] Clyde V. Cessna was buried next to his parents at the Belmont, Kansas, cemetary. Europa Cessna is also interred there.

CHAPTER TWELVE
Cessna - A Master's Expression

To aid the reader, historian, researcher, aircraft owner, modeler and Cessna enthusiast, this chapter will serve as a reference to aircraft built by Clyde V. Cessna, the Cessna-Roos Aircraft Company and the Cessna Aircraft Company from 1911 until 1955.

Section One covers the airplanes that received an Approved Type Certificate. Section Two discusses the models that were given Group Two Approval.

Wherever applicable, footnotes will be referenced to enhance the history of that particular ship or give some interesting bit of data that may previously have been unknown.

All of the information in this chapter has been obtained from official Cessna Aircraft Company records and documents. It is believed to be extremely accurate and reliable, having been cross-checked and corroborated over the years by Bob Pickett, who has done extensive research into all phases of Cessna Aircraft Company history. The author wishes to thank Mr. Pickett for making this information available for publication.

CESSNA MODEL AA
APPROVED TYPE CERTIFICATE #65
AUGUST, 1928

Model AA was the first production Cessna, powered with a 120 hp Cessna/Anzani radial engine. This airplane is the first factory ship sold, registered 4156, c/n 114, delivered to Edmund A. Link in February, 1928. Device on gear strut is an air-driven siren. (Bob Pickett Collection/Cessna Aircraft Company)

Engine - Cessna-modified Anzani, 10-cylinder, 120 hp
Wingspan - 40 feet, 2 inches
Wing area - 224 square feet
Airfoil - M-12 (modified by Cessna)
Chord at root/tip - 86 inches/58 inches
Length - 25 feet, 6 inches
Height - 7 feet, 2 inches
Empty weight - 1,304 pounds
Gross weight - 2,260 pounds

Useful load - 956 pounds
Payload - 510 pounds
Fuel capacity - 40 gallons
Oil capacity - 4.5 gallons
Maximum speed - 120 mph
Cruising speed - 102 mph
Landing speed - 45 mph
Rate of climb - 670 feet per minute (sea level)
Ceiling - 9,500 feet
Range - 550 miles
Total built - approximately 15
Production era - 1927-1929
Price - $5,750 with Hamilton wood propeller, later raised to $6,300 and $6,500 with Standard steel propeller.

CESSNA MODEL AW
APPROVED TYPE CERTIFICATE #72
SEPTEMBER, 1928

Model AW with its 110 hp Warner Scarab radial engine was sales champion, selling more than any other Cessna model. NC6448, c/n 148, was the third AW built. Truly a classic airplane design. (Bob Pickett Collection/Cessna Aircraft Company)

Engine - Warner 'Scarab', seven-cylinder, 110 hp at 2050 rpm
Wingspan - 40 feet, 2 inches
Wing area - 224 square feet
Airfoil - M-12 (modified by Cessna)
Chord at root/tip - 86 inches/58 inches
Length - 24 feet, 8.5 inches
Height - 6 feet, 11 inches
Empty weight - 1,225 pounds

Gross weight - 2,260 pounds
Useful load - 1,035 pounds
Payload - 550 pounds
Fuel capacity - 40 gallons
Oil capacity - 4.5 gallons
Maximum speed - 128 mph
Cruising speed - 105 mph
Landing speed - 42 mph
Rate of climb - 620 feet per minute (sea level)
Ceiling - 12,000 feet
Range - 630 miles
Total built - 48-50
Production era - 1928-1930
Price - $6,900 with Hamilton wood propeller, $7,115 with a Standard steel propeller, later raised to $7,500.

CESSNA MODEL DC-6
APPROVED TYPE CERTIFICATE #207
AUGUST, 1929

Second-generation Cessna DC-6 led the way for larger cabin size and comfort, more power and greater speed. This is the DC-6 prototype, 8142, c/n 157, with 170 hp Curtiss Challenger engine. (Bob Pickett Collection/Cessna Aircraft Company)

Engine - Curtiss "Challenger", six-cylinder, 170 hp at 2,000 rpm
Wingspan - 40 feet, 8 inches
Wing area - 265 square feet
Airfoil - M-12 (modified by Cessna)
Chord - 78 inches mean aerodynamic chord (MAC)
Length - 27 feet, 11 inches
Height - 7 feet, 8 inches
Empty weight - 1,767 pounds
Gross weight - 2,988 pounds

Fuel capacity - 66 gallons
Useful load - 1,221 pounds
Payload - 633 pounds (with 66 gallons of fuel)
Oil capacity - 5 gallons
Maximum speed - 130 mph
Cruising speed - 105 mph
Landing speed - 48 mph
Rate of climb - 780 feet per minute (sea level)
Ceiling - 16,000 feet
Range - 575 miles (at 10 gallons per hour)
Total built - 5
Production era - 1929
Price - $9,250 Note: Curtiss Flying Service bought all five DC-6 airplanes built. Four were later converted to Wright J-6-7 engines.

CESSNA MODEL DC-6A
APPROVED TYPE CERTIFICATE #243
SEPTEMBER, 1929

DC-6A 9864, c/n 199, was the first "Chief" built. It was sold to G.H. Rudd of New York City in 1929 and, as of 1985, is undergoing complete restoration to flying condition. (Bob Pickett Collection/Cessna Aircraft Company)

Engine - Wright J-6-9, nine-cylinder, 300 hp at 2,000 rpm
Wingspan - 41 feet
Wing area - 268 square feet
Airfoil - M-12 (modified by Cessna)
Chord - 78 inches mean aerodynamic chord (MAC)
Length - 28 feet, 2 inches
Height - 7 feet, 8 inches
Empty weight - 1,932 pounds
Gross weight - 3,180 pounds, later approved to 3,350 pounds
Useful load - 1,248 pounds
Payload - 606 pounds (with 66 gallons of fuel)
Fuel capacity - 66 gallons
Oil capacity - 9.5 gallons
Maximum speed - 161 mph
Cruising speed - 130 mph
Landing speed - 54 mph
Rate of climb - 1,300 feet per minute (sea level)
Ceiling - 18,500 feet
Range - 600 miles (at 13 gallons per hour)
Total built - 22
Production era - 1929-1930
Price - $11,500, later reduced to $11,000

CESSNA MODEL DC-6B
APPROVED TYPE CERTIFICATE #244
SEPTEMBER, 1929

DC-6B "Scout" was powered with a 225 hp Wright J-6-7 radial engine. C631K, c/n 211, originally went to Curtiss Flying Service of Texas. (Bob Pickett Collection/Cessna Aircraft Company)

Engine - Wright J-6-7, seven-cylinder, 225 hp at 2000 rpm
Wingspan - 41 feet
Wing area - 268 square feet
Airfoil - M-12 (modified by Cessna)
Chord - 78 inches mean aerodynamic chord (MAC)
Length - 28 feet, 2 inches
Height - 7 feet, 8 inches
Empty weight - 1,871 pounds
Gross weight - 3,100 pounds
Useful load - 1,229 pounds

Payload - 607 pounds (with 66 gallons of fuel)
Fuel capacity - 66 gallons
Oil capacity - 7 gallons
Maximum speed - 148 mph
Cruising speed - 120-125 mph
Landing speed - 52 mph
Rate of climb - 900 feet per minute (sea level)
Ceiling - 17,500 feet
Range - 685 miles (at 11 gallons per hour)
Total built - 22
Production era - 1929-1930
Price - $10,000, later reduced to $9,750
NOTE: Cessna records indicate c/n 275, c/n 276, c/n 290 were built in 1934-1935, with 250 hp J-6-7 engines.

CESSNA MODEL C-34
APPROVED TYPE CERTIFICATE #573
JUNE, 1935

NC15462, c/n 301, was the fourth C-34 built, rolling off the line in September, 1935. Warner radial of 145 hp gave the ship a maximum speed of 162 mph. (Bob Pickett Collection/Cessna Aircraft Company)

Engine - Warner Series 40/50, seven-cylinder, 145 hp at 2,050 rpm
Wingspan - 34 feet, 2 inches
Wing area - 180.5 square feet
Airfoil - NACA 2412
Chord at root/tip - 84 inches/58.6 inches
Length - 24 feet, 8 inches
Height - 7 feet, 3 inches
Empty weight - 1,380 pounds
Gross weight - 2,250 pounds
Useful load - 980 pounds
Payload - 514 pounds (with 35 gallons of fuel)
Baggage - 64 pounds maximum

Fuel capacity - 35 gallons
Oil capacity - 3.5 gallons
Maximum speed - 162 mph
Cruising speed - 143 (at 1,925 rpm)
Landing speed - 54 (flaps retracted) 47 (flaps extended)
Rate of climb - 800 feet per minute (sea level)
Ceiling - 18,900 feet
Range - 550 miles (at five gallons per hour and 1,925 rpm)
Total built - 42 First flight - 8-10-34, pilot: George Harte
Production era - 1935-1936

Price - $4,985 (standard aiplane) NOTE: C-34 also approved for Edo 44-2425 floats and Curtiss-Reed propeller. Empty weight-1,476 pounds, gross weight-2,500 pounds.

CESSNA MODEL C-37
APPROVED TYPE CERTIFICATE #622
FEBRUARY, 1937

The C-37 featured a four-inch wider cabin and could be purchased with the optional wheel fairings shown here on NC17086, c/n 346. Ship was originally a Cessna company demonstrator. (Bob Pickett Collection/Cessna Aircraft Company)

Engine - Warner Series 50, seven-cylinder, 145 hp at 2,050 rpm
Wingspan - 34 feet, 2 inches
Wing area - 182 square feet
Airfoil - NACA 2412
Chord at root/tip - 84 inches/58 inches
Length - 24 feet, 8 inches
Height - 7 feet, 3 inches
Empty weight - 1,304 pounds
Gross weight - 2,250 pounds
Useful load - 946 pounds
Payload - 540 pounds (with 35 gallons of fuel)

Fuel capacity - 35 gallons
Oil capacity - 3.5 gallons
Maximum speed - 162 mph
Cruising speed - 143 mph
Landing speed - 56 mph (flaps retracted), 48 mph (flaps extended)
Rate of climb - 800 feet per minute (sea level)
Ceiling - 18,000 feet
Range - 540 miles (at 9 gallons per hour and 1,925 rpm)
Total built - 46 First flight - 12-22-36, pilot: Dwane Wallace
Production era - 1937
Price - $5,490 (standard airplane), $6,000 (Deluxe model) NOTE: C-37 also approved for Edo 44-2425 floats and Curtiss-Reed propeller. Empty weight-1,560 pounds, gross weight-2,500 pounds.

CESSNA MODEL C-38
APPROVED TYPE CERTIFICATE #668
OCTOBER, 1937

Introduced in 1938, the C-38 featured a wider landing gear that improved ground maneuvering and crosswind handling. NC18048, c/n 400, was the prototype. Note Hartzell wooden propeller; production airplanes were fitted with Curtiss metal propellers. (Bob Pickett Collection/Cessna Aircraft Company)

Engine - Warner Series 50, seven-cylinder, 145 hp at 2,050 rpm
Wingspan - 34 feet, 2 inches
Wing area - 181 square feet
Airfoil - NACA 2412
Chord at root/tip - 84 inches/58 inches
Length - 24 feet, 8 inches
Height - 7 feet
Empty weight - 1,370 pounds
Gross weight - 2,350 pounds
Useful load - 980 pounds
Payload - 574 pounds

Fuel capacity - 35 gallons (standard), 45 gallon tanks (optional)
Oil capacity - 3.5 gallons
Maximum speed - 162 mph
Cruising speed - 143 mph (at 1,925 rpm)
Landing speed - 49 mph (drag-type flap extended)
Rate of climb - 800-1,000 feet per minute (sea level)
Ceiling - 18,000 feet
Range - 525 miles (standard tanks), 675 miles (optional tanks)
Total built - 16 First flight - 9-29-37, pilot: Dwane Wallace
Production era - 1938
Price - $6,490
NOTE: C-38 also approved for Edo 44-2425 floats and Curtiss-Reed propeller. Empty weight-1,626 pounds, gross weight-2,500 pounds.

142

CESSNA MODEL C-145/C-165
APPROVED TYPE CERTIFICATE #701
OCTOBER, 1938

Engine - Warner Series 50, seven-cylinder, 145 hp/165 hp
Wingspan - 34 feet, 2 inches
Wing area - 181 square feet
Airfoil - NACA 2412
Chord at root/tip - 84 inches/58 inches
Length - 24 feet, 8 inches
Height - 7 feet
Empty weight - 1,380 pounds (C-145), 1,400 pounds (C-165)
Gross weight - 2,350 pounds
Useful load - 970 pounds (C-145), 950 pounds (C-165)
Payload - 574 pounds (C-145), 544 pounds (C-165)
Fuel capacity - 35 gallons (standard), 45/52.5 gallons (optional)
Oil capacity - 3.5 gallons
Maximum speed - 162 mph (C-145), 169 mph (C-165)
Cruising speed - 143 mph (C-145), 157 mph (C-165)
Landing speed - 49 mph
Rate of climb - 800/925 feet per minute (sea level)
Ceiling - 18,000 feet (C-145), 19,300 feet (C-165)
Range - 525 miles (standard tanks), 725 miles (optional tanks)
Total built - 79 First flight - C-145, 9-11-38/C-165, 4-25-39
Production era - 1938-1941
Price - $7,875 (C-145), $8,275 (C-165)
NOTE: C-145/C-165 approved for Edo 44-2425 floats with Curtiss- Reed propeller.
Gross weight - 2,550 pounds.

Airmaster development reached its zenith in the 1939-41 Model 145/165. NC19464, c/n 450, was the prototype C-145, built in September, 1938. (Bob Pickett Collection/Cessna Aircraft Company)

AIRMASTER SUPPLEMENTAL DATA
C-34, C-37, C-38, C-145, C-165
Optional Equipment:

The Airmaster series offered a long list of options for the customer to choose from, including Curtiss-Reed metal propeller (standard on seaplane version), custom cabin appointments, cabin heater, paraflares, communications radio, bonding straps, camera apertures, stretcher installation, skis, wheel fairings, custom colors, pilot escape hatch, 22x10-4 Goodyear airwheels, 52-gallon fuel capacity.

The C-37 and C-38 could be ordered as specially-built cargo airplanes known as the "Freighter". Modifications made to the standard aircraft were:
1. Rear seat removed
2. Co-pilot seat designed for quick removal
3. Heavy-duty, increased thickness floorboards
4. Sheet metal sidewalls 18 inches up from floor level
5. Four freight tie-down lugs for the cargo space
6. Rear cabin windows deleted
7. Empty weight of 1,234 pounds
8. Gross weight of 2,250
9. Useful load (maximum) of 1,016 pounds
10. Heavy-duty landing gear shock struts

According to Cessna records, no freighters were built. An aerial ambulance version was also available, with seats that were quickly removed or installed, and special stretcher hangers for one patient, plus room for a doctor, nurse and the pilot.

CESSNA MODEL T-50
APPROVED TYPE CERTIFICATE #722
MARCH, 1940

Cessna expanded their product line in 1939 with introduction of the Model T-50. Two, 225 hp Jacobs L4MB radials gave the ship a maximum speed of 190 mph. (Bob Pickett Collection/Cessna Aircraft Company)

Engine - Two, Jacobs L4MB, seven-cylinder, 225 hp at 2,000 rpm
Wingspan - 41 feet, 11 inches
Wing area - 295 square feet
Airfoil - NACA 23014 (root), NACA 23012 at tip
Chord at root/tip - 105 inches/70 inches
Length - 32 feet, 9 inches
Height - 9 feet, 4 inches
Empty weight - 3,500 pounds
Gross weight - 5,100 pounds
Useful load - 1,600 pounds
Payload - 635 pounds (with 120 gallons of fuel)

Baggage capacity - 300 pounds
Fuel capacity - 120 gallons (standard), 160 gallons (optional)
Oil capacity - 10 gallons
Maximum speed - 185 mph
Cruising speed - 170 mph
Landing speed - 55 mph (flaps extended)
Rate of climb - 1,200 feet per minute (sea level)
Ceiling - 18,000 feet
Range - 850 miles (at 7,500 feet, 27 gallons per hour)
Total built - 40 First flight - 3-26-39, pilot: Dwane Wallace
Production era - 1939-1942
Price - $29,675, later reduced to $28,000
NOTE: 290 hp Lycoming engines were available as an option.

144

CESSNA MODEL 120/140
APPROVED TYPE CERTIFICATE #768
MARCH, 1946

The 1946 Model 120 proved to be a popular and hard-working airplane, well suited to pleasure flying or training student pilots. Many are still airworthy today. (Bob Pickett Collection/Cessna Aircraft Company)

Engine - Continental C-85-12, C-90-12, 85-90 hp at 2,575 rpm
Wingspan - 32 feet, 10 inches (120/140), 33 feet, 4 inches (140A)
Wing area - 159.3 square feet
Airfoil - NACA 23012
Chord - 60.5 inches
Length - 21 feet, 6 inches
Height - 6 feet, 3 inches
Empty weight - 785 pounds (Model 120), 860 pounds (Model 140)
Gross weight - 1,450 pounds
Useful load - 665 pounds (Model 120), 590 pounds (Model 140)
Payload - 295 pounds (Model 120), 262 pounds (Model 140) (with 25 gallons of fuel, two parachutes or 1 passenger and 80 pounds of baggage)
Fuel capacity - 25 gallons
Oil capacity - 4.5 quarts
Maximum speed - 123 mph (Model 120), 120 mph (Model 140)
Cruising speed - 106 mph (Model 120), 105 mph (Model 140)
Landing speed - 42 mph (Model 120), 40 mph (Model 140 with flaps)
Rate of climb - 640 feet per minute (sea level)

Ceiling - 15,500 feet
Range - 420 miles (at 5.9 gallons per hour)
Total built - Model 120- 2,172, Model 140- 4,904, Model 140A- 525
Production era - 1945-1951 (includes Model 140A production)
Price - Model 120 - $2,845, Model 140 - $3,385

The popular Model 140A was the last version of the highly successful 140. Major changes for the 140A were single lift strut and all-metal wing. (Bob Pickett Collection/Cessna Aircraft Company)

CESSNA MODEL 170
APPROVED TYPE CERTIFICATE #799
JUNE, 1948

One of the cleanest, most esthetic airplanes to come out of the Cessna factory was the Model 170. This 170A version shows off its classic profile. 145 hp Continental engine gave the 170- series a cruising speed of 120 mph. (Bob Pickett Collection/Cessna Aircraft Company)

Engine - Continental C-145, six-cylinder, 145 hp at 2,700 rpm
Wingspan - 36 feet
Wing area - 174.8 square feet
Airfoil - NACA 2412
Length - 25 feet
Height - 6 feet, 7 inches
Empty weight - 1,200 pounds
Gross weight - 2,200 pounds
Useful load - 1,000 pounds
Payload - 590 pounds (with 37.5 gallons of fuel)

Fuel capacity - 37.5 gallons
Oil capacity - 8 quarts
Maximum speed - 140 mph
Cruising speed - 120 mph (at 5,000 feet, 2,450 rpm)
Landing speed - 52 mph (flaps extended)
Rate of climb - 690 feet per minute (sea level)
Ceiling - 15,500 feet
Range - 500-550 miles (at 8 gallons per hour)
Total built - 5,000 (including Model 170A and Model 170B)
Production era - 1948-1956
Price - $8,295 (1956 Model 170B)
NOTE: Approved Type Certificate for Model 170A issued on December 15, 1948 and the Model 170B was approved September 28, 1950. Both certificates were based on ATC#799.

CESSNA MODEL 190/195
APPROVED TYPE CERTIFICATE #790
JUNE, 1947

A Model 190 with its big 240 hp Continental radial rips through the clear, winter sky on a business trip. With lots of room for four people and a cruise speed of 150 mph, the 190 was a popular airplane and has carved a niche for itself in the classic aircraft movement. (Bob Pickett Collection/Cessna Aircraft Company)

The robust Model 195 boosted available horsepower to 300 with its Jacobs radial, increasing the cruising speed to almost 160 mph while providing Cadillac comfort for its passengers. (Bob Pickett Collection/Cessna Aircraft Company)

Engine - Continental, seven-cylinder radial, 240 hp (Model 190) Jacobs, seven-cylinder radial, 300 hp (Model 195)
Wingspan - 36 feet, 2 inches
Wing area - 218 square feet
Airfoil - NACA 2412 (modified)
Chord - 84 inches
Length - 27 feet, 2 inches (190), 27 feet, four inches (195)
Height - seven feet, 2 inches
Empty weight - 2,030 pounds (190), 2,050 pounds (195)
Gross weight - 3,350 pounds
Useful load - 1,320 (190), 1,300 pounds (195)
Payload - 633 pounds (with 80 gallons of fuel)
Fuel capacity - 80 gallons
Oil capacity - 5 gallons
Maximum speed - 170 mph (190), 180 mph (195)
Cruising speed - 150 mph (190), 159 mph (195)
Landing speed - 60 mph (flaps extended)
Rate of climb -
    1,050 feet per minute (sea level) (Model 190)
    1,135 feet per minute (sea level) (Model 195)
Ceiling - 16,000 feet (190), 18,300 feet (195)
Range - 700-725 miles (at 13.9 and 16.0 gallons per hour)
Total built - 1,206
Production era - 1947-1954
Price - $13,250 in 1949 (190), $14,950 in 1950 (195)

SECTION TWO
GROUP TWO APPROVALS

The Department of Commerce created the Group Two Approval as a secondary channel for aircraft manufacturers who did not want to seek a complete ATC for a particular design.

Many Group Two Approvals were given to aircraft that were one-of-a-kind or factory-modified versions of an airplane that already had a valid Approved Type Certificate. In Cessna's case, both single and multiple examples of an approved airplane were built and sold under the Group Two system, differing primarily in powerplant, gross weight and passenger capacity. Generally, the aircraft approved under the Group Two category were airworthy and safe when operated in strict accordance with the approval's limitations.

After a government inspector viewed the craft and witnessed a flight (or performed it himself), a written authorization was issued to the builder, stipulating the limitations under which the aircraft could be manufactured and operated.

Five Cessna airplanes that were granted Group Two Approval are listed in this section, including their specifications, number built, constructor number eligible and date of manufacture. The term "PCLM" used in the description indicates: "P" for number of occupied seats, "C" for cabin, "L" for land and "M" for monoplane.

CESSNA MODEL BW
GROUP TWO APPROVAL #2-7
DECEMBER, 1928

Model BW sported a powerful 220 hp Wright J-5 radial engine, had spectacular performance and was used by air lines like Robertson based in St. Louis, Missouri. NC6442, c/n 138, was delivered in September, 1928. Pilot is believed to be Bud Gurney. (Bob Pickett Collection/Cessna Aircraft Company)

Engine - Wright J-5, nine-cylinder radial, 200-220 hp
Wingspan - 40 feet, 2 inches
Wing area - 224 square feet
Airfoil - M-12 (modified by Cessna)
Chord at root/tip - 86 inches/58 inches
Length - 25 feet, 10.5 inches
Height - 7 feet, 2 inches
Empty weight - Approximately 1,400 pounds

Gross weight - 2,435 pounds
Useful load - Approximately 800 to 900 pounds
Payload - Approximately 500 pounds
Fuel capacity - 40 gallons
Oil capacity - 7 gallons
Maximum speed - 160 mph
Cruising speed - 140-150 mph
Landing speed - Approximately 50 mph
Rate of climb - Over 1,000 feet per minute (sea level)
Range (estimated) - 500-550 miles
Ceiling (estimated) - 18,000 feet
Total built - 13 - Eligible c/n were: 113, 116, 117, 118, 120, 121, 125, 135, 138, 142, 143 and 147.
Production era - 1927-1928
Price - $9,800 (in 1928) NOTE: Model BW was approved as a 4PCLM, but often flown as 3PCLM.

CESSNA MODEL AS
GROUP TWO APPROVAL #2-8
JANUARY, 1929

Cessna Model AS was powered with the 128 hp Siemens-Halske radial of German design and manufacture. This ship, 4157, c/n 115, was sold to Beacon Airways, Kansas City, Missouri, in April, 1928 and was the first example built. (Bob Pickett Collection/Cessna Aircraft Company)

Engine - Siemens-Halske SH-12, nine-cylinder radial, 128 hp
Wingspan - 40 feet, 2 inches
Wing area - 224 square feet
Airfoil - M-12 (modified by Cessna)
Chord at root/tip - 86 inches/58 inches
Length - 25 feet, 2.25 inches
Height - 7 feet, 5.5 inches
Empty weight - Approximately 1,300 pounds
Gross weight - 2,260 pounds

Useful load - Approximately 950 pounds
Payload - Approximately 500 pounds
Fuel capacity - 40 gallons
Oil capacity - 5 gallons
Maximum speed - 120 mph
Cruising speed - 105 mph
Landing speed - 40 to 45 mph
Rate of climb - 650 to 700 feet per minute (sea level)
Ceiling - 10,000 feet
Range - 500 to 550 miles
Total built - 4 - Eligible c/n were: 115, 123, 136, 139
Production era - 1928
Price - $7,500
NOTE: The Siemens-Halske SH-12 engine was imported from Germany and marketed by T. Claude Ryan.

CESSNA MODEL AF
GROUP TWO APPROVAL #2-237
JULY, 1930

Cessna's Model AF featured a 150 hp Axelson radial engine, formerly FLOCO. C7462, c/n 141, was the second AF built, delivered in September, 1928. (Bob Pickett Collection/Cessna Aircraft Company)

Engine - FLOCO (1928), seven-cylinder radial, 150 hp at 1,800 rpm
Wingspan - 40 feet, 2 inches
Wing area - 224 square feet
Airfoil - M-12 (modified by Cessna)
Chord at root/tip - 84 inches/58 inches
Length - 24 feet, 10.5 inches
Height - 7 feet, 5.5 inches
Empty weight - 1,354 pounds
Gross weight - 2,262 pounds

Useful load - Approximately 950 pounds
Payload - Approximately 500 pounds
Fuel capacity - 40 gallons
Oil capacity - 5 gallons
Maximum speed - 125 to 130 mph
Cruising speed - 110 to 115 mph
Landing speed - 45 mph
Rate of climb - 750 to 800 feet per minute (sea level)
Range - 500 to 550 miles
Total built - 3 - Eligible c/n were: 137, 141, 149
Production era - 1928
Price - $7,500
NOTE: FLOCO became Axelson in the summer of 1928, but all three airplanes built with this engine are referred to as Model AF.

CESSNA MODEL AC
GROUP TWO APPROVAL #2-407
MAY, 1932

The only known AC built by the factory was c/n 150, NC6450, delivered to Atlantic Air Service, Inc., in January 1929. (Truman C. Weaver via Bob Pickett)

Engine - Comet, seven-cylinder radial, 130 hp at 1,825 rpm
Wingspan - 40 feet, 2 inches
Wing area - 224 square feet
Airfoil - M-12 (modified by Cessna)
Chord at root/tip - 84 inches/58 inches
Length - 25 feet, 5 inches
Height - 7 feet, 5.5 inches
Empty weight - Approximately 1,300 pounds
Gross weight - 2,260 pounds

Useful load - Approximately 900 pounds
Payload - Approximately 500 pounds
Fuel capacity - 40 gallons
Oil capacity - 4.5 to 5 gallons
Maximum speed - 120 mph
Cruising speed - 105 to 110 mph
Landing speed - 45 mph
Rate of climb - 650 to 700 feet per minute (sea level)
Ceiling - 10,000 feet
Range - 500 to 550 miles
Total built - 1 - Eligible c/n was: 150
Production era - 1928
Price - $7,500
NOTE: c/n 150 was approved as a 4PCLM.

CESSNA MODEL C-3
GROUP TWO APPROVAL #2-473
MARCH, 1934

The attractive C-3 was built for Walt Anderson from the fuselage of a Model AA, c/n 124, and a new wing. Powered by a 125 hp Warner radial, it featured DC-6-type landing gear. (Robert Gilmore via Bob Pickett)

NOTE: Specific information on the Model C-3 is uncertain. Only data known to be accurate is presented.

Engine - Warner, seven-cylinder radial, 125 hp at 2,050 rpm

Empty weight - 1,387 pounds (December, 1933)
Gross weight - 2,260 pounds
Fuel capacity - 44 gallons
Oil capacity - 4.5 gallons
Cruising speed - Approximately 120 mph
Production era - 1933
Total built - 1 - Eligible c/n: 4

APPENDIX

This index contains references to only primary characters, airplanes and organizations in the Cessna story, the page numbers where they initially appear and the chapters in which they form an integral part of the narrative.

BIBLIOGRAPHY

NEWSPAPER REFERENCES
1. Eagle and Beacon, The Wichita; 1924 through 1948. Articles and supplements thereto.

2. The Tulsa Democrat, Enid Daily Eagle, Jet Visitor, Waynoka Tribune and Kingman Leader-Courier; 1911 through 1915. Articles and supplements thereto.

CITY DIRECTORIES
1. Enid, Oklahoma and Wichita, Kansas, city directories, 1910 through 1936; R.L. Polk, publisher.

HISTORICAL PUBLICATIONS
1. Weaver, Truman C.; The Cessna Racers, Air Progress Magazine; Spring, 1961.

2. Weaver, Truman C. and S.H. Schmid; The Golden Age of Air Racing, Volume 1; EAA Aviation Foundation, Inc.

3. Smith, Herschel; Aircraft Piston Engines; McGraw-Hill Book Company, 1981.

4. DeVries, Col. John A.; Alexander Eaglerock, A History of Alexander Aircraft Company; Century One Press, 1985.

5. Deneau, Gerald; An Eye To The Sky, First Fifty Years; Cessna Aircraft Company, 1961.

6. Juptner, Joseph P.; U.S. Civil Aircraft, Volume 1 through 8; Aero Publishers, Inc. 1962-1980.

7. Pickett, Robert and Mayborn, Mitch; Cessna Guidebook; Flying Enterprise Publications, 1973.

8. Bowers, Peter M. and Mayborn, Mitch; Stearman Guidebook; Flying Enterprise Publications, 1972.

9. Crouch, Tom D.; Bleriot XI - The Story of a Classic Aircraft; Smithsonian Institution Press, 1982.

10. Brooks-Pazmany, Kathleen; United States Women in Aviation 1919-1929; Smithsonian Institution Press, 1983.

11. Oakes, Claudia M.; United States Women in Aviation through World War One; Smithsonian Institution Press, 1978.

12. Aviation and Aero Digest Magazine; 1924 through 1933.

13. Cessna Aircraft Company files; 1927 through 1948.

14. Stress analysis, notes and correspondence of Joseph S. Newell to Clyde V. Cessna/Cessna Aircraft Company, 1928.

15. Aeronautics magazine; Elbridge "Aero Special"; February, 1911.

16. Cessna, Howard, Esq.; The House of Cessna, Howard Cessna, 1935.

17. Allard, Noel; Speed - The Biography of Charles W. Holman; Noel E. Allard, 1976.

18. Cessna Aircraft Company Aircrafter, 1941-1942.

INTERVIEWS AND CORRESPONDENCE
1. Cessna, Eldon Wayne; interview and correspondence from 1980 to 1985.

2. Wallace, Dwane L.; interviews and correspondence, 1984-1985.

3. Phelps, Bob; interviews, 1980-1985.

4. Brown, Morton W.; interview, 1984.

5. Boyd, Karl Miller; interview, 1984.

6. Quick, Tom; interview, 1984.

CESSNA FAMILY HISTORY
1. Herman, Hazel Dell Cessna; notes and family history, 1947, 1974.

2. Dotzour, Grover; notes and family history with Roy Cessna, 1963.

NOTE TO READER: For persons desiring more information on Cessna airplanes, constructor number 112 through 591, than has been included in this publication, the author will make available a complete or partial listing which includes:

Engine/propeller make, model and serial number, date of manufacture/delivery, original owner, exterior/interior colors, upholstery colors and fabric vendor, special equipment, factory modifications and, when known, a service life summary.

Address correspondence to: Edward H. Phillips
924 Seashore Road
Cape May, New Jersey 08204